An Introduction to Buddhist Philosophy

In this clear and accessible book, Stephen Laumakis explains the origin and
development of Buddhist ideas and concepts, focusing on the philosophical
ideas and arguments presented and defended by selected thinkers and
sutras from various traditions. He starts with a sketch of the Buddha and
the Dharma, and highlights the origins of Buddhism in India. He then
considers specific details of the Dharma with special attention to Buddhist
metaphysics and epistemology, and examines the development of Buddhism
in China, Japan, and Tibet, concluding with the ideas of the Dalai Lama
and Thich Nhat Hanh. In each chapter he includes explanations of key terms
and teachings, excerpts from primary source materials, and presentations
of the arguments for each position. His book will be an invaluable guide for
all who are interested in this rich and vibrant philosophy.

STEPHEN J. LAUMAKIS is Associate Professor in the Philosophy
Department at the University of St. Thomas, St. Paul.

An Introduction to Buddhist Philosophy

STEPHEN J. LAUMAKIS

University of St. Thomas, Minnesota

CAMBRIDGE
UNIVERSITY PRESS

CAMBRIDGE UNIVERSITY PRESS
Cambridge, New York, Melbourne, Madrid, Cape Town, Singapore, São Paulo

Cambridge University Press
The Edinburgh Building, Cambridge CB2 8RU, UK

Published in the United States of America by Cambridge University Press, New York

www.cambridge.org
Information on this title: www.cambridge.org/9780521670081

First published 2008

Printed in the United Kingdom at the University Press, Cambridge

A catalogue record for this publication is available from the British Library

ISBN 978-0-521-85413-9 hardback
ISBN 978-0-521-67008-1 paperback

For Mary, Maggie, Molly and Stephen

Contents

Acknowledgments

This is a welcome opportunity to thank and publicly acknowledge those who have helped bring this book into being. First, I must thank Hilary Gaskin of Cambridge University Press for the invitation to write it, and Roger Ames of the University of Hawaii for his confidence in recommending me to Hilary. Second, I want to thank Peter Hershock of the East-West Center and the anonymous reviewers of both the initial proposal and the draft chapter of the book for their insightful comments and criticisms, as well as their helpful suggestions. I know that this is a better book because of their recommendations. Third, I want to thank my "Indian and Buddhist" teachers, especially those whose books I have read that appear in the bibliography, as well as John Kronen, Ramdas Lamb, George Tanabe, and in particular, David West, who first taught me that there might be something to Buddhist thought. Fourth, I owe a great debt of gratitude to my colleagues at the University of St. Thomas who have read drafts of its chapters, especially, Bernie Brady, David Landry, Mark Neuzil, and Greg Robinson-Riegler. Fifth, I want to thank David Wemhaner for his helpful comments and suggestions. Sixth, I want to thank my former Dean, Tom Connery, my former department Chair, Sandy Menssen, and the Faculty Development Committee for a grant and release time to finish the manuscript. Seventh, I want to thank my former students who have studied Buddhism with me, especially, Laurel Stack and Jake Tuttle, for pushing me to better understand what I was teaching. Eighth, I am grateful to my parents, Jack and Peg, my brothers and their wives, Pete, Paul and Marlena, Mark and Christi, and John and Juliana, and my in-laws Dick and Margaret Thomas, for their emotional support throughout the process. Ninth, I want to thank my long-time friends Bernie DeLury and Tim McTaggart for their continuing support and friendship. Tenth, and last, but above all, I thank my wife Mary, and my daughters, Maggie and Molly, and their unborn brother Stephen – without their love, support, and encouragement I would not be who I am and could not have written this book. I dedicate it to them as a small token of my love and affection.

"We are what we think. All that we are arises with our thoughts. With our thoughts we make the world."

> – *Dhammapada* (translation by Thomas Byrom)

"This is morality, this is concentration, this is wisdom. Concentration, when imbued with morality, brings great fruit and profit. Wisdom, when imbued with concentration, brings great fruit and profit. The mind imbued with wisdom becomes completely free from the corruptions, that is, from the corruption of sensuality, of becoming, of false views and of ignorance."

> – *Digha Nikaya, Mahaparinibbana Sutta*, 1.12 (translation by Maurice Walshe)

"The mind is that in the world by which one is a perceiver of the world, a conceiver of the world."

> – *Samyutta Nikaya*, IV, 95 (translation by Bhikkhu Bodhi)

"Do not go by oral tradition, by lineage of teaching, by hearsay, by a collection of scriptures, by logical reasoning, by inferential reasoning, by reflection on reasons, by the acceptance of a view after pondering it, by the seeming competence of a speaker, or because you think 'The ascetic is our teacher.' But when you know for yourselves . . . then you should do or do not."

> – *Anguttara Nikaya*, III, 65 (translation by Nyanaponika Thera and Bhikkhu Bodhi)

"Both formerly and now what I teach is suffering and the cessation of suffering."

> – *Majjhima Nikaya, Alagaddupama Sutta*, 38 (translation by Bhikkhu Nanamoli and Bhikkhu Bodhi)

"No other thing do I know, O monks, that is so intractable as an undeveloped mind. An undeveloped mind is truly intractable . . . No other thing do I know, O monks, that brings so much suffering as an undeveloped and uncultivated mind. An undeveloped and uncultivated mind truly brings suffering . . . No other thing do I know, O monks, that brings so much harm as a mind that is untamed, unguarded, unprotected and uncontrolled. Such a mind truly brings much harm . . . No other thing do I know, O monks, that changes so quickly as the mind. It is not easy to give a simile for how quickly the mind changes."

> – *Anguttara Nikaya*, I, iii, iv, v (selections) (translation by
> Nyanaponika Thera and Bhikkhu Bodhi)

"Not to do any evil, to cultivate good, to purify one's mind, this is the Teaching of the Buddhas."

> – *Dhammapada*, 183 (translation by Walpola Rahula)

Preface

These are interesting and exciting times to be studying Buddhism and non-Western philosophy and religion. As we try to make sense of recent and ongoing events in the world, it is evident that many actions are inspired by ideas that are foreign to traditional Western beliefs and practices. Whether these ideas are political, religious, or philosophical in origin and motivation, it is clear that understanding our global world requires more than knowledge of one's own philosophical and cultural heritage.

In response to these needs, universities throughout the world have been working to broaden their curricula by emphasizing the value and necessity of multiculturalism and diversity in all areas of study. In the field of philosophy, for example, there is increasing interest, research, and teaching in both comparative philosophy and "world" philosophy. This growing interest and activity in the realm of comparative and "world" philosophy can be observed in the ever-increasing number of books published on non-Western thought. In fact, there has been a veritable explosion in the number of introductory texts, translations of primary source materials, and even new editions of classic publications. These same activities are happening in the area of Buddhist philosophy and religion.

Nevertheless, it is easy for anyone who is new to the study of Buddhism to feel somewhat overwhelmed by the size of the task at hand. The history of Buddhism spans some 2500 years and its teachings, in one form or another, are found on almost every continent in the world. From their beginnings in India, the teachings of the Buddha spread north (to China, Korea, Japan, and Tibet) and south (through most of South East Asia) and most recently to the West as well. At the same time, there are "liberal" and "conservative" interpretations of "his" teachings, and strict and less strict observers of "his" way – and almost every position in between. In fact, there are some strands of Buddhism that are, or at least appear to be, so far removed from what are

generally considered to be the earliest teachings and practices of the historical Buddha and his immediate followers, that one cannot help but wonder
both how the name "Buddhism" can be accurately applied across such a broad
spectrum of beliefs and practices, and whether the name itself refers to any
coherent and consistent set of ideas, propositions, beliefs, and practices.

Consider for a moment the quotations at the beginning of this book. Each
is supposed to be an accurate rendering of a teaching of the historical
Buddha, and each is only a few lines taken from traditional Buddhist
texts. Now stop and think about the breadth and complexity of the ideas
expressed in each quotation; consider their interrelationships, and realize
that there are literally thousands of sayings of the Buddha. One should, I
hope, begin to get a sense of the size of the problems involved in an
introductory text on Buddhism.

There are at least three possible responses to this situation. First, one
might espouse a kind of forlorn skepticism and claim that there is quite
literally no hope of getting a grip on "Buddhism." One could simply decide
that "Buddhism" is just too complex and too culturally and historically
diverse to be clearly and unambiguously specified and studied. On the
other extreme, one might maintain a position of naive and blissful ignorance with respect to these problems and either simply fail to recognize
them or uncritically accept everything that claims to be "Buddhist" as
authentically Buddhist. Yet neither of these positions seems to be intellectually satisfying. There is, however, a third response, or a "middle way"
between these extremes. One could simultaneously be critically aware of
the problems, limitations, and difficulties of one's study, and also work to
avoid the charges of naiveté and oversimplification as well. That is the path
this book attempts to take. It is also, I think, something like the "Middle
Way" the historical Buddha himself is said to have taught.

As far as we know, the man who became "the Buddha" or "the Awakened
One" was neither a skeptic nor a fideist (i.e., a blind-faith believer) in
religious and philosophical matters. He is said to have urged his followers
not to believe something because of who said it or where they heard it or
where they read it, but because it accorded with their own experiences. It is
precisely this standard that I urge the reader to use when considering the
claims and arguments in this book.

It is also important to keep in mind that no single-volume introduction to
Buddhism can cover everything in the Buddhist tradition; the historical

forms are simply too complex and diverse in time, language, culture, geography, and even doctrinal matters to be covered in anything more than a superficial way in one volume. As a result, one must make some difficult and perhaps controversial decisions about what topics, ideas, and figures to cover. And these decisions are further complicated by two important background questions: first, is Buddhism a *philosophy*, or a *religion*, or some kind of combination of both, or neither? And second, assuming one could isolate Buddhist *philosophy* from Buddhist *religion*, what divisions or branches of its *philosophy* ought one to consider?

These are obviously large and complex questions that could be the subjects of books of their own. The subject matter of this book is Buddhist *philosophy* – with a particular focus on its epistemology and metaphysics. In other words, unlike most introductions to Buddhism that focus on it as a *religion*, this book is an introduction to Buddhist *philosophy*. Moreover, this book will be concerned primarily with Buddhist theories of knowledge and reality, and only secondarily or peripherally with its ethical claims.

Given these initial considerations and decisions, the plan of the book is as follows. **Part I** presents a rough "Sketch of the Buddha and the *Dhamma*." Its four chapters are concerned with "The life of Siddhattha Gotama," "The contexts for the emergence of Buddhism," "The basic teachings of the Buddha," and the theoretical and practical question of whether there is "One Buddhism or many Buddhisms?" **Part II** fills in the "Details of the *Dhamma*." Its four chapters focus on the metaphysical and epistemological aspects of "*Kamma*, *Samsara*, and rebirth," "Interdependent arising," "Impermanence, no-enduring-self, and emptiness," and "*Moksa* and *Nibbana*." Finally, **Part III** traces the ongoing "Development of the *Dhamma/Dharma*" in "Bodhidharma's and Huineng's Buddhisms," "Pure Land Buddhism," "Tibetan Buddhism," and concludes with "Two contemporary forms of Buddhism" – the Buddhism of the Dalai Lama and the "engaged Buddhism" of Thich Nhat Hanh.

Following the advice of the Buddha himself, I encourage the reader to consider the evidence for the Buddha's teachings for yourself and to weigh and test it against your own experience. No other effort is requested or necessary – and none will be better repaid.

Part I

A sketch of the Buddha and the *Dhamma*

As the title suggests, **Part I** provides background information about both the society and culture, and philosophical and religious context in and from which the life and teachings of Siddhattha Gotama emerged. In this light, it considers how his experiences and teachings are both a product of and reaction to the "philosophies" and "religions" of his times.

While recognizing that our knowledge of the man who became known as "the Buddha" is based on limited historical evidence, the chapters of **Part I** try to piece together the basic strands of his biography and show how his life experiences shaped his philosophical views. They also propose a "philosophical reading" of the facts of the life of Siddhattha Gotama as an initial way to approach and understand the teachings of the historical Buddha. These chapters encourage the reader to consider why the fundamental beliefs and practices of this particular man were able to take root in India and flourish throughout Asia. They will also challenge the reader to consider why and how the cultural environments of India and Asia influenced and changed the teachings of the Buddha.

After initially considering "The life of Siddhattha" in **Chapter 1** and "The contexts for the emergence of Buddhism" in **Chapter 2**, **Chapter 3** presents the ideas, concepts, and terminology of "The basic teachings of the Buddha" as they are found in the earliest sources of the Pali texts and the Theravada tradition. The teachings to be covered include: the Middle Way, the Four Noble Truths, and the Eightfold Path. The key concepts to be introduced include: *dukkha*, *tanha*, interdependent arising, *anatta*, *nibbana*, wisdom, moral excellence, and meditation. Finally, **Chapter 4**, "One Buddhism or many Buddhisms?" presents a first, rough sketch of subsequent Buddhist philosophical developments – in the Theravada, Mahayana, and Vajrayana traditions. As its title indicates, this chapter also raises the intriguing question of whether "Buddhism" denotes a single philosophical system or a complex network of distinct yet interrelated philosophies.

1   The life of Siddhattha Gotama

Key terms and teachings

Abhidhamma/Abhidharma: Pali and Sanskrit terms for the "higher" *dhamma/dharma* or teachings of the Buddha. These texts are the philosophical and psychological explanations, clarifications, and commentaries on the teachings of the Buddha contained in the *suttas/sutras*.

Buddha: Pali and Sanskrit title, derived from the word "*budh*," meaning to awaken, it is used for anyone who has achieved enlightenment (*bodhi*) or awakened to the truth about the way things really are. According to the Theravada tradition, the Buddha was a human being who, as a result of sustained disciplined practice, underwent a profound religious and spiritual transformation. This conception was considerably expanded by the Mahayana tradition to include numerous Buddhas from other worlds. The central function of a Buddha is to teach the *Dhamma* to unenlightened beings.

Dassana/Darsana: Pali and Sanskrit words for "seeing" or "vision," they refer both to what is sought in ritual practices (i.e., seeing and being seen by the gods) and to what is sought from a teacher or spiritual guide. In a philosophical sense, these terms refer to the "system" or "view" of a given thinker and his followers.

Dhamma/Dharma: Perhaps the most ambiguous Pali and Sanskrit terms, they refer to the order of the universe, the nature and proper functioning of things, the basic elements of a thing, the moral law, ethical duties, and truth.

Four Sights: Traditional account of the cause or causes of Siddhattha's renunciation and great departure from his "princely" life to his search for enlightenment. After living a sheltered life, Siddhattha and his charioteer, Channa, leave his home and encounter an old man, a sick man, a corpse, and an ascetic wanderer. The vision of these sights led Siddhattha not only to question his original view of things but also to seek a solution to the suffering and dissatisfaction that are part of the human condition.

Jataka: The Pali term for "birth" and "pre-birth stories" that describe the former lives of the Buddha, Siddhattha Gautama. These tales contain more than 500 birth stories arranged in twenty-two books. Each claims to illustrate the qualities and actions that over the course of numerous lives prepared the way for the arrival of the historical Buddha.

Middle Way: Traditional English name for the enlightened path of the Buddha, *majjhima-patipada* and *madhyama-pratipad* in Pali and Sanskrit. At the most general level it is meant to capture the moral and ethical teaching of the Buddha that one's life and actions should steer a middle course between the extremes of hedonism and asceticism. In the metaphysical and epistemological realms, especially with regard to philosophical questions about human existence and human knowing, it refers to the fact that human souls are neither permanent and eternal nor annihilated, but *anatta* (i.e., lacking a fixed self) instead, and that the ultimate truth in all matters is always somewhere in the middle between extreme positions.

Samana/Sramana: Pali and Sanskrit terms for anyone who leads the life of a religious mendicant or homeless wanderer. As a group, they sought religious and/or philosophical knowledge about the meaning and purpose of life and the fundamental nature of reality. They also rejected the authority and teachings of the Brahmins or the Vedic "vision." The Buddha and his followers were part of this group of religious seekers or strivers.

Samgha: Sanskrit word for "group," this term designates the followers of the Buddha or the Buddhist community. The Buddhist community includes ordained monks and nuns, and male and female lay followers.

Siddhattha Gotama/Siddhartha Gautama: Pali and Sanskrit name of the man known as the historical Buddha. "Siddhattha" was his personal name and "Gotama" was his family or clan name. According to the Buddhist tradition he was born into a leading political family of the Sakya clan, and was also known as "Sakyamuni" – the sage or wise man of the Sakyas.

Sutta/Sutra: Pali and Sanskrit terms for "thread," they refer to the sayings or discourses of the historical Buddha, though they were neither written nor compiled by Siddhattha. In the Pali canon, they are gathered into five "collections" known as *Nikayas* (or *Agamas* in Sanskrit), and grouped according to their lengths. The Mahayana canon, on the other hand, includes many more texts and compilations than the Pali *Nikayas*.

Tipitaka/Tripitaka: Pali and Sanskrit terms meaning "three baskets," which refer to the texts of the Buddhist canon. These include, the

Sutta /Sutra Pitaka, or the basket of sayings or discourses of the Buddha, the *Vinaya Pitaka*, or the basket of monastic rules and discipline, and the *Abhidhamma/Abhidharma Pitaka*, or the basket of higher teachings.

Vedas: From the Sanskrit word, *veda*, meaning "knowledge," this term refers to the earliest collections of Indian religious texts. Strictly speaking, the *Vedas* include the *Rg Veda* (hymns to gods), the *Sama Veda* (songs and instructions based on the *Rg Veda*), the *Yajur Veda* (ritual verses and mantras), the *Atharva Veda* (hymns and magical formulae for ordinary life), the *Brahmanas* (ritual rules), and the *Upanishads*.

Vinaya: Name of the basket of teachings concerned with the monastic rules and discipline of the Buddhist community. These rules, which vary in number between 227 (for men) and 311 (for women), cover the day-to-day activities of the monastic community.

A disclaimer

Although there are many accounts of the life of the man who would become known as "the Buddha," and even more that continue to appear, almost every contemporary account of the life of the historical Buddha begins with a disclaimer about how little we actually know with certainty about even the most basic facts of his life. Although some scholars doubt his historical existence, most believe that we can be reasonably sure that Siddhattha Gotama did in fact exist. Yet aside from this most basic fact there are serious scholarly debates about many events in his life, including when he lived and when he died. Earlier scholars have dated his birth around 550–500 BCE. Recently, however, scholars have suggested a later date, perhaps as late as 350 BCE. Although the technical details of this debate need not detain us, it is important to be aware that scholars continue to study and investigate even this most basic question about his life.

For those who accept the actual historical existence of Siddhattha Gotama as the man who became "the Buddha," the basic facts of his life are really quite few. In fact, one of the most succinct accounts of his life can be found in Michael Carrithers book, *The Buddha*.

According to Carrithers:

The Buddha was born the son of a king, and so grew up with wealth, pleasure and the prospect of power, all goods commonly desired by human beings. As he reached manhood, however, he was confronted with a sick man, an old man and a corpse. He had lived a sheltered life, and these affected him profoundly, for he realized that no wealth or power could prevent him too from experiencing illness, old age and death. He also saw a wandering ascetic, bent on escaping these sufferings. Reflecting on what he had seen, he reached the first great turning-point of his life: against the wishes of his family he renounced home, wife, child and position to become a homeless wanderer, seeking release from this apparently inevitable pain.

For some years he practiced the trance-like meditation, and later the strenuous self-mortification, which were then current among such wanderers, but he found these ineffective. So he sat down to reflect quietly, with neither psychic nor physical rigours, on the common human plight. This led to the second great change in his life, for out of this reflection in tranquility arose at last awakening and release. He had "done what was to be done," he had solved the enigma of suffering. Deriving his philosophy from his experience he then taught for forty-five years, and his teaching touched most problems in the conduct of human life. He founded an order of monks who were to free themselves by following his example, and they spread his teaching abroad in the world. When he died, he died of mortal causes and was wholly dead. But unlike other mortals he would never be reborn to suffer again.[1]

Interestingly enough, Carrithers himself admits that there are good reasons to doubt even this very compressed account of the Buddha's life. Nevertheless, he and many scholars believe that at least the outline of the events in Siddhattha's life must be roughly true. Why do they think this, and what does that outline look like?

An "ordinary" life

If we assume that Siddhattha Gotama was an ordinary human being like the rest of us (and not a divine being or god, as some forms of the later Buddhist tradition hold), we know he had a father, Suddhodana, and a mother, Maya, and came into the world in the usual way humans are conceived and born – postponing for the time being questions about *kamma* and rebirth. He is reported to have had a privileged youth, a sound moral upbringing, and a good education. Having enjoyed the benefits of a good family life, he married and had a son, but at some point, he began to question both the meaning and purpose of his life. Unlike most of us, however, he seems to

---

[1] Carrithers (1983), pp. 2–3.

have had experienced serious misgivings and even existential angst over the prospects of his life as he saw it unfolding. For reasons that were known only to himself (though the Buddhist tradition tried to capture them with its stories of the "Four Sights"), he renounced his wife, son, and family, his friends, his possessions, and his way of life in search of answers to life's greatest problems and questions: Who am I? Why am I here? What is the purpose of my life? Why must I die? What happens after death? Why are things the way they are or seem to be?

The *samanas*

At first, having lived a life full of worldly comforts, Siddhattha decided to try the other extreme and pursued a life of ascetic practices. This was a viable option during his lifetime because many of his contemporaries were renouncing both the traditional forms of life as well as the emerging possibilities of the newly developing urban centers. These wandering philosophers and religious seekers were known as *samanas*.

Conceived of as a whole, the *samanas* can best be thought of as those who held the "heterodox" views of what I shall be describing as the "post-Vedic vision" in the next chapter. As a group, they not only rejected the authority and teachings of the *Vedas* and the Vedic tradition (i.e., the "orthodox" Indian view of life), but they also rejected the new kinds of life developing in the big cities. They wandered about free from the usual family commitments and obligations of ordinary householders, practiced ascetic austerities, and lived on alms. This kind of unencumbered life gave them the opportunity to think about, explore, study, and debate among themselves about the relative truth and value of various views of the meaning and purpose of life and how to live appropriately.

Among the more famous *samanas* were Mahavira and the Jains, Gosala and the Ajivaka fatalists, as well as other groups of materialists, skeptics, and yoga ascetics. Each group had its recognized leaders and teachers to whom others went for advice and guidance. It was to men such as these that Siddhattha first went for help with his religious and philosophical questions and problems.

According to the Buddhist tradition, Siddhattha is reported to have outdone even his most renowned teachers in his efforts to embrace a life of serious self-denial and rigorous austerities. At first, he sought the help and advice of two yoga masters, Alara Kalama and then Uddaka Ramaputra both of whom taught and practiced different systems of meditation and mental concentration. Although Siddhattha quickly mastered both systems, in fact so quickly that each teacher asked him to lead their respective group of followers, he rejected their leadership offers because, while helpful with calming and stilling his mind, their meditative practices did not produce the goal he was eagerly seeking, i.e., enlightenment and the realization of the end of suffering. In fact, the early Buddhist tradition reports that the results of his ascetic practices were no better, and in some ways because of both their physical and psychological consequences, far worse than the outcomes of his earlier life choices and decisions. He continued to experience the same nagging doubts, questions, and uncertainties about his life but now they were exacerbated by grave physical problems.

The "Middle Way"

After six years of experiencing firsthand the frustrating futility of searching for answers at both ends of the material and psychological spectrum of goods and pleasures, Siddhattha, whose name means "one who has achieved his goal," subsequently renounced both his ascetic and hedonistic practices in favor of what the Buddhist tradition has called the "Middle Way" and achieved or realized enlightenment, i.e., he found or discovered what he took to be the answers to his questions. He then decided, or was persuaded by a god (as some early traditions hold), to offer his insights to others who were, like himself, willing to try and test his teachings against their own thoughts and experiences. Having taught a large number of people over the course of a long life, he eventually grew old and died. His effectiveness as both a teacher and a model of the kind of life that he thought was available to all of us, if only we were willing to try and diligently persevere in it, is vouched for by both the sheer number of his followers after his death as well as the durability of his teachings. Indeed, very few human beings have had the kind of impact or left the kind of legacy that Siddhattha Gotama did.

Living in a time of crisis

As we shall see in the next chapter, Siddhattha Gotama lived during the transition from what I shall call the "Vedic vision" to the "post-Vedic vision" in classical Indian thought. The features of each of these visions as I shall outline them are meant to help capture, in a general way, the intellectual environment – the philosophical and religious contexts – in which and against which Siddhattha tried to formulate his own *dassana* or "vision."

As I have already tried to indicate, Siddhattha and his contemporaries found themselves living during an intellectually exciting, but challenging and demanding time. On the one hand, the material and social conditions of ordinary life were undergoing radical changes, as small kin-based and village-based communities were being absorbed and replaced by regional kingdoms and concentrated urban centers. At the level of the community, this meant that a rural, agriculturally based form of social life was gradually beginning to make way for an organized trade-based money economy localized in crowded and impersonal cities. What these changes meant for each individual is difficult to say, but there can be little doubt that there was a loss of traditional forms of living and social relationships, and a demand for specialized skills to survive and succeed in the changing economic marketplace. It does not take a great deal of imagination to see how these kinds of changing material and social conditions would produce both excitement and concern and unease for people.

On the other hand, the intellectual environment was, presumably in response to these changing social conditions, alive with vigorous debate, discussion, and disagreement about the purpose and meaning of life, the value and place of traditional religious rituals and practices, and the long-term moral and ethical effects of new social roles and relationships. At the most personal level, there can be little doubt that individuals engaged in these kinds of philosophical debates were also concerned with questions about their personal destinies and the "karmic" consequences of their own thoughts, words, and deeds. It should not be difficult to imagine Siddhattha Gotama, the historical Buddha, as such an individual.

I want to suggest that if we join the social and intellectual contextual features we have just been considering with the individual facts of the life of Siddhattha, we will get a more complete picture of the man and a better understanding of his teachings. In order to do this, however, we must consult the texts of his followers, since Siddhattha left no personal writings. What, we might ask, did the historical Buddha's immediate followers and the subsequent Buddhist tradition think was important to know about his life in order to understand and believe his claims?

An outline of Siddhattha's life

The basic outline of facts about his life seems clear and easy enough to understand. First, we can see that Siddhattha lived a privileged life. He clearly was not immediately concerned with the basic worries over food, clothing, and shelter. These practical concerns were taken care of by his father and his family. Second, he seems to have had an education in the basic knowledge of his culture and beliefs and he also seems to have been quite naturally curious and critical about the "why" of things. Third, he seems to have fulfilled his duty or obligation as an Indian man and good son to marry and produce a son of his own – so in that respect, at least, he was like any other "ordinary" Indian male. Fourth, despite all of his advantages in life, he seems to have experienced a profound dissatisfaction, perhaps bordering on depression, with the way things were arranged and how his life was proceeding. By some kind of fortuitous, fortunate, or simply karmic juxtaposition of personal qualities and worldly reality Siddhattha experienced a deep and profound unrest with both his life and the ways of the world. Fifth, his dissatisfaction was deep enough to lead him to renounce all of the pleasures and benefits of his comfortable life and to seek his own answers and solutions to the puzzles and questions about life, its purpose, and meaning. Sixth, his initial steps in the search for an answer led him to the opposite extreme of his early life. Having lived a life of worldly pleasure and satisfaction, Siddhattha turned away from these things, to a life of ascetic rigor and sustained self-mortification. Seventh, his experiences at the other end of the pleasure–pain spectrum eventually led him to search for a solution somewhere in the "middle" between hedonism and asceticism. Eighth, his personal commitment and spirit of determination to seek and not rest until the answers were obtained was finally rewarded with his enlightened realization of the truth about the world and himself. Ninth, having considered both his ability to teach his message and his audiences' abilities to understand him, and perhaps with the timely persuasion of a god, he decided to spend the last half of his life teaching others how to find their own way to the truth and liberation. Tenth, and finally, having lived to the ripe old age of eighty, he departed this earthly life and left his teachings as a guide to future seekers and followers of the *Dhamma* path.

When we place these facts of his life against the background of the culture and society in which he was born and raised, and consider the context and conditions in which he lived, a clearer picture of who the historical Buddha was should begin to emerge. In order to help clarify and fill in the details of that picture, however, I want to return to his social situation and ask the reader to imagine, by way of a thought experiment, what it would be like to have the same experiences as Siddhattha or to be in Siddhattha's place. What would you be thinking, feeling, and doing, and why?

Thinking like the Buddha

As we have seen, the historical circumstances during the life of Siddhattha were characterized by significant shifts and changes in basic social, economic, political, cultural, religious, and philosophical ideas and structures. In order to help convey some sense of the excitement as well as the uncertainty, unease, and upheaval these changes were causing Siddhattha and his contemporaries, imagine, for a moment, moving to a new part of town, or to a new part of the country, or even to a new part of the world. Or recall if you can, your own educational and social transitions from the elementary grades to high school to college or the university and graduate school, and finally the move from "school" to the "real world" of gainful employment. Each of these changes and transitions is, to a greater or lesser degree, experienced simultaneously with both excitement and trepidation, with exhilaration and with concern.

On the one hand, these situations are exciting because of their freshness, uncertainty, and their latent possibilities. On the other hand, they are also times of fear, doubt, and anxiety, precisely because their very newness takes us beyond the comfort zone of our ordinary, everyday habitual experiences. In fact, even the slightest changes in our daily routines can sometimes be rather disconcerting because they force us to think and respond to the world in new, creative, and unusual ways. In these types of circumstances, as the current sayings go, we are forced to "think outside the box," and we must "respond in the moment" to unfamiliar situations. Yet what exactly do these sayings mean and how do they help us get a clearer picture of the life and teachings of the historical Buddha?

I want to suggest that if you reflect for a moment on the spectrum of experiences described above, or on the imagined scenarios of moving to other places, and also keep in mind the events in the outline of the life of

Siddhattha Gotama and the social conditions in which they occurred, then I think a number of common features of these events and his life will present themselves for consideration.

There can be little doubt that these events and experiences are unsettling. It also seems rather obvious that rapid and significant personal and social changes upset people. Human beings tend, for better or worse, to be creatures of habit. Most of us are disposed to like things (assuming they are at least tolerable) to remain as they are. After all, there is order and predictability and comfort and safety when things in the world tend to follow regular patterns. The same can also be said about ourselves, and our relationships with other people. Stability, constancy, dependability, and reliability are almost universally recognized as positive qualities of people and their relationships. No one, or very few people, would want or have a friend who was consistently unstable, inconstant, undependable, and unreliable. Nevertheless, the fact remains that our friends and we are often precisely that.

Despite our best efforts to have and make things be the way that we want them to be, we and the things around us tend not to meet our expectations. In fact, if only we stopped and thought about it for a moment, we would soon realize that the most basic, if often overlooked, fact about the world and the people and things in it is that all of it is constantly changing. Somehow our natural and habitual tendency to recognize and seek consistency and dependability overrides both the reality and our awareness of the mutability and impermanence of all things. Our basic awareness of these facts, however, is usually, if only, brought to our attention when things stop being the way they were or have always been, and we are forced to confront the reality of this in our current circumstances. As a result, it is events like those that I have described above that serve as catalysts to wake us from our usual, habituated unawareness and lack of attention to the way things really are. The same kinds of things were happening to the man who would become "Buddha," a title that means "awakened" or "enlightened."

I want to suggest that something similar to these types of experiences is precisely what happened to Siddhattha Gotama, and that it was his particular personal responses to these events and experiences that led him to pursue and ultimately realize the answers to his own philosophical problems and questions.

A philosophical reading of his life

Although neither the Buddha's immediate followers nor the Buddhist tradi-tion ever saw fit, whether accidentally or by design, to preserve and present the facts of his life as a continuous biography, the fact remains that what we do know about his life is that at some point, rather precipitously and unexpectedly, he completely and irrevocably abandoned his safe, orderly, and predictable life for the life of a homeless and wandering *samana*. Moreover, every recent account[2] of the historical Buddha's life includes a detailed description of his renunciation and radical departure from his former way of life and his subsequent quest for enlightenment in a com-pletely new and different kind of life. What this seems to indicate, among other things, is that at least one of the most important facts of his life and character was his willingness to change his thinking and not accept the usual, common, habitual, and expected way of living that seemed to him and many of his contemporaries to lead inevitably to suffering, pain, anxi-ety, and frustration. In other words, at the level of his own life, the Buddhist tradition thought it important to point out that the historical Buddha abandoned what any ordinary Indian male would have desired and pursued as a good and successful life, in order to realize the most basic truth about the world and himself – the most fundamental truth of the *Dhamma* – that both we and the things we perceive are a function of how we see them, and not the other way around.

Understood in that way, the life of the Buddha and the context in which he lived it both serve as points of instruction to help us see what the Buddha himself saw, that "things," including ourselves and the people and the material objects around us, do not exist in the ways we ordinarily think they do, at least not as we take them to be according to common sense. They are not, strictly speaking, even "things" (i.e., discreet, self-contained, independently existing units or beings or substances) in the ordinary sense of that word. They literally are or at least minimally ought to be thought to be, instead, events or processes or happenings that causally interact with other "events" or "processes" or "happenings" in the same ways that the Mississippi river is a happening, or members of a community interacting

[2] Armstrong (2001), Carrithers (1983), Kalupahana and Kalupahana (1982), Nanamoli (1972), Rahula (1974), and Strong (2001).

with each other and the environment in which they live are processes or events. We shall be examining the details of this account of the being of "things" (i.e., the Buddha's metaphysics) as well as the explanation of how we know its truth (i.e., the Buddha's epistemology) in **Chapters 6 and 7**. In the meantime, however, I want to suggest that this "philosophical reading" of the life of Siddhattha Gotama is one way of understanding the facts of his life and their relationship to the social context and conditions in which they happened as well as the teachings or *dassana* they gave rise to.

The benefits of this reading

According to this reading of his biographical facts, at least one of the things that the Buddhist tradition wanted to convey about Siddhattha Gotama was that his very life and the social and cultural conditions and environment in which he lived it could be seen as an object lesson in the teaching of the *Dhamma*. Taken together, they not only provide an important lesson about the kind of person the historical Buddha was, but they also convey what I shall attempt to defend (in **Chapter 2**) as "the Buddha's most basic philosophical insight" as well as his important complementary teaching on interdependent arising – *paticca-samuppada*.

What I want to suggest is that if we look at the outline of facts of Siddhattha's life from this perspective, the individual elements begin to take on a deeper and more complex kind of narrative unity and logical coherence than they otherwise would seem to have at first glance. I also want to suggest that we can begin to make more rational sense of both the *Jataka Tales* and the other elements of his historical biography if we understand them as conveying simultaneously truths about the man Siddhattha as well as the truth of the *Dhamma* itself.

On the one hand, the outline we have constructed can be read as conveying the basic biographical facts of a certain Indian man living around 500 BCE. On the other hand, the individual elements of the outline can be read together as forming a philosophical account of the meaning and purpose of life and the fundamental nature of reality. On this latter reading, we can tell a coherent story about how the parts of the outline fit together to present and explain both the life of the Buddha as well as the Buddha's *dassana*.

Although there are obviously many other ways to read and understand the elements in the life story of the historical Buddha, this "philosophical reading" of them has a number of advantages. These advantages include: its ease of understanding, its simplicity, order, coherence, consistency, agreement with common sense and other ordinary beliefs, its explanatory power, and finally, its appropriateness.

The most obvious advantage is directly related to the question of why the early followers of the Buddha even bothered or did not bother to ask or worry about his biography. I have already noted that neither the Buddha's immediate followers nor the Buddhist tradition ever saw fit to preserve and present the facts of his life as a continuous, self-contained biography. What they did record, the *Tipitaka*, is a collection of the words or teachings of the Buddha, the *Suttas*, the disciplinary rules, or *Vinaya*, for the monastic community of his followers, the *Samgha*, and later, the "higher," and much more detailed philosophical and psychological commentaries on the Buddha's teachings, the *Abhidhamma*. What this seems to indicate, if we take the texts we do have seriously and at their word, is that what the Buddha and his early followers thought was most important was the actual teaching or *Dhamma*, and not the story of how it came to be realized or (re)discovered.

The early followers of the historical Buddha preserved his teachings orally at first, and only years later were they written and compiled as texts. It is not difficult to imagine in these circumstances that the primary goal of both activities was an accurate recollection of the teachings themselves first, and, secondarily, a desire for appropriate practice in response to the teachings. Understood in this way, it is also easy to imagine and understand appealing to instructive examples and situations from the life of Siddhattha Gotama himself as both useful mnemonic devices and also fitting and persuasive ways to convey and reinforce important points of the *Dhamma*. The facts of the life of Siddhattha become, as a result, an easy way of imparting the teachings, which is, interestingly enough, precisely what the Buddha was up to in the last forty-five years of his life.

A clearer picture

If we turn our attention back again to the traditional elements in the life story of Siddhattha, we see that the ten facts of the outline themselves have the advantage of being simple because they present the life of Siddhattha in a straightforward and uncomplicated way. We learn about his family situation, his education and upbringing, his personal experiences and his dedicated search for answers to his questions, his realization of the *Dhamma*, and his subsequent teaching of it.

The facts of the outline are also orderly, coherent, and consistent. They provide a beginning, middle, and an end to the life of the man who would come to be called "Buddha." They offer an account of his life that harmonizes with other things we know about the historical, social, economic, political, religious, intellectual, and cultural contexts in which Siddhattha lived. They not only agree with common sense, but they also help make elements of the later tradition more understandable (i.e., they have explanatory power), as we shall see in **Chapter 4** and **Chapters 9–12**. Moreover, interestingly enough, the story they tell provides a perfect opportunity for the "prequel" karmic account of his previous lives in the *Jataka Tales*.

From the point of view of philosophy, however, the greatest advantage of a "philosophical reading" of the outline of the facts of the life of Siddhattha Gotama is its usefulness and appropriateness as a way of conveying a significant and manageable set of the most important ideas and teachings of the *Dhamma*.

As I said in the **Preface**, we are investigating the teachings of the Buddha and Buddhism as a *philosophy*, with special attention given to its metaphysics and epistemology, and only limited consideration given to its ethics. Given these restrictions, it might appear that there really is no important connection between the events in the life of Siddhattha Gotama and the teachings of the historical Buddha. However, I want to reiterate my earlier claim that knowing something about the story of a philosopher's life and its historical context can help to make the philosopher's thoughts and ideas both real and more readily and easily understandable. It is precisely in this respect, in conjunction with our philosophical approach to the teachings of the Buddha and Buddhism, that I am proposing this "philosophical reading" of his biography.

The ultimate justification for this approach is the simple fact that it is some of the most basic and important metaphysical and epistemological features of his teaching that are captured for the first time and in a preliminary way in the facts of his biography. In other words, what I am suggesting is that the life of Siddhattha Gotama can be usefully read as embodying the very same philosophical ideas that he tried to teach his followers. In short, he lived the principles and ideas he tried to teach and he taught the principles and ideas he lived. This fact was not lost on his immediate followers or the later Buddhist tradition, and they preserved it in the elements of his life story.

Given this reading of his life, I would maintain that the most important metaphysical and epistemological ideas that we are introduced to in this "philosophical reading" of his biography include: *Dhamma*, interdependent arising, *rta*, duty, *kamma*, impermanence, *dukkha*, non-attachment, meditation, the "Middle Way," wisdom, enlightenment, and *nibbana*. We shall be considering each of these ideas in more detail in subsequent chapters.

I should also note, however, that this is not meant to be a complete or exhaustive list of the philosophical ideas and concepts that may be found in the particular facts of the life of Siddhattha Gotama. Rather, they are presented as the more obvious teachings that appear in the outline of the events of his life that we have been considering in this chapter.

Finally, I think it goes without saying that there are clearly other ways[3] of reading and understanding the facts of the biography of the historical Buddha – ways that I have not considered. In fact, I invite and challenge the reader to think about and reflect on these possible alternative readings in order to generate plausible explanations for why the fundamental philosophical ideas and beliefs of this particular man were able, rather easily, to take root in India and flourish throughout Asia and even the rest of the world. Before exploring these subsequent developments, it would be useful to consider in more detail the historical, cultural, and intellectual contexts in which and from which the life and teachings of the man who would become "the Buddha" first emerged. It is to a more detailed account of these contexts that we turn our attention in **Chapter 2**.

Things to think about

1. What effect, if any, does our lack of knowledge about the life of the Buddha have on your understanding of his teachings?
2. Who were the *samanas* and why was their way of life appealing to Siddhattha?

---

[3] Ibid.

3. Why is the Buddha's teaching referred to as the "Middle Way?"
4. Which event(s) in his life contributed the most to the Buddha's teachings? Why?
5. What are the strengths and weaknesses of a "philosophical reading" of the Buddha's life? In addition to the "philosophical reading" of his life proposed in this chapter, how else might one read and understand the story of his life?

2 The contexts for the emergence of Buddhism

Key terms and teachings

Aranyakas: Collection of texts from the *Vedas* compiled by forest ascetics, these texts offer reflections on the meaning of ritual symbols and practices.

Aryans: Traditional name of the people who settled in northern India and whose religious beliefs and practices were recorded in the *Vedas*.

Brahman: Name for ultimate reality or source of power behind all of the gods and rituals spoken of in the *Vedas*.

Brahmanas: Collection of texts from the *Vedas* that explain the meaning and purpose of the Vedic rituals.

Dasyus: Name for one of the groups or tribes of people from northern India who were assimilated by the Aryans.

Interdependent arising: One English translation of the Pali and Sanskrit terms *Paticca-Samuppada* and *Pratitya-Samutpada*, these terms have been variously translated as, "dependent origination," "conditioned co-production," "co-dependent origination," "inter-dependent-origination," or "interdependent arising." Each of these is an attempt to capture the Buddha's account of causality.

Kamma/Karma: Pali and Sanskrit terms for "act" or "action," they refer to the connection between actions and their consequences that affect one's life both in this world and after death.

Moksa: The ultimate goal of many forms of Indian religious and philosophical practices, this term means liberation or release from the cycle of *samsara*.

Nibbana/Nirvana: Literally, "to extinguish" or "blow out," these Pali and Sanskrit terms refer initially to release from *samsara* and the end of suffering. The Buddha reinterprets these terms to mean the extinguishing of the fires of greed, hatred, and delusion.

Rta: Name for the underlying structure and ordering of the universe and events taking place in it. It is the law-like regularity and harmony of both the moral and physical aspects of the universe.

Samsara: Literally, "wandering on," this term refers to the cycle of birth, life, death, and subsequent rebirth in ancient Indian philosophy and religion.

Upanishad: Literally, "to sit down near," this word refers to the last part of the *Vedas*. The texts of this part of the *Vedas* consist of more purely philosophical reflections on the nature of self and the ultimate nature of reality.

Varna: Literally, "color," this term refers to the four main social classes in ancient India: the priestly Brahmins, the warrior Kshatriyas, the merchant Vaishyas, and the peasant Shudras. This term is often mistaken for *jati* (birth status), which refers to one's caste or station in society.

Vedas: From the Sanskrit word, *veda*, meaning "knowledge," this term refers to the earliest collections of Indian religious texts. Strictly speaking, the *Vedas* include the *Ṛg Veda* (hymns to gods), the *Sama Veda* (songs and instructions based on the *Ṛg Veda*), the *Yajur Veda* (ritual verses and mantras), the *Atharva Veda* (hymns and magical formulae for ordinary life), the *Brahmanas* (ritual rules), and the *Upanishads*.

Yoga: Literally, "to yoke, or bind," this term refers to ascetic meditative techniques for disciplining the mind and body in order to achieve "higher" knowledge and escape the bondage and suffering of *samsara*.

A reminder

Given our preliminary sketch of the life of Siddhattha Gotama outlined in **Chapter 1** and my suggestion that we pursue a "philosophical reading" of the story of his life in order to understand the phenomenon of Buddhism more clearly, it is now necessary to provide a richer and more detailed account of the various contexts in which and from which his life and teachings emerged. In this chapter we shall explore these contexts as a series of "visions" or "ways" of looking at the world and reality.

Indian "visions" of reality

One way of analyzing the basic elements of classical Indian thought is to think of them as the intellectual products or insights of a series of transitions in what we might call the "Indian Way"[1] of encountering reality.

---

[1] This designation is inspired, in part, by John M. Koller's (2006) excellent text, *The Indian Way: An Introduction to the Philosophies and Religions of India.*

Conceived of in this way, we can think of the ancient Indians as offering us at least three distinct "visions" of reality. The first "vision," what we might call the vision of the Dasyus or the pre-Aryan or pre-Vedic view of things, seems to have countenanced belief in many gods, nature worship, fertility rituals, concerns about purification, and some basic ideas about both an afterlife and the possibilities of reincarnation. According to some scholars, the last two points, in particular, appear to be anchored in simple observations about the cycle of birth–life–death in nature and obvious family resemblances. Recent archaeological evidence also supports the claim that the Dasyus appear to have been vegetarians who engaged in ascetic practices and yogic meditation.

The second Indian "vision," the vision of the Aryans and the *Vedas*, builds upon this early view of things and seems to have formalized it with ritual sacrifices and celebrations, the production of sacred texts concerned with the "wisdom" of poet-seers, and liturgical formulae and chants about what had been heard and seen. This view also contains the "philosophical" reflections and speculations of the *Upanishads*.

The third and final "vision," what we might, for the sake of simplicity, call the post-Vedic vision, is actually a more sustained, careful, and detailed working out of the individual elements of the pre-Vedic and Vedic views of things. This rather complex vision includes a clarification and specification of the roles of the gods (or a denial of their existence) and their relation to the ultimate, single source of all things (i.e., Brahman), a delineation of the details of the *varna*/color and caste systems, as well as an account of the stages of life and the various aims of life. It also contains more serious reflection on the cyclical nature of birth–life–death and the notions of rebirth and the prospects of release or liberation from this cosmic cycle. At a more fine-grained level of consideration, this third "vision" includes what scholars have identified as the nine *dassanas* of classical Indian thought, i.e., Samkhya, Yoga, Mimamsa, Vedanta, Nyaya, Vaisheshika, Jain, Carvaka, and Buddhist views.[2] Finally, it involves an elucidation of the notions and relations of the self and society and social regulation through the ideas of norms, duties, obligations, virtues, *kamma*, and *dhamma*.

What begins to emerge from this series of "visions" is, I think, a rather rich and complex understanding of reality that includes features that are

---

[2] Following Mohanty (2000), pp. 153–158.

both "philosophical" and "religious"/"theological"[3] in our Western senses of these terms. In fact, before delving into the details of these visions, I think it is possible at this point at least to get some preliminary sense of the intellectual and cultural milieu that supported the social and intellectual development of Siddhattha Gotama and his emergence as the historical Buddha.

If, at first glance, we use the conceptual categories of "philosophy" (i.e., a bottom-up activity that moves from human experience and rational reflection on it to a reasoned explanation of reality, or a way of life focused on the search for an organized body of knowledge about whatever exists, seeking an ultimate explanation of reality through the use of reason alone) and "religion" (i.e., a top-down enterprise that moves from divine existence and revelation to an understanding of creation, or a way of life concerned with "divine," "transcendent," or "superhuman" agencies [whether one or many in number] and our human responses to it or them as these are understood in the West), then I think we can classify the elements of each of the three visions we have distinguished as either "Indian philosophy" or "Indian religion" or both. For example, the Dasyu beliefs in many gods, nature worship, and fertility and purification rituals are clearly "religious" kinds of beliefs. These same "religious" or "theological" beliefs are also part of the Vedic vision of the Aryans who formalized them with ritual texts and the Brahminical priesthood. But it is also important to recall that this same Vedic vision includes the purely "philosophical" reflections and arguments of the *Upanishads*. In fact, when conceived of as a whole, it is useful to think of the *Vedas* themselves as a complex, simultaneously religious and philosophical reconciliation, merging the pre-Vedic and Aryan views of reality. The *Vedas* contain virtually every element and theme of the pre-Vedic vision of the Dasyus as well as the wisdom of their own seers and hearers: hymns for deities, rules for fire sacrifices, music, poetry, magic rituals, and ideas about *rta*, *kamma*, *samsara*, and the afterlife. The *Upanishads*, on the other hand, continue to develop these themes in a more strictly "philosophical" way. In fact, it is this philosophical working out of the same themes and their logical implications as the post-Vedic vision that provides the immediate historical, cultural, and intellectual context within which the life and

---

[3] For an interesting and persuasive analysis of this distinction see Fitzgerald (2000). For more on the ongoing debate about the status of religious studies and for other views of the matter see *Religious Studies Review* (volume 27, number 2/April 2001 and volume 27, number 4/October 2001).

teachings of Siddhattha Gotama were formed. As a result, I think it is safe to say that the post-Vedic vision that was formed both during and after the life of the historical Buddha is what we in the West would call "Indian philosophy" strictly or properly speaking.

Siddhattha's cultural context

Siddhattha, like many great thinkers, was born into a rich, complex, and dynamic social and historical setting. On the one hand, he inherited an Indian culture rich in philosophical and religious beliefs and practices. Not only were his contemporaries interested in securing the material goods necessary for subsistence, such as food, clothing, and shelter, but they were also profoundly interested in trying to understand the purpose and meaning of life and the fundamental nature of reality. In fact, Sue Hamilton[4] has pointed out that in India it was traditionally believed that the activity of philosophizing was directly associated with one's personal destiny. She also notes that what we in the West tend to distinguish as religion and philosophy were actually combined in India in people's attempts to understand both the meaning and structure of life and the nature of reality. In other words, in India, especially at the time when Siddhattha was alive, the two activities of practicing philosophy and religion were actually two interrelated or interdependent aspects of the same inner or spiritual quest.

On the other hand, in addition to his personal and cultural wealth, Siddhattha was born into a society in the midst of great social and political changes. His was a time when the certainties of traditional ways of thinking and living were being challenged by the new and unsettling problems arising out of the breakdown of tribal federations and the development of powerful monarchies and emerging urban centers. Siddhattha lived in the midst of a transition from an agrarian, village-based economy to a city-based form of life with all of its attendant problems and possibilities.

Like many great thinkers, Siddhattha's life may be seen as the fortuitous coming together of the right man with the right abilities at the right time in the right circumstances, bringing about a truly amazing solution to a very serious situation. It is precisely this image of an appropriately qualified person and a portentous opportunity fortuitously (and/or karmicly?) coming together – what Peter Hershock[5] refers to as "virtuosity" – that I want to

---

[4] Hamilton (2001), p. 1.   [5] Hershock (1996), p. 110.

employ as a heuristic to help present and explain the conceptual and historical context for the emergence of Buddhism. I want to do this for three
reasons: first, it is a helpful pedagogical device; second, it is, as far as we
know, historically true; and third, it perfectly captures one of the most basic
and important ideas of the Buddha's own teachings – interdependent arising.[6]

As far as Indian thought is concerned, I have already indicated that India
had a rich history of "philosophical" and "religious" debate about the purpose and meaning of life and the fundamental nature of reality. In fact, I
have suggested that one way of considering the basic elements of classical
Indian thought is to think of them as the intellectual products or insights of
a series of transitions in the "Indian Way" of encountering or viewing
reality. In short, these "visions" formed the intellectual and cultural matrix
in which and from which the teachings of the historical Buddha arose.

Details of the pre-Vedic vision

As we have seen, the Dasyu or pre-Vedic "vision" of reality (circa 2500 BCE),
which is not supported by primary texts but rather by archaeological evidence and the writings of their successors, is rooted in nature worship and
beliefs in multiple gods. Other features of this *dassana* include purification
and fertility rituals, vegetarianism, asceticism, yoga, and some rudimentary
ideas about an afterlife and the possibility of rebirth. Although it is not
possible to be certain about how these basic beliefs were formed, it is not
difficult to imagine an ancient agricultural people and their ordinary problems and concerns.

To begin, it is obvious that the basic facts of every human life include
practical concerns about food, clothing, and shelter. There are also environmental concerns about one's life and safety in the face of nature and its
power as well as concerns about wild animals and other human beings.
Once these basic biological needs and environmental concerns are met and
addressed, it is natural to assume that ancient people turned their attention
to deeper "metaphysical" questions about the point and purpose of living
and dying since presumably these were the basic facts of ordinary life.

Little reflection is required for one to realize that many things in the world
are beyond human control, and it is often difficult, if not impossible, to know
or predict future events and circumstances, such as the weather and seasons

[6] See Chapter 6.

and natural disasters. However, it is also quite clear that many of these very same forces and events in nature seem to follow patterns, even predictable cyclical patterns. The sun rises and sets, the moon waxes and wanes, the tides rise and fall, and the seasons come and go in relative order and stability. It should not be difficult to imagine ancient Indians being concerned with questions about what the source or sources of this apparent order and pattern are. Furthermore, it is easy to imagine them asking if the order itself is real or merely apparent. Finally, if things are not in their control, then one could imagine them asking themselves whether there is some thing or things that does or do control or explain the order and pattern.

The best available evidence seems to indicate that the ancient Dasyu way of understanding and dealing with the ordinary questions and problems of life was to recognize some superhuman or divine sources of power behind or in the forces and events in nature. They also seem to have realized that nature itself exercised a kind of control over human affairs. The Dasyus recognized the immutable and inexorable truth that humans are born, live, and die, but they also appear to have held the view, based on their burial practices, that death was not the end of life. It is, however, unknown whether they clearly distinguished between rebirth in a different world in some other location or simply rebirth in this world at some future time. Whether they had considered some kind of causal (i.e., karmic) explanation of either possible rebirth scenario is unclear as well. Nevertheless, it is intriguing and important to those interested in philosophy to consider just why someone might think that there is some kind of life or existence after this life and what its causes and conditions might be. What kind of case could be made?

The question of life after death

Traditionally, there have been two kinds of cases for believing that there is life or existence after death. The first kind of case, a religious or theological case, is anchored in some kind of revelation from a god or gods about the, or an afterlife. In this scenario someone claims to have heard or received a message about what awaits or happens to those who die, and others choose to believe both the message and the person who has received the revelation. The second kind of case, a philosophical or scientific case, is justified by observations about the way things appear to happen in nature or the world, and logical inferences to the best explanation as a way to make sense out of the data of experience. In this kind of case, one recognizes through observation that things and events in nature appear to follow regular and orderly patterns or cycles: the rising and setting of the sun, the waxing and waning of the moon, the movements of the tides, and the changes of the seasons, all of which occur in relative order and stability. In addition to these obvious facts, plants and crops seem to follow seasonal and annual patterns of growth, maturation, fruition, and death; in the cases of perennial flowers and plants, the "same" plants and flowers appear to return year after year after year. Similarly, few would deny that animal offspring often look very much like their parents. The same is also true for human beings, especially in cases where a child is the "spitting image" of a deceased parent or grandparent or other relative. How can such likenesses be rationally explained?

One ancient Indian account, that I am ascribing to the Dasyus or the pre-Vedic "vision," is to claim that the similarities and patterns or cycles that we experience in our interactions with nature and other human beings are best explained by appealing to the idea of rebirth: that it is literally the exact same individual who has been born, lived, died, and then been reborn all over again. This kind of inference is justified as being the best explanation for the puzzling and sometimes overwhelming experience of observing someone who not only looks, and acts, but also speaks and sounds like another deceased human being.

The same kind of inference and justification can be used to explain causal activity in the world. Without going into all of the details of *kamma* as a physical, metaphysical, and ethical theory of causation (which we shall do in **Chapter 5**), we can at this point, at least, say something about how the idea might arise.

Kamma?

Consider the same data of experience that we have been considering, especially in an agricultural community setting. The sun rises and sets, the moon waxes and wanes, the tides rise and fall, and the seasons come and go in relative order and stability. Humans, plants, and animals are born, grow, mature, and die. Humans interact with one another and the world around themselves, and events and outcomes seem to follow regular patterns. The same kinds of seeds produce the same kinds of trees, which in turn produce the same kinds of fruit and the same seeds all over again. The same kinds of animals produce the same kinds of offspring and the results of similar kinds of human actions tend, always or almost always, to be the same, and for that matter, even predictably so. In general, when I do action X to object Y at time T, the result is always, or nearly always, the same. How can one make sense of this?

One ancient Indian account, whose origin and roots are unknown, is to claim that the similarities in outcomes that we experience in our interactions with nature and other human beings are best explained by appealing to the agricultural idea of seeds and their fruits. Actions, whether human or natural, like seeds, produce fruits or outcomes or effects, based on the kinds of seeds they are. Apple seeds produce apple trees that produce apples that once again produce apple seeds. Cows produce cows that produce more cows. Humans produce humans that produce more humans. So by extension, human actions, whether "morally good," "morally bad," or "morally neutral," produce outcomes or results that are causally determined by the kind of actions they are. "Good" actions produce good effects and "bad" actions produce bad effects. In general, effects follow from their causes in the same way that fruit comes from seeds. In other words, the world and events happening around us seem to follow law-like, regular patterns.

Whether this regularity is real, or apparent and merely perceived, whether it is a necessary relation or merely a statistical probability or correlation, whether it is a real feature of the world or the result of a psychological habit built up over time in human observers, the fact remains that the ancient Indians used the idea of *kamma* to make sense out of and explain what was happening around them. Like the idea of rebirth, the idea of *kamma* provides a plausible and rational explanation for things and events that are happening around us. Moreover, for the ancient Indians, these ideas seem to have been among the most basic insights of their "vision" and understanding of reality. Whether and how these two basic insights are related to one another we shall consider in more detail in **Chapter 5**. For the time being, I am introducing them as important elements of an ancient Indian vision of the world, and I am suggesting that early on in the Indian philosophical attempts to understand the meaning and purpose of life as well as the nature of reality it was not thought irrational or illogical to appeal to the ideas of rebirth and *kamma* as a first and perhaps best and only explanation of the data of experience.

As a matter of fact, it is important to keep in mind that we are here dealing with one of the first sustained attempts to make "philosophical" sense of the world. The tools of rational justification and critique were just being forged in response to questions and problems that arise only when the basic biological requirements for food, clothing, and shelter have been satisfactorily met. We should also keep in mind that it is unclear, and perhaps ultimately unknowable, exactly how the other elements of this pre-Vedic "vision" of things relate to one another.

While it is certainly interesting to speculate on the logical possibilities of a unified Dasyu "vision" of the world that includes a coherent conception of the relationships among their supposed beliefs (i.e., in vegetarianism, asceticism, polytheism, and an afterlife) as well as their yogic meditation practices, such an exercise can only be conducted as a thought experiment. Moreover, we should remember that this "vision" itself is not only reconstructed from inferences based on archaeological evidence, but it is also supported by reports from those who succeeded and, in all likelihood, conquered the originators of the view. It is to this second, Aryan Vedic "vision" that we now turn our attention.

Details of the Vedic vision

What I am calling the Vedic "vision" of reality (circa 1500–500 BCE), which, for my purposes, is found in both the *Vedas* and the *Upanishads*, is an understanding of life and reality that emerged from a complex cultural and intellectual process of absorption, assimilation, rejection, and revision of Dasyu beliefs and practices. Although there is much historical ignorance and uncertainty about both the geographical origins of the Aryans as a people and culture, and their subsequent arrival and impact on the Indus Valley civilization of the Dasyus, there is no doubt that during the second millennium BCE the Aryans, who spoke and wrote a form of proto-Sanskrit, replaced the Dasyus as the dominant people of the Indus Valley. The basic elements of their account of the purpose and meaning of life and the fundamental nature of reality are recorded in the *Vedas*, the *Brahmanas*, *Aranyakas*, and later the *Upanishads*. These elements, which were "heard" and "remembered" by poet-seers and sages, include an initial polytheism (later replaced by the monism/monotheism of the *Upanishads*), and formalized ritual fire sacrifices performed by priests. Other features of this *dassana* include a gradual acceptance of vegetarianism, non-violence, asceticism, yoga, *kamma*, and belief in rebirth and the cyclical nature of reality and existence.

Just as there are serious scholarly doubts and uncertainties about the formation of the pre-Vedic "vision," there are similar problems and questions about exactly how the basic features of the Vedic "vision" were formed. Without getting bogged down in the details of these academic debates, we should point out that regardless of worries about their origins and production, the fact remains that the elements of what I am calling the Vedic "vision" have the notable advantage of being recorded in texts.

The texts themselves seem to indicate that the religious and philosophical beliefs and practices of the Aryans underwent two distinct but related types of development. On the one hand, they appear to have absorbed and eventually replaced Dasyu beliefs and practices. On the other hand, they seem, gradually over time, to have undergone an internal development and deepening penetration of vision and understanding. In other words, what I want to suggest is that the Vedic "vision" sublated, in the sense of retained yet transcended, the pre-Vedic Dasyu "vision" while simultaneously, over a period of some 500–1000 years, deepening its own insight and vision of reality and the meaning and purpose of life. This development, from the *Vedas* themselves to the later *Upanishads*, can be captured schematically, following Koller,[7] as follows:

Vedic "vision"	Upanishadic "vision"
Texts: *Vedas, Brahmanas, Aranyakas*	Texts: *Upanishads*
Many gods	Brahman
This-worldly focus	Other/Spiritual-world focus
Primary value: earthly success	Primary value: liberation/*moksa*
Key to perfection: ritual	Key to perfection: knowledge
Emphasis on community	Emphasis on the individual seeker
Importance of prayer	Importance of meditation/yoga
Cycle of nature and perhaps rebirth	*Samsara* as fundamental problem
Kamma recognized but not important	*Kamma* as all-important
Emphasis on plurality of existence	Emphasis on unity of existence
"Self" is body and mind	"Self" is *Atman* that is *Brahman*
Existence as conflict/struggle	Non-violence
Sharing in divine power	Being divine
Rta	*Kamma* and *Dhamma*
Supported by Mimamsa philosophy	Supported by Vedanta philosophy

[7] Koller (2006), p. 58.

What this table tries to capture in simple form is the rather complex notion of what I am referring to as the Vedic "vision." It is a schematic version of the fundamental ideas contained in the *Vedas* and the *Upanishads*.

At first glance, it should be rather obvious that what I am calling the Vedic "vision" is in reality something far more complex and complicated than the single vision name I am employing to denominate it. In fact, as the table indicates, this "vision" includes a relative spectrum of historically distinct beliefs about important philosophical concepts and ideas. Despite the apparent oversimplification, I think this way of presenting the Vedic "vision" has the advantage of capturing most, if not all, of the important religious and philosophical ideas that came to form the immediate historical, intellectual, and cultural context from which and against which the teachings of Siddhattha arose. I shall have more to say about the specific elements of this vision when we consider them as features of the nine classical *dassanas* or philosophical schools of ancient India. Before considering the nine schools, however, I first want to complete my account of the three "visions" of Indian thought by outlining a third, post-Vedic "vision" as the immediate contemporary of and successor to the teachings of the historical Buddha.

Details of the post-Vedic vision

The post-Vedic "vision" (after 500 BCE) was a more careful, rigorous, and systematic working out of the details of the Vedic and pre-Vedic "visions" of things. It was also, simultaneously, the source of the nine classical systems or schools of Indian philosophy. In fact, it is instructive and helpful to think of this third vision as being constituted by the individual visions of its nine schools in the same way that white light is the product of the seven colors of the visible spectrum. Each individual color/school has its own unique features and history, and when appropriately harmonized they interdependently give rise to the post-Vedic view of things.

This rather complex "vision" included a clarification and specification of the roles of the various deities of the pre-Vedic and Vedic "visions" (or their non-existence) and their relations to the ultimate, single source of all things (i.e., Brahman of the *Upanishads*), a delineation of the details of the *varna/*color and social caste systems, and the enumeration of the stages of life, and the various possible aims of individual lives. It also contained more serious and sustained philosophical reflection, and, in fact, vigorous disagreement over the possible outcomes of the cyclical nature of birth–life–death as well as the notions of rebirth and the prospects of release or liberation from this cosmic cycle. Finally, it involved more sustained philosophical debate about the notions and relations of the "self" and society (i.e., metaphysical and epistemological thinking) and social regulation (i.e., ethical thinking) through the increasingly complex ideas of norms, duties, obligations, virtues, *kamma*, and *Dhamma*.

It goes without saying that the living and social reality of all of this was clearly far more complex and complicated than my simple distinguishing of Indian thought into three "visions" would indicate. In fact, the division of Indian thought into the nine classical *dassanas* is itself a simplification of a richer and more complex spectrum of historically and philosophically distinct set of views. Moreover, when we turn our attention to these various "schools" or systems we encounter a number of ideologically distinct and mutually exclusive accounts of the meaning and purpose of life and the fundamental nature of reality. In short, what is commonly designated as the teachings of Siddhattha Gotama is actually just one of these nine classical systems.

It is important to realize that the systems or *dassanas* themselves represent, in rather broad strokes, a full spectrum of both logical and real possible positions with respect to the fundamental ideas contained in the pre-Vedic, Vedic, and post-Vedic "visions." In the light of the initial outlines of the three visions already presented, we may now consider these other systems in more detail as a prelude to our account of Buddhism.

Nine *dassanas*

It may be helpful to begin our consideration of the nine classical systems of Indian thought by noting that the Buddhist tradition[8] itself refers to no fewer than sixty-two kinds of wrong views on matters as diverse as the past, the self, the world, pleasure, the mind, good and bad, chance, the future, life after death, *nibbana*, and even the teaching on interdependent arising. The Buddha himself not only compares these wrong views to a fishnet, but he also actually refers to them as a net of views – a net that catches and holds

---

[8] *Digha Nikaya*, *Brahmajala Sutta*: *The Supreme Net*, pp. 67–90.

those who hold them. It should be clear from these facts that there were many more than nine systems or views with regard to the topics just mentioned. For the sake of clarity and simplicity, however, we shall divide these views into just nine major systems or *dassanas*.

From what has already been said about the history of the three "visions," it should not be surprising that the roots of Indian philosophical orthodoxy are traced to the *Vedas* and the *Upanishads*. In fact, the traditional and perhaps easiest way of capturing the distinctions among the classical systems of Indian philosophy is to categorize them as "orthodox" and "unorthodox" or "heterodox" based on whether they accept or reject the basic "truth" of the *Vedas* and the *Upanishads*. It should be noted, however, that even though it is somewhat misleading to suggest that both sets of texts share the exact same "vision" of reality, for our purposes, I have combined them as part of the "Vedic vision" in order to simplify and clarify a rather complex situation. These are, after all, the first written texts that convey the basic elements of what one might call "the Indian view of the world." Not only were these texts and their words regarded by the religious leaders of ancient India, the Brahmins, as the primary sources of truth about the ultimate meaning and purpose of life and the fundamental nature of reality, but they also were compiled by those with the power, both materially and spiritually, to confirm their truth and ensure their acceptance and continuing influence. It should not be surprising, therefore, to see the religious and philosophical landscape of India, especially at the time of the Buddha, defined by one's relationship to the Vedic "vision."

Six "orthodox" *dassanas*

According to the Indian tradition six systems or *dassanas* are recognized as "orthodox." These include: the Samkhya, Yoga, Mimamsa, Vedanta, Nyaya, and Vaisheshika systems.

According to the Samkhya view, whose name means reason or discriminating knowledge, reality, which is ultimately dualistic (i.e., consists of two irreducible modes of being or existence) in nature, can be classified into twenty-five categories of matter (*prakriti*) and spirit (*purusha*) – the two most basic principles of being. This view also maintained that reality consists of three elements – water, fire, and air – as well as three qualities (*gunas*) that helped to explain the material constitution of things – lightness or mental activity (*sattva*), energy or activity (*rajas*), and inertia or dullness (*tama*). This vision, which is sometimes described as an atheistic naturalism,[9] admitted an eternal self, numerically distinct for each individual. As Mohanty claims, "In its mature form, it developed a theory of evolution of the empirical world out of the original, undifferentiated nature."[10] In fact, the three qualities or *gunas* of material being, which were originally in a state of equilibrium, were disturbed by contact with spirit or *purusha*. The subsequent evolution of the physical world is a progressive and uneven scattering or intermingling of the three *gunas* and spirit. The causal mechanism of this activity is explained by arguing that effects pre-exist in their causes, in order to avoid the logical and metaphysical problem of something coming from nothing. At the same time, each unique, individual spirit experiences attachment to its materially composite body as a result of failing to distinguish its true "spirit-self" from the composite that is itself a product of nature and its causes. According to this view, release or *moksa* from this condition, which is a return to the state of an unmixed spirit, is achieved by realizing or understanding or knowing that the "spirit-self" is really metaphysically different from matter and nature.

Subsequently, over time, this rather speculative metaphysical view of the world came to be paired with the more practical or ethically focused system of Yoga. According to the Yoga view of things, ontological dualism is metaphysically correct, but there is also a recognition that in addition to matter and individual spirits, there is a divine or supreme being, a God or Self that exists. Following the Samkhya idea that there is a real metaphysical difference between spirit and matter, the Yoga view insists that the composite being leads the true spirit-self to mistake itself for the composite. The solution to this misidentification, and ultimately to release or *moksa*, is the development of discriminating insight or knowledge that is achieved through the disciplined meditation of yoga. It is the practice of yoga meditation that enables the true self to overcome its ignorance and liberate itself from its bondage and attachment to the material and physical.

The third (and fourth) classical Indian system is called Mimamsa, which means exegesis. Without getting too detailed, it should be noted that this system is traditionally divided into an early (Purva Mimamsa) and later (Uttara Mimamsa or Vedanta) version.

---

[9] Mohanty (2000), pp. 4–5.   [10] Ibid., p. 5.

In general, holders of this view, at least in its earliest version, disagree with the Samkhya and Yoga belief that knowledge alone is sufficient for release from bondage. According to the early version of this *dassana*, ritual practice is what is essential for *moksa*. At the same time, however, those who maintain this early view appear to be ambivalent about the existence of God or a supreme being. On the one hand, they reject typical arguments for God's existence, but on the other hand, they also recognize an ontological category of potency or power that seems to include supernatural agency. Nevertheless, the most important element of the Mimamsa vision of reality (taken as a whole) is its rather elaborate system for understanding and interpreting the *Vedas*.

As part of their science of interpretation, Mimamsa thinkers believe that words themselves are the ultimate source of knowledge and that they serve as a direct means of truth. They also argue that true cognition originates from multiple sources, including: perception, logical inferences, verbal utterances, simple comparison, and postulation. As Koller[11] points out, the chief concern of Mimamsa philosophers, at least in its early version, is to work out a theory of knowledge that accommodates scriptural testimony as a valid means of knowledge and, on that basis, to provide a science of scriptural interpretation that captures and explains the meaning and truth of the *Vedas*, especially the ritualistic *Brahmanas*.

The later Mimamsa or Vedanta philosophers focused their attention on the more philosophical and non-ritualistic *Upanishads*. While initially accepting the authority of the early *Vedas*, the Uttara Mimamsa emphasized knowledge, instead of ritual, as the means to liberation. However, at least some Vedanta thinkers insisted that ritual-type devotion was a means of relating to and knowing Brahman. Not surprisingly, following the *Upanishads*, they argued that Brahman is the ultimate reality, and that the "true self" is, in the final analysis, the same as Brahman, and that knowledge of this truth was essential for *moksa*.

Taken together, the two versions of the Mimamsa exegetical system represent the ritual and gnostic branches of the Brahminical tradition whose roots can be traced back to the fifth century BCE. These complementary halves of the Vedic and post-Vedic vision ultimately came to be known as the action/*kamma* and knowledge/*jnana* interpretations of the *Vedas*.

---

[11] Koller (2006), p. 247.

The fifth and sixth classical systems of Indian thought are the Nyaya, and Vaisheshika views. The Nyaya *dassana* is basically concerned with questions and problems in logic. Its roots may be traced back to the non-theistic belief that faulty reasoning and/or logical mistakes are the cause of suffering and attachment, and that one can arrive at the truth and ultimately liberation by correcting fallacious reasoning. In order to root out mistakes in reasoning, Nyaya thinkers analyzed reality into various logic-based categories, all of which could be proven to exist. In fact, the philosophers of this school worked out an entire epistemological theory of logic, rational argumentation, and proof, as well as an account of valid knowledge. Their ideas in logic and epistemology were subsequently adopted by their "sister system," the Vaisheshika, from whom the Nyaya borrowed their metaphysical views of reality and the self. This sharing of ideas led in time to a nominal joining of the views as the Nyaya-Vaisheshika.

The Vaisheshika contribution to the union was an account of the particularities of all real things. Their pluralistic realism, which involved an atomistic theory of the material world, was rooted in six ontological categories, including: substance, quality, action, universal, particularity, and inherence. They employed these categories to demonstrate the incompatibility of spirit and matter. They also claimed that "God" made the physical world out of pre-existent elemental substances. More importantly, they argued that through logical analysis one could arrive at a sound knowledge of all things, including the mind and the true eternal self, and that such knowledge was the only source of liberation from attachment and enslavement to matter.

These six *dassanas* or interpretations of the *Vedas* and the *Upanishads* are collectively referred to as the *astika* – "so-sayers"[12] – systems because they are in general agreement, despite their particular differences, with respect to their acceptance of the authority and truth of what I am calling the "Vedic vision" of the purpose and meaning of life as well as the fundamental nature of reality. Their acceptance of the *Vedas* and the *Upanishads* also justifies their designation as the "orthodox" schools. The remaining three classical systems of Indian thought, the Jain, the Carvaka, and the Buddhist *dassanas*, are collectively referred to as the *nastika* – "deniers or rejecters"[13] – systems because they all, in their own unique ways, reject the authority and truth of the Vedic scriptures and tradition.

[12] Renard (1999), p. 90.   [13] Ibid.

Three "heterodox" *dassanas*

According to the Jain view of things, there is a sharp distinction between spirit and matter or souls and bodies. The first kind of beings, spiritual beings (*jiva*) are beings that are alive, and the second kind of beings, material beings or non-spiritual beings (*ajiva*) are not alive. Bondage to the cycle of birth, life, death, and rebirth for spiritual beings is caused by their karmic actions. The specifics of this account of rebirth involve the idea that karmic actions by spiritual beings causally produce material particles that are attracted to the soul's spiritual energy and thereby bind themselves to the spiritual self. The continuing union of the soul and matter that results from karmic action is itself caused by both ignorance and attachment that results from the passions, wants, and desires of spiritual beings. There is, however, a way out of the soul's bondage through the practice of moral living, meditation, and great ascetic austerities. In fact, the ultimate cause of release is the acquisition of knowledge or insight into the soul's samsaric situation by way of a kind of awakening or extraordinary insight into the true, pure, and unsullied nature of the soul or self. This profound insight also includes the recognition that the only way to experience liberation is to destroy, by ascetic mortification – preferably in a monastic setting – the accumulated "material" karmic consequences of prior actions and avoid all future karmic action. In addition to these ethical and metaphysical claims, Jain thinkers also reject the sacrificial rituals of the *Vedas* as well as the monism of the *Upanishads*.

From the epistemic point of view, the Jains claimed that reality has an infinity of aspects, and that all truth claims can be confirmed by perception, logical inferences, or verbal testimony. As a result of their ontological pluralism, they also claimed that all truths are relative to a specific frame of reference. In other words, every claim or proposition is true from a certain point of view and false from some other point of view.

Given this account of the basic features of the Jain view of reality, it should not be surprising that they deny the existence of a single "God" or divine being, but simultaneously affirm the existence of multiple gods or divine beings. In fact, Jain thinkers insist that each individual soul or spirit has the capacity, through severe ascetic practice, to develop infinite consciousness or omniscience, infinite power or omnipotence, and absolute happiness or eternal bliss. All that is necessary for this ultimate achievement is sufficiently severe ascetic practices that eliminate impure and harmful thoughts, words, and deeds.

The second "heterodox" classical Indian view is the Carvaka *dassana*. According to this materialist system, only material things exist, and as a result, there are no immaterial beings and hence no spiritual selves. Since matter is the only reality, there is no afterlife (precisely because there is no existence beyond the physical, material world), and consequently, no *kamma*, no karmic bondage, and no possibility of *moksa* or *nibbana*. Like all materialists, Carvaka thinkers maintained that the only reliable source of knowledge is sense experience, and the goal of life is the pursuit of pleasure and the avoidance of pain.

While individual materialists disagreed about the number and kind of basic material elements from which all material things are composed, they appear to be unanimous in their denial of *moksa* or *nibbana* and affirmation of causal determinism. Their argument for the latter view appears to be anchored in their belief that true knowledge is justified by sense experience only.

Without going into the details of their specific arguments, it is easy to imagine oneself defending causal determinism by appealing to the evidence of the senses. For example, experience teaches us that where there is smoke, there is fire. Where there is fruit, there are plants and trees. Where there are actions, there are results or consequences. In these and many other cases like them, it is obvious, at least at the level of direct observation, that what we ordinarily think of as causes and effects are joined in ways that are more intimate than simple constant conjunctions or mere temporal succession. Moreover, since we also fail to have any direct empirical evidence of any immaterial kinds of beings (whether they be souls or other kinds of meta-physical "powers" or "forces") – either in ourselves or outside of ourselves – it seems perfectly reasonable to conclude that material objects interact according to causally determined and necessitated patterns. If that is true, then it is easy to see why some materialists would be determinists and fatalists.

One such thinker, Gosala, claimed that human beings have no freedom to act precisely because all outcomes are causally predetermined by fate, or the laws of material interactions. According to this view, despite the internal introspective experience of choice, the actual outcome of events is necessitated by the prior physical conditions that give rise to it – like the balls on a pool table, whose paths are determined (assuming no external interference) by the forces and impacts of the other moving balls and the friction of the table.

Such a view, however, is rather obviously at odds with the hedonistic claim that suggests that the purpose of life is to pursue pleasure and avoid pain, because the notions of pursuit and avoidance seem to presuppose or assume choice or at least some form of non-determinism. Perhaps it was this inconsistency and other uncertainties about the metaphysics of the self and *kamma* and *moksa* that led some materialists to defend a complete skepticism with regard to any true knowledge about the meaning and purpose of life as well as the fundamental nature of reality.

Regardless of their individual differences, it is clear that the one unifying belief of Carvaka thinkers as a group was their rejection of the authority of the *Vedas*. In this respect, at least, they agreed with the Jains and the Buddha. On the other hand, their basic difference with the Jains and the Buddha and the other "orthodox"[14] thinkers was their rejection of *moksa*. We have already considered the Jain view of *moksa* or liberation, and we shall consider the Buddhist view of things in more detail shortly.

The Buddha's appeal

Before concluding this chapter I want to raise one more subject for consideration. I also want to challenge the reader to formulate, over the course of their reading of the book, his or her own view on this topic. What I want to consider is why Siddhattha's teachings were able to take root and flourish in the kind of social, economic, political and, most importantly, philosophical environment of ancient India.

Richard Gombrich[15] has speculated, and argued rather persuasively, that the social conditions prior to and at the time when Siddhattha Gotama lived

---

[14] At this point, it is important to keep in mind that the "orthodox"/"heterodox" distinction is just one of many different ways of clarifying and understanding the relationships among the various philosophical systems of ancient India. There are obviously other possible ways of distinguishing the numerous *dassanas*, for example, according to their metaphysical beliefs (about the whole of reality, or about its parts, i.e., the nature of the human person, the soul or spirit or self, *nibbana*, etc.), or their epistemological beliefs (about the nature, origin, and limits of knowledge), or their ethical beliefs (about the goals of human living, the elements of the good human life, the standards of morality, *kamma*, etc.). I leave these distinctions for the reader to investigate and make.

[15] Gombrich (1988).

contributed much to the *Dhamma*'s success. According to Gombrich, and as should be clear from this chapter's consideration of the Indian context of Siddhattha's teaching, the Buddha owed much to his predecessors and to his social and cultural context. What were the conditions that contributed to the success of his message?

Gombrich[16] maintains that it was the material and social conditions of those living at the time of Siddhattha that paved the way for both the appeal of his teaching as well as his followers' acceptance of it. In other words, the basic elements of his teachings appealed to those in the social, economic, and political situation of ancient India. These people and conditions included: a new and growing class of wealthy town and city dwellers, householders, manual laborers, merchants and business people, and ascetic *samanas* or renouncers, as well as increased opportunities for individual choice and success in different forms of life, social displacement, new commercial markets, professional specialization, a developing bureau-cracy, and public health and environmental issues and problems.

As we have seen throughout this chapter, in addition to these material and social conditions, there were also intellectual and ideological factors that formed the "spiritual" conditions and environment in and from which the teachings of the man who came to be called "the Buddha" emerged and flourished. Beyond the eight *dassanas* that we have already outlined, espe-cially with respect to their acceptance of the *Vedas* and the priestly activities of the Brahmins, other intellectual conditions at work at the time of Siddhattha included, according to Gombrich: a developing sense of reli-gious individualism, a need for an ethic for the socially mobile, as well as an ethic for those who were both politically active and ultimately dominant (i.e., kings and rulers), and finally, an open and lively environment for vigorous philosophical and religious discussion and debate. In the language of the Buddha and the Buddhist tradition, these conditions provided the causal nexus from which his ideas interdependently arose.

Although it is clear, and presumably beyond dispute, that both material and spiritual conditions played their parts in the interdependent arising, development, and flourishing of the teachings of Siddhattha Gotama, I want to suggest that a plausible, and in fact persuasive case can be made, that the most basic explanation for the success of Buddhism over its extended

---

[16] Ibid., pp. 32–86.

history in various social, economic, political, religious, philosophical, cultural, and geographical areas, is the simple fact that at least some of its teachings are true. In fact, Aristotle insisted that many people over an extended period of time believing something to be true surely counts as both support for its truth and also stands as something in need of explanation. As a result, we shall examine in more detail some of the most basic elements of the Buddha's *Dhamma* and the subsequent historical developments of his account of the meaning and purpose of life, and the fundamental nature of reality, in order to see how and whether his teachings can stand up to a philosophical test of their truth.

The Buddha's most basic philosophical insight

Given the preceding account of classical Indian thought in terms of its three overarching "visions," what I hope to make clear in the remaining chapters of this book is that while the Buddha and the other eight *dassanas* share many thoughts and ideas in common, it is their differences in outlook that are most interesting and instructive. In fact, I shall argue that it is in response to the conception, articulation, and elucidation of the elements of what I have been calling the post-Vedic "vision" that Siddhattha Gotama and his contemporaries worked out their own philosophical "visions."

In the case of the Buddhist vision, in particular, the central thesis of this book is that the single most important or most basic insight of the historical Buddha is the claim that who we are and what we think exists is a function of our mind and its cognitive powers. In other words, it is our mind and our uses of it that determine how we see and understand our self, the world, and other things. In order to help clarify what I take the Buddha to be claiming, let me propose an analogy and a story from the Buddhist tradition. The analogy is straightforward; the moral of the story is open to interpretation – it depends on how you understand it.

In the same way that I can maintain, shape, and transform my physical body through a proper diet and a serious weight-training and exercise program, I also can maintain, shape, transform, and indeed, strengthen, improve, and perfect my mind and its powers by meditative practices and exercises. In other words, the Buddha's most basic insight is that it is my mind and how I develop and use it that determine how I understand, think about, and interact with the things around me. It is precisely this insight and power that the Buddha himself is said to have experienced and exercised while under the *Bodhi* tree. In fact, I would suggest that it was Siddhattha's experiences with his first teachers after his renunciation, Alara Kalama and Uddaka Ramaputta, and their yogic meditative practices, that formed the bedrock of both his enlightenment experience and his own understanding of the value of meditative practices for the mind and its operations.

The story[17] (in brief), whose origins are unknown, involves a woman named Kisa Gotami, who like Cinderella, manages to overcome a dreadful situation and eventually has everything she could want in life – i.e., a loving husband, a beautiful son, a supportive family, etc. Unfortunately, and somewhat like Job in the Hebrew Scriptures, she suddenly and tragically loses her son, her family, and her mental health. She refuses to accept her son's death and carries his lifeless body about while asking her neighbors for medicine. Eventually, a wise man recommends that she go to see the Buddha for help. The Buddha agrees to help her but only after she has visited every house in her town and obtained a mustard seed from those who have not been touched by death. Kisa Gotami eagerly tries to fulfill the Buddha's command but sadly she soon realizes that she cannot collect any mustard seeds because every house has been visited by death. Finally, she returns to the Buddha and he heals her with the medicine of his teachings about the impermanence of all things, the universality of death, and the necessity of compassion for all beings.

What is particularly relevant about this story for my purposes is the fact that there are at least two different and competing interpretations of it,

[17] There are various names and versions of the story, and just as many interpretations of it. For example, Peter Hershock and Roger Ames (via public lectures and an email exchange) offer an interpretation that they say is based on oral traditions passed down through the Chan/Son Lineage. In fact, Hershock reports that he has heard of Chinese commentaries that reflect his (relationship) interpretation of the story, but he cautiously sites his own reading as simply "culturally informed." George Tanabe, on the other hand, could not find any textual evidence of Kisa Gotami in pre-modern Japanese Buddhist literature or standard dictionaries, and he suggests that she might appear in popular tale (*setsuwa*) literature and cites Hiro Sachiya (a popular contemporary writer) who uses the story of Kisa Gotami as an example of Sakyumuni's public preaching material. Whatever the ultimate source of the story may be, there can be little doubt that it conveys important Buddhist ideas, and that one's understanding of these ideas depends in no small part on both one's own way of "seeing and hearing" them and one's cultural sensibilities (be they Indian, Chinese, or other) as well.

both of which are supported by the "facts" of the story, and both of which depend, quite crucially, on how one reads and understands the story. The first, and most obvious or standard Indian Buddhist interpretation is that the Buddha was simply trying to get Kisa Gotami (and his audience) to recognize and accept the fact of impermanence and the reality of suffering and death. In other words, he simply wanted her (and them) to see the truth of his *Dhamma*. A second, less obvious interpretation and one sometimes ascribed to Chinese Buddhists is that the Buddha was trying to get Kisa Gotami reconnected with her community (and hence back to mental and physical wellbeing) by sharing her story and re-establishing her relationships with others. On this interpretation, what really matters, or at least what one might claim the Buddha was trying to convey, is the importance of one's relationships with others rather than the ubiquity of death and change. Both interpretations are supported by the traditional elements of the story. The difference, I would suggest, depends on how you "see" or "undertand" the point of the story. In that respect, at least, the story and its different interpretations are a perfect example of the Buddha's insight that it is our mind and our uses of it that determine how we see and understand our self, the world, and the things around us. Moreover, I shall be arguing throughout this book that it is precisely this insight and the subsequent historical development of Buddhist understandings of this simple yet profound idea that form the heart of the Buddhist "vision" of reality. At the same time, the teachings of the Buddha did not stop there.

According to the Buddhist tradition, the historical Buddha went further and insisted that one's understanding of the self, the world, and others, when fully perfected, leads to actions whose moral qualities are commensurate with the level and depth of insight or "vision" of one's mind. That is, the greater one's intellectual penetration into the fundamental nature of reality, the greater the virtuosity of one's actions. In short, moral action is the fruit of intellectual insight, or as Socrates once said, to know the good is to do the good. Put differently, I want to suggest that the Buddha and Socrates seem to share the view that lack of vision or insight in the realms of epistemology and metaphysics leads inevitably to failure in the moral sphere.

What follows is an attempt to trace the arc of development of the basic insight of the Buddha while under the *Bodhi* tree to the interests of the current Dalai Lama and Thich Nhat Hanh and their studies of the mind, life, and consciousness. As previously indicated, the starting point of this arc is the various responses to the conception, articulation, and elucidation of the elements of what I am calling the post-Vedic "vision" by Siddhattha Gotama and his contemporaries. It is to the specific details of Siddhattha's lived response that we turn in the next chapter.

Things to think about

1. What are the basic features of the intellectual and cultural context into which Siddhattha was born and raised? In what ways are the Buddha's teachings a product of his culture?
2. What kinds of philosophical reasons can be given to support the view that there is existence after death?
3. What is the classical Indian conception of *kamma*? Do you accept it? Why or why not?
4. How is the Buddha's most basic philosophical insight related to the three "visions" distinguished in this chapter? Do the different "visions" represent an improvement in the Indian view of reality? Why or why not?
5. Which features of the Buddha's teachings allowed it to flourish in contexts outside of India? Why?

3 The basic teachings of the Buddha

Key terms and teachings

Anatta/Anatman: Literally "no-self," this term refers to the denial of a fixed, permanent, unchanging self or soul (*atta/atman*). On a more general level, it refers to the Buddha's denial of any fixed or permanent substantial nature in any object or phenomenon. According to the Buddha, everything lacks inherent existence, because all things arise in dependence on impermanent causes and conditions.

Dukkha/Duhkha: The subject of the Four Noble Truths, whose root meaning refers to an off-center wheel hub, "*dukkha*" captures the fact that life never quite lives up to our expectations, hopes, dreams, and plans. Usually translated as "suffering," it includes the broader psychological ideas of dissatisfaction, lack of contentment, discontent, pain, misery, frustration, and feeling ill at ease.

Eightfold Path: A basic summary of the Buddha's teachings in morality/*sila* (right or appropriate speech, action, and livelihood), mental concentration or meditative cultivation/*samadhi* (right or appropriate effort, mindfulness, and concentration), and wisdom/*panna* (right or appropriate view or understanding, and thought or intention).

Four Noble Truths: The Buddha's insight into *dukkha*; the source or arising or coming to be or cause of *dukkha* (*tanha*); the cessation or ceasing of *dukkha* (*niroda*); and the path or way (*magga*) leading to the extinction of *dukkha*.

Kamma/Karma: Literally "action" or "deed," this term refers to the fact that actions and intentions have or produce consequences. The basic Buddhist account of it is that both appropriate and inappropriate tendencies or habits lead to actions that ultimately produce fruits or consequences.

Middle Way: In metaphysics, or matters relating to being, becoming, and non-being, the Middle Way of interdependent arising lies between the extremes of eternalism (things or selves or substances exist) and

---

annihilationism (no-thing or self or substance exists). The Middle Way recognizes "things" as processes or events or happenings arising from prior conditions. In epistemology, or matters relating to knowledge, truth, belief, and ignorance, the Middle Way of ultimate truth may be said to lie between the extremes of ignorance (neither truth nor knowledge) and conventional belief (what is thought and said to be true but is not). In ethics, or matters relating to proper living, the Middle Way of the Eightfold Path lies between the extremes of sensual indulgence and ascetic mortification.

Nibbana/Nirvana: Literally "to blow out" or "extinguish," this term refers to both the final release from *samsara* and the ultimate liberation from *dukkha*. Understood in this way, it refers to the quenching of the fires of *tanha*, and thus may be thought of as the goal of Buddhist practice.

Panna/Prajna: In the traditional presentation of the teachings of the Eightfold Path, "wisdom" refers to the liberating knowledge of truth achieved in awakening or enlightenment. Right or appropriate view or understanding, and right or appropriate thought or intentions are the first two elements of the path to insight into the true nature of existence.

Paticca-Samuppada/Pratitya-Samutpada: Variously translated as, "dependent arising," "dependent origination," "conditioned co-production," "co-dependent origination," "inter-dependent-origination," or "interdependent arising," all of these refer to the Buddha's account of causality. In short, this cluster of terms refers to the law-governed dynamics of change in which the events or happenings in the world are causally conditioned by and dependent on other processes, events, or happenings.

Samadhi: In the traditional presentation of the teachings of the Eightfold Path, "concentration" or "meditation" refers to the "right" or "appropriate" kinds of intellectual attitude required for sustaining one's practice of the path. The appropriate mental states include: right or appropriate effort, mindfulness, and concentration.

Samsara: Literally "wandering on/about," this term refers to the ongoing and seemingly endless cyclical process of birth, life, death, and rebirth. In a more general way, it refers to the conditioned world of this life, its *kamma*, and its concomitant *dukkha*.

Sila: In the traditional presentation of the teachings of the Eightfold Path, "moral excellence" or "morality" refers to the three kinds of virtues required for the "right" practice of the path. These include: correct speech, correct action, and correct livelihood.

Tanha/Trsna: Within the context of the Four Noble Truths, *tanha* or selfish craving, grasping, wrong desire, greed, lust, and attached wanting, is the cause or root condition of *dukkha*. At its most basic level it is the drive for selfish gratification and possessiveness that fuels the fires of our suffering.

Three teachings

Although the exact events in the life of Siddhattha Gotama will probably never be known, the outline sketch of **Chapter 1** provides the background against which his basic philosophical ideas and teachings may be considered.

As we have seen, the man who became "the Buddha" or the "Awakened One," underwent a radical re-visioning of life and his understanding of it. Whatever the specifics of his enlightenment were, there can be no doubt that according to his followers the Buddha's awakening consisted essentially of a "new way" of seeing the world and understanding its functioning. This epistemological paradigm shift may be likened to the experience of awakening from a dream and realizing that what one thought was real was not. According to the Buddha's followers, this awakening is captured in the three most basic teachings of Sakyamuni: the "Middle Way," the Four Noble Truths, and the Eightfold Path.

First, the Buddha teaches the "Middle Way" between the extremes of the sensual pleasure of self-indulgence and the rigors of ascetic self-mortification.

> Bhikkhus, these two extremes should not be followed by one who has gone forth into homelessness. What two? The pursuit of sensual happiness in sensual pleasures, which is low, vulgar, the way of worldlings, ignoble and unbeneficial; and the pursuit of self-mortification, which is painful, ignoble and unbeneficial. Without veering towards either of these extremes, the Tathagata has awakened to the middle way; which gives rise to vision, which gives rise to knowledge, which leads to peace, to direct knowledge, to enlightenment, to Nibbana.
>
> And what, bhikkhus, is the middle way awakened to by the Tathagata, which gives rise to vision, which gives rise to knowledge, which leads to peace, to direct knowledge, to enlightenment, to Nibbana? It is this Noble Eightfold Path; that is, right view, right intention, right speech, right action, right livelihood, right effort, right mindfulness, right concentration. This,

bhikkhus, is that middle way awakened to by the Tathagata, which gives rise to vision, which gives rise to knowledge, which leads to peace, to direct knowledge, to enlightenment, to Nibbana.[1]

Having lived and experienced both the excesses and deficiencies of the extremes of pleasure and deprivation, the Buddha was painfully aware of their debilitating consequences. On the one hand, the pleasurable excesses of his princely life were not satisfying for at least two reasons. While enjoying them he was poignantly aware of their imminent passing, and while not enjoying them he found himself longing for what he knew could not truly satisfy him because of their inherent transience. On the other hand, his experiments with extreme ascetic practices left him physically emaciated and mentally unfulfilled. Moreover, these practices failed to produce their advertised and promised ends; in fact, they left him both mentally distracted and physically enfeebled. So his followers insisted that one of the most basic teachings of the "Awakened One" was his insistence on the "Middle Way" between the two extremes of pleasure and pain.

A second basic teaching of the Buddha involves a new philosophical outlook or "truth" – a new way of seeing and understanding the world and its metaphysical structure. This way of knowing and being in the world is set forth in what is traditionally referred to as his First Sermon and is succinctly summarized in what is commonly referred to as the Four Noble Truths. According to the Buddha,

> Now this, bhikkhus, is the noble truth of suffering: Birth is suffering; aging is suffering; illness is suffering; death is suffering; sorrow and lamentation, pain, grief and despair are suffering; union with what is displeasing is suffering; separation from what is pleasing is suffering; not to get what one wants is suffering; in brief, the five aggregates subject to clinging are suffering.
>
> Now this, bhikkhus, is the noble truth of the origin of suffering: it is this craving which leads to renewed existence, accompanied by delight and lust, seeking delight here and there; that is, craving for sensual pleasures, craving for existence, craving for extermination.
>
> Now this, bhikkhus, is the noble truth of the cessation of suffering: it is the remainderless fading away and cessation of that same craving, the giving up and relinquishing of it, freedom from it, non-reliance on it.

---

[1] *Samyutta Nikaya, Saccasamyutta, Setting in Motion the Wheel of the Dhamma*, p. 1844.

Now this, bhikkhus, is the noble truth of the way leading to the cessation of suffering: it is this Noble Eightfold Path that is, right view, right intention, right speech, right action, right livelihood, right effort, right mindfulness, right concentration.

"This is the noble truth of suffering": thus, bhikkhus, in regard to things unheard before, there arose in me vision, knowledge, wisdom, true knowledge, and light.

"This noble truth of suffering is to be fully understood": thus, bhikkhus, in regard to things unheard before, there arose in me vision, knowledge, wisdom, true knowledge, and light.

"This noble truth of suffering has been fully understood": thus, bhikkhus, in regard to things unheard before, there arose in me vision, knowledge, wisdom, true knowledge, and light.

"This is the noble truth of the origin of suffering": thus, bhikkhus, in regard to things unheard before, there arose in me vision, knowledge, wisdom, true knowledge, and light.

"This noble truth of the origin of suffering is to be abandoned": thus, bhikkhus, in regard to things unheard before, there arose in me vision, knowledge, wisdom, true knowledge, and light.

"This noble truth of the origin of suffering has been abandoned": thus, bhikkhus, in regard to things unheard before, there arose in me vision, knowledge, wisdom, true knowledge, and light.

"This is the noble truth of the cessation of suffering": thus, bhikkhus, in regard to things unheard before, there arose in me vision, knowledge, wisdom, true knowledge, and light.

"This noble truth of the cessation of suffering is to be realized": thus, bhikkhus, in regard to things unheard before, there arose in me vision, knowledge, wisdom, true knowledge, and light.

"This noble truth of the cessation of suffering has been realized": thus, bhikkhus, in regard to things unheard before, there arose in me vision, knowledge, wisdom, true knowledge, and light.

"This is the noble truth of the way leading to the cessation of suffering": thus, bhikkhus, in regard to things unheard before, there arose in me vision, knowledge, wisdom, true knowledge, and light.

"This noble truth of the way leading to the cessation of suffering is to be developed": thus, bhikkhus, in regard to things unheard before, there arose in me vision, knowledge, wisdom, true knowledge, and light.

"This noble truth of the way leading to the cessation of suffering has been developed": thus, bhikkhus, in regard to things unheard before, there arose in me vision, knowledge, wisdom, true knowledge, and light.

So long, bhikkhus, as my knowledge and vision of these Four Noble
Truths as they really are in their three phases and twelve aspects was not
thoroughly purified in this way, I did not claim to have awakened to the
unsurpassed perfect enlightenment in this world with its devas, Mara, and
Brahma, in this generation with its ascetics and Brahmins, its devas and
humans. But when my knowledge and vision of these Four Noble Truths as
they really are in their three phases and twelve aspects was thoroughly
purified in this way, then I claimed to have awakened to the unsurpassed
perfect enlightenment in this world with its devas, Mara, and Brahma, in
this generation with its ascetics and Brahmins, its devas and humans.
The knowledge and vision arose in me: "Unshakable is the liberation
of my mind. This is my last birth. Now there is no more renewed
existence."[2]

According to this passage, the path to liberation from the cycle of rebirth
and *kamma* begins with a reorientation in one's knowledge, understanding,
and causal interaction with the world. The specifics of his Truths will be
discussed shortly, but for now we may summarize them as follows:

1. Everything involves *dukkha*.
2. *Dukkha* has an origin or cause and condition.
3. *Dukkha* can be overcome or cured.
4. There is an Eightfold Path for reorienting one's practices and life.

Third, the Buddha teaches the Eightfold Path as a practical method of
thinking, living, and relating to the world that leads to the cessation of
dukkha. According to his First Sermon, the steps of the Path, which may be
seen as a basic outline of ethical advice, are:

1. Right or appropriate view.
2. Right or appropriate thought.
3. Right or appropriate speech.
4. Right or appropriate action.
5. Right or appropriate livelihood.
6. Right or appropriate effort.
7. Right or appropriate mindfulness.
8. Right or appropriate concentration.

---

[2] Ibid., pp. 1844–1846.

The Buddha as doctor

One of the most common and helpful ways of presenting and understanding the teachings of the Buddha is to consider them as analogous to the best
practices of a medical doctor. Imagine, for a moment, that you are ill and in
need of medical attention. According to this method of presentation, the
Buddha should be seen as a "healing physician" (as he was for Kisa Gotami)
who can diagnose your sickness, identify its cause or causes, prescribe a
treatment plan, and finally help you overcome your illness. Your illness in
this scenario is not, however, a bodily disease like cancer, a pulled muscle,
or a broken leg. Your illness is *dukkha*.

Following his enlightenment, the Buddha set in motion the wheel of
truth of his teaching by returning to his fellow ascetic practitioners to
convey the fruits of his experience and *Dhamma*. Although we cannot be
sure about the exact content of this sermon, it seems both plausible and
appropriate in the light of the traditional stories of his life that the compassionate Buddha would begin his teaching by returning to the band of
ascetics with whom he had spent so much time.

As we have seen, the Buddha informed them that those who have already
set out on the path of spiritual enlightenment and renounced the ordinary
life of a householder must avoid the extremes of indulgence in sensual
pleasures and rigorous self-mortification. He was speaking from experience. The Buddha had initially devoted himself to a life of self-indulgent
pleasure and found it unsatisfying and hollow. He had also recently devoted
himself to the common practices of ascetic self-mortification and found
them unbearably painful. According to the Buddha, both extremes were
"unworthy and unprofitable," precisely because he experienced them as
inappropriate to the goals of enlightenment and *Nibbana*. He informed the
"ailing" ascetics that his realization of the "Middle Way," and not the
experience of the two extremes, was what produced the vision, knowledge,
calm, insight, enlightenment, and *Nibbana* that they sought. He had experienced the release that he and they had been seeking, and he insisted that it
was to be found in the Eightfold Path of the "Middle Way."

One can only imagine the reaction of the ascetics. On the one hand, they
needed to overcome their anger, disappointment, resentment, and suspi-
cion of Siddhattha for having abandoned their way of life, and on the other,
they were probably curious about his experiences because he was known to

be quite adept at ascetic practices. One can also imagine the compassion of the Buddha for his fellow seekers. He had finally realized the truth of the "Middle Way," and he was now in a position to offer help, guidance, and "medical attention" to those still bound by the ignorance and dissatisfaction of unfulfilling practice. The "patients," who rather paradoxically, were both painfully aware and blissfully ignorant of their ongoing sicknesses, were finally in the presence of a real "doctor." What did the doctor recommend?

The Buddha's diagnosis: the First Noble Truth

According to his First Sermon, the Buddha's diagnosis of the sickness of the ascetics, in particular, and humans, in general, is called the First Noble Truth. This truth is the realization that everything involves *dukkha*. Being born, growing up, and aging all involve *dukkha*. We come into the world in a way that produces *dukkha* for our mothers and fathers and *dukkha* for ourselves. We go through the processes of growth and maturation and the experiences of *dukkha* are multiplied and enhanced. We continue to age, and life becomes increasingly difficult as we encounter the debilitating consequences of physical, mental, and emotional sicknesses. And finally, inevitably, we die.

The Buddha's First Truth is the medical and spiritual diagnosis that our condition is dire. The lives of the ascetics (and our lives too) are full of sorrow, lamentation, pain, grief, and despair. All of it is *dukkha*. And who could deny it? Every one of us has experienced the *dukkha* of unpleasant things, like sickness, physical pain, hunger, sleeplessness, frustration, and anxiety. Every one of us has also experienced the *dukkha* of losing pleasant things, like friends, and pets, and possessions. Who could truthfully deny that not getting what one wants is *dukkha*? No one, says the Buddha.

The problem is that we fail to realize all of this is due to blissful ignorance of our own ignorance. We are neither awakened to nor aware of the way things really are, and so we continue the mindless pursuit of our own dissatisfaction – which simply produces more *dukkha*. The ultimate explanation of all of this is, according to the Buddha, our ignorance of our true selves. We simply do not realize that our ordinary, habitual, and ignorant way of conceiving of our selves is part of the problem of *dukkha*. In short, the Buddha teaches that how we conceive and understand who and what we are is basic to our disease – it, too, leads to *dukkha*. Why and how do we get things wrong?

The First Noble Truth as the Buddha's diagnosis of the human condition has traditionally been understood to involve important metaphysical and epistemological claims about both the nature of the human person and our knowledge of the ontology of our selves and other things in the world. As the sermon says, "the five aggregates of attachment" are *dukkha*. Although we shall be considering the features of the Buddha's metaphysical claims in more detail in **Chapter 6** and **Chapter 7**, for now, we shall try to clarify what he means by these "aggregates."

Recall for a moment that the most prominent Indian schools of religious and philosophical thought at the time of the Buddha argued for the existence of a substantial or essential self – an immaterial being, which transmigrated from past lives into this life and into the next life as well. We shall be considering the Buddha's detailed response to these claims in **Chapter 5** and **Chapter 7**. For now, we need only recall that they had posited such a being for at least two reasons: first, to explain one's metaphysical identity in this life as well as in past and future lives, and second, to explain the obvious unity of our perceptual experience. This *atman* or immaterial self was required, according to the Indian tradition and the Buddha's contemporaries, to explain how both our personal identity and our unified perceptual awareness remained the same in the face of the unending changes of our daily experience.

The Buddha and his followers, however, categorically denied the existence of such a being for at least two reasons: first, it involved a metaphysical hypothesis that was patently unverifiable, and second, it was unjustified because it was ultimately unnecessary for explaining either the phenomena of experience or the truths of rebirth and *kamma*. Let's look at each of these reasons more carefully.

We have seen that the Buddha himself denied the existence of *atman* because he refused to posit the existence of an entity whose very being was not verifiable by direct experience. He had personally engaged in the kinds of introspective meditative experience that presumably could and would have confirmed the continuing and ongoing existence of his own *atman*, but he had failed to discover any fixed inner essence of himself. At least initially, he and his followers denied the existence of enduring selves underlying the ever-changing flux of daily experience precisely because there simply was no empirical evidence of abiding selves. Instead, the Buddha taught *anatman* or the no-enduring-self view of the human person. At the same time, the Buddha also rejected the existence of *atman* as logically necessary to explain the Indian teachings on rebirth and *kamma*. We shall be considering his reasons for this in more detail in **Chapter 5**.

According to the Buddha, there is an ongoing series or cycle of rebirths that does in fact occur, but there is no fixed and unchanging self, soul, or *atman* that undergoes the transmigration. So, how, one might ask, do I, or more precisely, what "I" take "myself" to be, reconcile the constantly changing world of experience with my obviously unified experience of "self"? The Buddha explains it in terms of his teaching of *paticca-samuppada*, or his account of causality.

Variously translated as "dependent arising," "dependent origination," "conditioned co-production," "co-dependent origination," "inter-dependent-origination," and "interdependent arising," *paticca-samuppada* refers to the Buddha's teaching about the law-governed dynamics of daily change in which the events or happenings of the world and experience are causally conditioned by and dependent on other processes, events, or happenings. In the *Nidanasamyutta* or *Connected Discourses on Causation* he says:

> And what, monks, is interdependent arising? With ignorance as condition, volitional formations come to be; with volitional formations as condition, consciousness; with consciousness as condition, name and form; with name and form as condition, the six sense bases; with the six sense bases as condition, contact; with contact as condition, feeling; with feeling as condition, craving; with craving as condition, clinging; with clinging as condition, existence; with existence as condition, birth; with birth as condition, aging-and-death, sorrow, lamentation, pain, dejection, and despair come to be. Such is the origin of this whole mass of suffering. This, monks, is called interdependent arising.
>
> But with the remainderless fading away and cessation of ignorance comes cessation of volitional formations; with the cessation of volitional formation, cessation of consciousness . . . Such is the cessation of this whole mass of suffering.[3]

This network of interdependent happenings is the Buddha's way of making sense of the basic features of our ordinary experience of both the world and ourselves without appealing to or positing the existence of either enduring substances (on the part of the "objects" out in the world that we are experiencing) or enduring selves who are undergoing or having the experiences. Unlike those who insist on either enduring selves and

---

[3] *Samyutta Nikaya, Nidanavagga Sutta, The Book of Causation*, pp. 533–534.

substances, or at least enduring selves, in order to make sense of both the world of flux and our experiences of it, the Buddha and his followers categorically deny a fixed essence or unchanging substance in any being. Instead, they teach that reality and our experiences of it are best seen as continuous and ongoing dynamic processes of becoming in which each "part" or "element" is itself both constantly conditioned by and causally contributing to the endlessly cyclical processes of the whole. The traditional Buddhist terms for this are *samsara* and the "twelve-fold chain of interdependent arising," and it is these terms and their referents that help clarify the Buddha's meaning of "the five aggregates of attachment" in the First Noble Truth.

Against the background of interdependent arising, what the Buddha meant by "the five aggregates of attachment" is that the human person, just like the "objects" of experience, is and should be seen as a collection or aggregate of processes – *anatman*, and not as possessing a fixed or unchanging substantial self – *atman*. In fact, the Buddhist tradition has identified the following five processes, aggregates, or bundles as constitutive of our true "selves":

1. *Rupa* – material shape/form – the material or bodily form of being;
2. *Vedana* – feeling/sensation – the basic sensory form of experience and being;
3. *Sanna/Samjna* – cognition – the mental interpretation, ordering, and classification of experience and being;
4. *Sankhara/Samskara* – dispositional attitudes – the character traits, habitual responses, and volitions of being;
5. *Vinnana/Vijnana* – consciousness – the ongoing process of awareness of being.

The Buddha thus teaches that each one of these "elements" of the "self" is but a fleeting pattern that arises within the ongoing and perpetually changing context of process interactions. There is no fixed self either in me or any object of experience that underlies or is the enduring subject of these changes. And it is precisely my failure to understand this that causes *dukkha*. Moreover, it is my false and ignorant views of "myself" and "things" as unchanging substances that both causally contributes to and conditions *dukkha* because these very same views interdependently arise from the "selfish" craving of *tanha*. It is the causal process of this desiring that the Buddha addresses in his Second Noble Truth.

The Second Noble Truth

The Buddha teaches that the Second Noble Truth of the origin of *dukkha* involves *tanha*, or selfish wanting and possessiveness that fuel the fires of *dukkha*. As the First Sermon reports, *tanha* and the passionate greed bound up with it causally contribute to "our" rebirth and ongoing participation in the cycle of *samsara*. This happens in three ways: first, by continuously experiencing new and exciting delights in our senses, we mindlessly develop a habitual drive or lust to fulfill our unquenchable thirst for more and varied sense-pleasures; second, this attached wanting produces a desire and craving for existence in which we seek to preserve our "selves" by trying to be some fixed thing, or imagine our "selves" as becoming some fixed thing; and third, we also simultaneously experience the thirst to remove and overcome the obstacles to our satisfaction, including our "selves" if necessary.

Understood in this way, it is easy to see why *tanha* is the source and origin of *dukkha*. In the first case, who would deny that the constantly changing flux of the world and our "selves" is a sure recipe for frustration? Just when we think things are perfect, along comes a new source of distraction and desire. You finally get the new car you have always wanted, and before you know it, next year's model is even bigger and better. You finally get a date with the person you have been admiring from a distance, and before long you see some new person who captures your attention. Even when you get exactly what you want, there is always some new thing that you do not currently have, and so you experience the hunger of being unfulfilled.

In the second case, you begin to take the steps that you think are necessary to satisfy your desires and help you be what you want to be, and before you know it the karmic consequences of your actions and intentions lead to attachment to *samsara*. And finally, when things get in the way of our plans, like the slow driver in front of you, or things simply do not go the way that we want them to, when our favorite team loses again, who could deny the often overwhelming frustration and pain of these situations? All of it is *dukkha*, according to the Buddha, and all of it is caused by *tanha*. So, you may wonder, what's the point?

Just when you may be tempted to throw in the towel and call it quits, the "Awakened One" tells us to hold on. There is hope and a way out of our predicament and suffering. The lifeline is the subject of the Third Noble Truth.

The Third Noble Truth

The Third Noble Truth is concerned with the cessation of *dukkha* and is rather straightforward and obvious in theory, if not in practice. According to the Buddha, the way to stop *dukkha* is to stop its cause, *tanha*. In short, if you want to avoid the fruit of an action or intention, avoid the action or intention. Said another way, if you want to remove an effect, remove its cause. So the Buddha says that the cessation of suffering depends on the complete cessation of the very craving that causes and conditions it. In short, stop *tanha*, stop *dukkha*. It seems rather obvious, but perhaps there is more to this truth than first meets the eye. Where is the Buddha leading us with this line of reasoning?

If we recall again that the First Sermon is addressed to his fellow ascetics, the Buddha's point may be more obvious. He is, both literally and figuratively, hitting them where they live. The Third Noble Truth asserts that the cessation of *dukkha* depends on the complete and total cessation of *tanha*. Although the ascetics think they are making such a sacrifice, they are not. One must not simply give up *tanha*, like giving up candy during Lent or skipping TV for the evening or even renouncing the world and its pleasures. "Giving up" involves much more than doing without. The Buddha seems to be insisting that one must fully renounce *tanha*, entirely emancipate oneself from *tanha*, and in the end completely detach oneself from *tanha*. What he is talking about in a nutshell is both the release from *samsara*, and the ultimate realization of *Nibbana*.

The Buddha seems to be telling his fellow ascetics that the ultimate goal of their practice is only attainable when there is complete and total non-attachment – even to the practice itself. He had achieved the goal himself and now he was trying to teach them how to do it as well. In order to achieve *Nibbana*, the Buddha says, the ascetics need first to recognize the paradox of its realization. In other words, the Buddha seems to be asserting a self-referentially inconsistent claim. If you desire to be free of *dukkha*, then you must want to stop *tanha*. This would seem to entail, however, that one must desire to not-desire, and that after all is desire – *tanha*. What is a good ascetic to do?

One solution is to disregard the Buddha's truth as fatally flawed in its logic. Another solution is to admit that the Buddha actually does require a desire, presumably of a different sort from ordinary *tanha*, in order to overcome *tanha*. A third solution is to consider another possibility. Perhaps what

the Buddha is teaching is that the final release from *samsara* and the ultimate liberation from *dukkha* can only be realized beyond the quenching of
the fires of *tanha* itself.

What he is telling the ascetics is that they must not only stop the particular
desire for sensual pleasures if they want to stop *dukkha*, but they must also
stop the more general desire of *tanha* itself. In short, they must transcend
tanha itself – completely and totally – in order to realize *Nibbana*. He was not
asking them to do the impossible. He had done it himself, and now he was
letting them know that they too could realize it if only they would let go of
their attachment to their own ways and follow a new path.

The Fourth Noble Truth

The Fourth Noble Truth is a specification of the Path leading to the cessation
of *dukkha*. As we have seen, the Eightfold Path includes: right or appropriate
view, thought, speech, action, livelihood, effort, mindfulness, and concentration. Traditionally these eight elements have been arranged into three
subsets concerned with wisdom/*panna* (view or thought), virtue or moral
excellence/*sila* (speech, action, and livelihood), and concentration/*samadhi*
(effort, mindfulness, and concentration). Although the actual order of presentation of the groupings is moral excellence, concentration, and wisdom,
most scholars do not think that there is any real significance to the ordering
of either the elements of the Eightfold Path or its subsets. The reason for this
is that elements of each are continuously and iteratively reinforcing one
another throughout the day. What is significant, however, is that the
Buddha has proposed a specific and manageable ethical plan for eliminating *dukkha* and realizing *Nibbana*. In fact, the *Majjhima Nikaya* reports that the
Buddha insists, "Both formerly and now what I teach is suffering and the
cessation of suffering."[4]

As we have seen, the first three Noble Truths are basically concerned
with metaphysical and epistemological claims related to the realization of
Nibbana. The First Noble Truth is concerned with the way things are in our
"selves" and the world and how they ought to be seen. The Second Noble
Truth focuses on the cause of the First Truth. The Third Noble Truth specifies that the cause can in fact be eliminated. The Fourth Noble Truth then

---

[4] *Majjhima Nikaya, Alagaddupama Sutta*, p. 234.

offers the practical moral advice necessary to remove both *tanha* and *dukkha* and achieve the ultimate goal, *Nibbana*.

According to the earliest Buddhist tradition, the Fourth Noble Truth's path to *Nibbana* begins with an initial acceptance of the Buddha and his teachings as provisionally true. In other words, one must first hear and then commit themselves to the Buddha and what he teaches as the starting point of the path. In order to begin the path, one must at least provisionally believe in *kamma*, *samsara*, rebirth, and one's responsibility for the consequences of one's actions and intentions. One must also be committed to the appropriateness of the Buddha's view. In short, one must take the Buddha at his word and then follow his advice. Second, one's thoughts and emotions must be directed to the "Middle Way" between the extremes of sensuous pleasure and aggravating want. Third, one must employ appropriate forms of speech. One must avoid lying and all forms of harmful speech and instead speak, like the Buddha himself, with compassion and kindness toward all beings. Fourth, one must always act in the appropriate or morally correct way. Fifth, one ought to make one's living by morally praiseworthy means that do not cause harm and suffering for others. Sixth, one must be fully committed to the effort involved in pursuing the path. One must be consciously and mindfully aware, at all times and in all places, of the thoughts and responses one is having to the way things are going both in our selves and in the world around us. Seventh, one must be continuously cultivating the motivation and mental awareness required to practice the path in the appropriate way at all times. Finally, one must foster the various levels of mental calmness and collectedness that are the fruits of appropriate mental concentration.

At the same time, it is important to point out that the Buddha imagines pursuit of the path as taking place in different ways and at different levels or stages for different followers. In the *Anguttara Nikaya* he says:

> Just as the great ocean slopes away gradually, falls gradually, inclines gradually, not in an abrupt way like a precipice; even so, Paharada, is this *Dhamma* and Discipline: there is a gradual training, gradual practice, gradual progress; there is no penetration to final knowledge in an abrupt way.[5]

This quote and the remaining part of the First Sermon seem to support the idea of the Buddha as a skillful teacher who recognized that his

---

[5] *Anguttara Nikaya*, p. 203.

audiences and followers were going to be at various levels or stages of preparation for following his advice. In fact, the last part of the First Sermon clearly recognizes a three-step process or threefold perspective on each of the Four Noble Truths. First, each Truth must simply be heard or made available. Second, its full import and meaning must be grasped and understood. Third, the Four Noble Truths must be followed, lived, and realized. Only when all of these had been fully understood and diligently practiced did the Buddha report his own realization of perfect enlightenment and release from *samsara*, and promise this to his followers as well.

Taken together, the First Sermon and the quotation from the *Anguttara Nikaya* seem to complement and reinforce one another. On one hand, they introduce the newcomer to Buddhism to the most basic teachings of the Buddha, and on the other they inform the beginner of the gradual process of initiation, development, and realization open and available to anyone willing to follow the Buddha's Path – the path to the cessation of *dukkha*. This early technique of the Buddha adapting his message to his audience eventually became known as *upaya* or skillful means. This method of practice is one of the fundamental teachings in the latter Mahayana tradition, and a perfect example of the kind of "seed of truth" first found in "Mainstream" or early Buddhism that is later cultivated by the developing Buddhist tradition. We shall be examining similar "seeds" in the remaining chapters of **Part II**, and then study their fruit in the chapters of **Part III**.

Things to think about

1. What are the Four Noble Truths and how are they related to one another?
2. What is the most important step of the Eightfold Path and why?
3. What are the strengths and weaknesses of presenting the Buddha's teaching as analogous to the practices of a medical doctor?
4. What are the traditional Indian reasons for believing in the existence of a substantial self or soul? What is the Buddha's argument against these reasons? Which account seems better to you and why?
5. What are the "five aggregates of attachment" and what evidence is there for the Buddha's conception of the human person as an "aggregate"?

4   One Buddhism or many Buddhisms?

Key terms and teachings

Arahant/Arhat: Pali and Sanskrit for "worthy one," these terms designate an enlightened individual who has overcome the cognitive and spiritual impurities that cause rebirth and has attained *Nibbana* as the result of following the teachings of the Buddha, as opposed to having done it on their own.

Bodhisatta/Bodhisattva: Literally, "enlightenment being," these terms refer to the ideal of Buddhist practice in Mahayana Buddhism. This ideal is derived, in part, from the *Jataka Tales*, where the activities of the Buddha prior to his ultimate enlightenment are described. According to the Mahayana tradition, the *Bodhisattva* forgoes his own final enlightenment or realization of *Nibbana* until he has helped all other beings escape *samsara*. In this respect, the *Bodhisattva* is considered superior to the *Arahant* who pursues his own individual enlightenment.

Mahasiddha: Sanskrit term meaning "Great Master" or "Fully Perfected One," it refers to the ideal of Buddhist practice in the Vajrayana tradition, to one who has mastered the *Tantras*.

Mahayana: Sanskrit word meaning "the greater way" or "greater vehicle," followers of this version of Buddhism used this term to distinguish themselves from their earlier predecessors, the Hinayana or "lesser way" or "lesser vehicle," most notably, the Theravada. It is now generally thought that this form of Buddhism developed within some Buddhist communities between 100 BCE and 200 CE. Its teachings, which are located in its own *Perfection of Wisdom* (*Prajnaparamita*) literature, represent a major revision and reinterpretation of many fundamental ideas, concepts, and practices of "early" Buddhism. Among its most basic teachings are: emphasis on wisdom or insight (*prajna*) and compassion (*karuna*), espousal of the *Bodhisattva* ideal, and development of the idea of emptiness (*sunyata*) as a way of expressing the truth that things do not have fixed or inherent natures or essences.

Mainstream Buddhism: Descriptive name used by Paul Williams, Paul Harrison, and others, to designate non-Mahayana Buddhism. As Williams notes, this designation helps avoid the pejorative "Hinayana" and the technically incorrect and too narrow "Theravada" to refer to the general form of early Buddhism outside the Mahayana tradition.

Siddha: Sanskrit term for "accomplished one," this term refers to an enlightened master, teacher, or *guru* in the Tantric tradition.

Sunnatta/Sunyata: Pali and Sanskrit terms meaning "emptiness" or "nothingness," these terms refer to the Mahayana interpretations of interdependent arising and the original state of mind.

Tathagata-garbha: Sanskrit for "womb of the thus come one," this term refers to the Mahayana notion that all beings intrinsically possess the potential to become a Buddha or have a Buddha-nature.

Tantras: Sanskrit term for both esoteric texts and the tradition of practices that developed around them. As a form of Mahayana Buddhism, these texts claimed to offer a particularly speedy means of enlightenment through a series of ritual and meditative practices guided by a *guru*.

Theravada: Pali term, whose meaning is literally "way of the elders," this word refers to the only one of several early branches of the Buddhist monastic community to have survived to the present day. It is the dominant form of Buddhism in much of South East Asia, especially in Burma, Cambodia, Laos, Thailand, and Sri Lanka. The followers of this form of Buddhism adhere to the Pali canon, the earliest complete set of Buddhist scriptures in a single canonical language. This version of Buddhism emphasizes the monastic community or *Samgha*, the life of monks and nuns, and the *Arahant* as the highest ideal of Buddhist practice.

Vajrayana: Literally, "diamond or thunderbolt vehicle," in Sanskrit, this third form of Buddhism emphasizes ritual and devotional practices, and is found today in the tantric traditions of Tibet. As a form of Buddhism, it combines elements of Mahayana philosophy with esoteric Tantric practices in order to help its practitioners achieve enlightenment. Special emphasis is placed on the role of the *guru* or spiritual master, who utilizes *mantras*, *mandalas*, and *mudras* to help his followers realize their inner Buddha-nature.

A question of approach

The purpose of this chapter is to provide a general overview of a fascinating yet immensely complicated subject – the spread and development of Buddhism from its native India to East and South East Asia. Obviously, it is not possible in a work of this length to give anything but a basic outline of such a complex topic. Nevertheless, I think it is appropriate, at this point in our sketch of the Buddha and the *Dhamma*, to raise the issue of whether the subsequent historical forms of Buddhism are logically consistent variations on specific older ideas and themes or the emergence of wholly new and different Buddhist philosophies.

There are many different ways to approach this topic. One could, for example, trace the historical routes of transmission as the teachings of the Buddha were carried by his followers to locations outside of India. According to this method of approach, one typically distinguishes two lines of transmission: a northern route and a southern route. The northern route extends from India through Nepal, Tibet, and China to Korea and Japan. The southern route runs from India to Sri Lanka and from Burma and Thailand through much of South East Asia, Indonesia, and eventually Vietnam and southern China. It is customary in this approach to designate the northern route as the spread of Mahayana Buddhism (subsuming Vajrayana Buddhism under it) and the southern route as the spread of Theravada or Hinayana Buddhism. It is also common to distinguish the various species of Mahayana Buddhism (and not Hinayana or Theravada) by their geographical and national locations. Hence, one can identify in Mahayana Buddhism, its Tibetan, Chinese, Korean, and Japanese versions. All of this is intended to help simplify and clarify what in reality were much more complex, dynamic, and complicated historical situations.

One advantage of this approach is that it makes it easy to keep track of what kind of Buddhism you are dealing with as you move from country to country in Asia. Another advantage is that it provides a satisfactory, rough approximation of the geographical and historical spread of Buddhism in Asia. Its shortcomings, however, are quite numerous.

First of all, it assumes that there really were just two distinct but related kinds of Buddhism and two completely independent lines of transmission. This simply was not the case in reality. Second, it assumes that each national form of Buddhism was a unique, self-contained, monolithic system of beliefs and practices. We shall see in **Part III** that this also was not the case. Third, it fails to recognize how and why Buddhism was changed and transformed as it adapted itself to new locations, cultures, and languages. Fourth, it also disregards the rather important question about what exactly one is required to believe and do in order to actually be an authentic

Buddhist. There are obviously other shortcomings that that reader may think of, but this last one, at least from the point of view of a philosophical assessment of Buddhism, shows the limitations of a purely historical and geographical account of the spread of Buddhism.

A second way to approach this topic is from the point of view of cultural anthropology by studying the social and religious practices of people who claim to be Buddhists. One advantage of this approach is that it actually studies what people do and how they live their lives as Buddhist practitioners. One disadvantage of this approach, however, is that individual and communal practices can be so numerous and so diverse, not only within a given location, but also across geographical regions, that it is almost or actually impossible to give a general account of just what is necessary and sufficient for one to be a practicing Buddhist. A second, related, disadvantage of this approach is that it may ignore or overlook, what from the point of view of philosophy is absolutely essential, namely, the nature of the beliefs that justify or support the kinds of practices one is engaged in and their relationship to one's actions.

A third, uniquely philosophical, way to try to answer the question of whether "Buddhism" denotes a single, unified philosophical system or a complex network of distinct but interrelated philosophies is to start with a rough account of each of the forms to be considered, note their ideological similarities and differences, and then decide, based on reasonable grounds or rational principles, whether the forms under consideration have enough essential ideas in common to be designated as a single philosophical view. In the interests of space (because the different historical forms of Buddhism are just too numerous to consider individually) and in order to help simplify the process, we shall be considering the question of the unity and development of the ideas and teachings of Buddhism with respect to its three broadest traditions: Theravada, Mahayana, and Vajrayana.

Multiple traditions

Chapter 3 was concerned with the most basic teachings and ideas of the Buddha as these were preserved in the Pali texts of just one of eighteen different kinds of early forms or "schools" of Buddhism – the Theravada tradition. According to this form of early or "Mainstream Buddhism," as it is now called to distinguish it from its Mahayana counterparts, the most fundamental teachings of the Buddha are the Middle Way, the Four Noble Truths, and the Eightfold Path. His most important philosophical ideas were concerned with *anatta*, *dukkha*, craving, *kamma*, interdependent arising, *samsara*, wisdom, meditation, morality, and *Nibbana*.

What is most striking about the Theravada view of the teachings of the Buddha, at least from the point of view of our motivating question, is that it is just one among many early forms of Buddhism. Moreover, the fact that there were anywhere from fifteen to twenty early "schools" or traditions of Buddhism should make us wonder why this was the case.

One obvious answer is that followers of the Buddha in different locations formulated their own local beliefs and practices based on how they understood his oral teachings. A second answer is that the historical Buddha actually gave different teachings to different groups of followers at different times (i.e., employed *upaya*/skillful means), and that is why different schools or traditions developed. A third possible answer is that the teachings themselves, as orally transmitted, were simply ambiguous, and hence they could be reasonably interpreted in different ways by different people.

A matter of interpretation

Whatever the actual historical answer was, the principal philosophical advantage that the Theravada Buddhists had over their predecessors was that their version of the Buddha's teachings was actually recorded and preserved as written texts. However, this advantage carries with it the simultaneous disadvantage that even written texts must be read, understood, and interpreted in order to be put into practice. As a result, one way of distinguishing the different kinds of Buddhism is to see how each version understands and interprets the most basic ideas and teachings of the Buddha, at least as these were captured in the written texts of an authentic and generally undisputed form of Buddhism, i.e., Theravada.[1] According to this test, one charitable way of reading Mahayana and Vajrayana or "non-Mainstream Buddhism" is to say that they accept the same basic teachings of the Buddha as their Theravada predecessors do, but that they reinterpret, or rather, highlight or emphasize

---

[1] We are, of course, prescinding from the question about whether the Theravada tradition (or any tradition for that matter) has completely and accurately compiled the authentic teachings and ideas of the historical Buddha.

certain features or ideas of the teachings that the Theravada Buddhists had either overlooked, disregarded, or simply neglected.

Different ideals

For example, one rather obvious difference among the Theravada, Mahayana, and Vajrayana traditions is that Theravada Buddhism proposes the individual or solitary *Arahant* as the ideal of Buddhist practice, while Mahayana Buddhism emphasizes the selfless compassion of the *Bodhisattva* as its ideal of practice, and Vajrayana Buddhism recognizes either the *Siddha* ("perfected one") or the *Mahasiddha*[2] ("the fully perfected one") as the pre-eminent model of accomplished Buddhist practice. All three forms of Buddhism propose an ideal of practice that leads to enlightenment and *Nibbana*, so in that respect, at least, they share a common end. Yet what, one might reasonably ask, does this difference in ideals amount to either in theory or in practice and is the difference great enough to justify the claim that we have a new kind of Buddhism?

Theravada Buddhists believe that the *Arahant* attains the same goal as the historical Buddha, enlightenment and *Nibbana*, but that he does so with the help of the teachings of the Buddha, who happened to attain enlightenment and *Nibbana* without any assistance. In this respect, at least, the *Arahant* achieves exactly the same goal as the historical Buddha, though he does it by a different means. Mahayana Buddhists, on the other hand, reject this "individual" or "selfish" *Arahant* ideal of practice as being morally inferior to the actual realization of true Buddha-hood, which they insist can only be achieved by the great compassion of a being (i.e., the *Bodhisattva*) who already personally merits *Nibbana*, but who, like the historical Buddha, postpones it instead, and dedicates himself selflessly to leading all other beings to *Nibbana* first. Finally, Vajrayana Buddhists insist that the *Mahasiddha* embodies the character and ideals of the Vajrayana tradition, with its emphasis on meditation, personal magical powers, the *guru*–disciple relationship, and the non-monastic practices of wandering ascetics. Each of these three ideals clearly involves differences in practice, if not in theory as well. Yet each tradition's view of the ideal of Buddhist practice might also arguably be taken as merely a difference in focus or approach,

---

[2] See "The Mahasiddha," by Reginald Ray in Kitagawa and Cummings (1989), pp. 389–394.

because while all three forms of Buddhism acknowledge the same end, they simply propose alternative paths to it.

Whether these changes of emphasis with respect to the ideal of the highest Buddhist practice, away from individual concerns to compassion for the entire community and back to the individual again, establish important philosophical differences and real distinctions among Theravada, Mahayana, and Vajrayana Buddhism is up to the reader to decide. Regardless of one's answer to this particular question about ideal practice, however, the fact remains that, in general, both Mahayana and Vajrayana Buddhists accept the same basic teachings (i.e., the Middle way, the Four Noble Truths, and the Eightfold Path) as Theravada Buddhists.

Extending the teachings: *anatta*

A second way to consider the relationships among the different kinds of Buddhism is to suggest that "non-Mainstream Buddhism" is simply an unpacking or a more rigorous working out of the details of earlier Mainstream Buddhist ideas. This way of considering the different kinds of Buddhism differs from the previous way, which was concerned with questions of emphasis, by extending the understanding of a concept or idea to new and different areas of application not previously considered. Understood in this way, we can talk about the domain of an idea commonly held by all Buddhists and then speak about their specifically different ranges of interpretation of it.

For example, it is clear from **Chapter 3** that Theravada Buddhists understood that the historical Buddha taught *anatta* or the no-enduring-self view of the human person, not only because he lacked any direct evidence of a fixed soul or *atman*'s existence but also because he did not think its existence was necessary to explain the Indian teachings on rebirth and *kamma*. Mahayana Buddhists, on the other hand, accepted and extended this teaching from human beings to all beings in existence. On this extended view, *anatta* is true, in the conventional sense, not because there is no direct introspective experience of *atman*, nor because *atman* is not required to explain rebirth and *kamma*, but rather, because it is both one of the three marks of all existing beings, and it is the "middle way" between "everything is" (eternalism) and "everything is not" (annihilationism). In a deeper, more profound, and ultimate sense, however, *anatta* is true for Mahayana

Buddhists, because of the truth of interdependent arising as well as the emptiness (*sunyata*) of all things. Without getting into all of the details of each version of this particular teaching, which we shall do in **Chapter 7**, it should be clear, in this case, that we have some real basis for distinguishing Theravada Buddhism and Mahayana Buddhism – at least with respect to the scope of their teachings. In fact, if we compare these two teachings on no-enduring-self with their Vajrayana counterpart, which we shall be examining in more detail in **Chapter 10** when we consider Tibetan Buddhism, we get our first real philosophical difference between a non-essentialist view of the human person and an essentialist, subtle stream of consciousness view of the person.

I want to suggest that the same kind of differences among the three traditions we are considering can be seen in a number of other ideas as well, including: the relationship between *samsara* and *Nibbana*, the value and role of meditation, the spheres of wisdom and morality, the domains of *dukkha* and *tanha*, and even the idea of interdependent arising.

Samsara **and** *Nibbana*

Consider, for example, the relationship between *samsara* and *Nibbana*. It should be clear from **Chapter 3** that Theravada Buddhists accept a real distinction between the present realm of *samsara* and its attendant *tanha* and *dukkha*, and the cessation of *dukkha* achieved in the release from *samsara* and realized in *Nibbana*. On this view of things, the realization of *Nibbana* is the *de facto* end of *samsara*, the condition to which it is directly and diametrically opposed. In other words, *Nibbana* is the ultimate cure for or resolution to the problems of *tanha*, *dukkha*, and *samsara*. Mahayana Buddhists, however, appear to hold a number of different views on the relationship between *samsara* and *Nibbana*.

On the one hand, they seem to downplay the importance of *Nibbana* as an individual, personal goal in life, because of their acceptance of the *Bodhisattva* ideal, i.e., a being that willingly postpones his own achievement of *Nibbana* in order to work for the collective realization of it. On the other hand, they also insist, as Madhyamaka thinkers do, that realizing emptiness allows one to see or understand that *samsara* and *Nibbana* are two sides of the same coin – they are literally the same thing. In fact, a similar kind of identification is taught by Yogacara thinkers as well, who maintain that the cessation of subject–object or dualistic thinking leads to the recognition that the seeming opposition between *samsara* and *Nibbana* is merely apparent or purely conceptual and not ultimately real.

Finally, Vajrayana Buddhists view their own form of Buddhism as both extending and developing the Mahayana account, especially with respect to the powers of the *Mahasiddha* when compared to the *Bodhisattva*. Not only do they conceive of the *Mahasiddha* as the ultimate personal realization of the *Bodhisattva* view, but they also understand him to possess unlimited freedom, power, and holiness in direct opposition to our ordinary experience of a finite and limited world. They also insist that the *Mahasiddha* is completely beyond our conventional conception of *samsara* precisely because he embodies timeless and universal aspects of universal Buddha-nature. In fact, his death is not strictly speaking a natural passing away or even the achievement of *Nibbana*, rather he continues to exist in an invisible, spiritual state or celestial realm from which he is able and available to appear at any subsequent time. Understood in this way, the powers of the *Mahasiddha* allow him to transcend both our ordinary conception of things such as life and death, as well as our conventional distinction between *samsara* and *Nibbana*.

We shall have the opportunity to examine the specifics of each of these accounts of *samsara* and *Nibbana* in more detail when we consider the ideas of *moksa* and *Nibbana* in **Chapter 8**. At this point, however, it should be clear that the three traditions appear to hold broadly divergent views of *anatta*, *samsara*, and *Nibbana*.

Paticca-samuppada

The same kind of differences and development in terms of working out the details of the earlier Mainstream Buddhist ideas can also be seen in the concept of *paticca-samuppada* or interdependent arising. As we have seen, the Theravada tradition teaches that Siddhattha Gotama became completely enlightened only after he fully realized the profound truth of interdependent arising, namely, that all phenomena are causally conditioned, and arise and cease to be in causally determinate ways. Theravada Buddhists maintain that the historical Buddha formulated his understanding and teaching on *paticca-samuppada* with the twelve-fold chain of interdependent arising. It is important to keep in mind, however, that this initial formulation explains interdependent arising with respect to a particular individual's birth, life, death, and rebirth only, and not in terms of the being of all phenomena. In this respect, this manner of presentation is consistent with the early Theravada view of *anatta* as being limited to human beings only. Later Theravada Buddhists, like Buddhaghosa, for example, extended their interpretation of the twelve-fold chain of interdependent arising over the past, present, and future lives of the same human being. It was not, however, until the Madhyamaka thinker Nagarjuna in the second century CE that the Mahayana tradition consciously extended the teachings on interdependent arising to all beings and phenomena and insisted that interdependent arising was synonymous with *sunyata* or emptiness. According to this line of thinking, the idea of interdependent arising can be metaphysically true only if all beings and all phenomena are devoid of fixed essences or self-being.

The Vajrayana interpretation of this teaching extends it through various ritual and esoteric practices to include realized identification between one's intrinsic Buddha-nature and the body of various cosmic Buddhas and *Bodhisattvas*. By practicing both ritual and meditative techniques one can achieve not only direct experience of one's Buddha-nature, but also receive the protection and empowerment of identification with a cosmic Buddha or *Bodhisattva*. These ritual practices provided a method of direct realization of Buddha-nature in this life, and they also helped one avoid the usual difficulties of ordinary religious practices. Finally, these practices served as a vehicle for the direct experience or realization of the unity and interpenetration of all beings and their Buddha-natures.

Once again, it seems clear that the three traditions hold broadly divergent views of one of the most basic ideas of the Buddha. We shall have the opportunity to consider more of the remaining ideological differences among the various form of Buddhism when we present a fourth way of distinguishing the different traditions below. Before considering this fourth way, however, we should examine a separate, third way of comparing the three main Buddhist traditions.

Different texts

A third way to consider the relationships among the different kinds of Buddhism is to focus on their respective texts. We have already considered some of the Pali texts of "Mainstream Buddhism" in **Chapter 3**.

"Non-Mainstream Buddhist" texts include: the *Prajnaparamita* or *Perfection of Wisdom Sutras*, the *Lankavatara Sutra*, the *Lotus Sutra*, the *Vimalakirti Sutra*, the *Heart Sutra*, the *Avatamsaka Sutra*, and the collection of *Pure Land Sutras*, to name just a few.

Vajrayana texts include: various *Tantras* (though it is not the case that Vajrayana is co-extensive with Tantric Buddhism[3]), *Vajrasattva's Fivefold Secret Meditation*, the *Mahavairocana Sutra*, the *Tattvasamgraha Sutra*, the *Vajrasekhara Sutra*, and the *Namasamgiti*.

It should be clear rather quickly to anyone who investigates these texts and their teachings that this third way of considering the relationships among the different kinds of Buddhism provides one of the easiest, if not the least controversial, ways of distinguishing the various forms of Buddhism. It is easy because it is immediately evident to the reader of any of these texts that they are concerned with different ideas and teachings. So one of the first ways to sort out and distinguish the various forms of Buddhism is to begin with the basic texts of each tradition. Yet, even this easy and ready solution has its critics.

According to one school of interpretation, the first justification for distinguishing the various forms of Buddhism cannot be the *sutras* of each tradition because the texts themselves not only can, but also must be read on multiple levels. In addition to this hermeneutical principle, the same school of interpretation insists that one's own ability to read and understand the *sutras* depends on the state of the mental faculties with which one approaches them. In this respect, at least, the reader should be reminded of the opening quotation from the *Dhammapada* where the Buddha is reported to have said that things are the way that we see them. In fact, this view goes further and insists that the teachings themselves have been skillfully given by the historical Buddha in order to accommodate his ideas and teachings to the cognitive or epistemic powers and abilities of his listeners. What this view seems to imply is that each of the different traditions is authentically Buddhist, but their respective messages have been adapted to suit their audiences.

For example, one can imagine different ways by which one could explain the games of baseball, football, or basketball to different audiences. Imagine three groups of listeners and players: beginners, intermediate, and advanced. Surely there is a certain sense in which all three groups will be talking about and participating in the same game. For each game

---

[3] See Williams and Tribe (2000), pp. 192–244.

there are established fields of play, rules governing one's conduct, limitations on the number of players, etc. Nevertheless, there are also accommodations (i.e., with respect to the balls and other rules) made for younger and more inexperienced players. By analogy, then, the same thing is true of the Buddha and his ideas and teachings.

According to this interpretation, the historical Buddha realized that his early audiences would not be able to understand or master the fullness of his ideas and teachings, so he skillfully adapted them to their level. Subsequently, more advanced practitioners were able to understand and study more technically complex forms of his ideas and teachings and that is what non-Mainstream (i.e., Mahayana and Vajrayana) Buddhism is – a richer and more complete version or the fullest expression of his ideas and teachings that audiences over time became able to understand and practice. These differences in skillful means of presentation are captured in the different teachings of the Theravada, Mahayana, and Vajrayana traditions.

At the same time, a second, different school of interpretation insists that the successive teachings of each tradition are in fact actual improvements on the earlier, provisional approximations of their predecessors. According to this Vajrayana view, there were three distinct but related turnings of the wheel of the *Dhamma*. The first turning was the Buddha's first public teaching at the Deer Park in Sarnath. This was his first presentation of the Four Noble Truths in the Pali canon. The second turning of the wheel was the *Perfection of Wisdom sutras* of the Mahayana tradition. This turning was concerned with the topic of emptiness and our experience of it. The third and final turning of the wheel of the *Dhamma* is the unique Vajrayana focus on the innate potential for enlightenment in all beings called their essence of Buddhahood or Buddha-nature. We shall have the opportunity to examine this latter view in more detail in **Chapter 11** and **Chapter 12** when we consider Tibetan Buddhism and the thought of the Dalai Lama. For the time being, however, it should be obvious that this third, supposedly easy, way of considering the relationships among the different kinds of Buddhism by studying their respective texts is more controversial and problematic than would first appear.

Different historical traditions

A fourth, and final way of considering the relationships among the different kinds of Buddhism is to focus on the historical traditions of their teachings.

Like the previously discussed textual way of classifying the different kinds of Buddhism, this way of distinguishing the historical forms of Buddhism rests on the simple fact that the basic teachings of various kinds of Buddhist traditions are at least, at first glance, nominally and conceptually different. Theravada or Hinayana Buddhism is not Mahayana Buddhism and neither form is exactly the same as Vajrayana Buddhism. Madhyamaka Buddhism is not the same as Yogacara Buddhism and neither is the same as Tantric Buddhism. Indian Buddhism is different from Chinese Buddhism and both are fundamentally different from Japanese Buddhism and Tibetan Buddhism. In fact, if we look at the development of the ideas and teachings of the historical Buddha from the elevated heights of both historical and geographical points of view we get a direct and immediate sense of the full scope and range of "the Buddha's" teachings.

We have already noted that within a very short time after the death of the historical Buddha there were no less than eighteen different forms of "Mainstream Buddhism." This should not be surprising. The Buddha had taught publicly for forty-five years, and he taught many different kinds of people, both educated and uneducated, in numerous locations. Having left no centralized authority, other than the *Dhamma* itself, to make judgments about matters of orthodoxy and right practice it should not be difficult to understand how various interpretations of his teachings would and did emerge, even within the same monastic communities.

The problem is only magnified if we extend these same considerations over large geographical distances and hundreds and thousands of years. It should come as no surprise, therefore, that there would be changes and developments in the understanding and interpretation of the basic ideas and teachings of the Buddha, and that is exactly what we see happening even shortly after his death. Without going into all of the details of the fascinating history of the early community of followers of the Buddha, it should not be difficult to imagine what happened.

What has traditionally been called the "First Council" or "First communal recitation" (*sangiti*) of Buddhism was held at Rajagaha only months after the Buddha's death. The purpose of the meeting (according to the early tradition), called and supervised by the monk Mahakasyapa, was to establish a standardized account of the authentic teachings of the Buddha. According to the historical record of the meeting, some five hundred *Arahants* gathered to recite and agree upon an oral record of the Buddha's ideas and teachings.

Two monks, Ananda and Upali, in particular, are traditionally credited with recalling the discourses or basic teachings of the Buddha (Ananda) as well as the rules of discipline for the monastic community (Upali). Once recited, these records were memorized and passed down over the next two hundred years until they were finally written down as the parts of the Pali canon of scriptures called the *Tipitaka*. At first, the oral tradition was divided into two collections or baskets (*pitakas*). The collected discourses of the Buddha were referred to as the *Sutta Pitaka*, and the rules of discipline for the monastic community was called the *Vinaya Pitaka*. A third collection of "Higher Teachings," also attributed to Ananda but probably the result of many years of philosophical reflection and systematization, was designated the *Abhidhamma Pitaka*. These oral traditions and their subsequent versions as three baskets or collections of written texts are the scriptural foundation of what I am calling the Theravada tradition. However, things were more complicated than I am indicating.

Not surprisingly, about one hundred years after the "First communal recitation" a "Second communal recitation" was convened at Vesali in the fourth century BCE. Unlike the first gathering, which was concerned with establishing and preserving the basic teachings of the Buddha, this meeting was concerned with a disagreement over particular monastic practices and disciplinary rules, especially those concerned with the handling of money and nine other practical matters. After a series of discussions, these matters were ultimately decided in favor of a stricter or more conservative reading of the *Vinaya*, but the seeds of future disagreement and fragmentation were already sown. Eventually, the community of Buddhists split into two main groups, the *theras/thaviras* or "elders," from which the Theravada tradition that we have been speaking about emerged, and the *mahasanghika* or "great community," from which, in ways that scholars continue to debate, the Mahayana tradition emerged or against which it defined itself. Whatever the exact history of the disintegration was, the once "unified" community of followers continued to split into more and more distinct factions and monastic communities.

At the same time that practical questions about disciplinary rules and monastic practice were being debated and decided, there were also doctrinal disputes and disagreements about the proper philosophical and theoretical understanding of many of the ideas and teachings of the Buddha. For example, although it is clear that the Buddha taught that there are "five aggregates of attachment" it is not clear exactly what the nature of each is or how they are metaphysically related to one another or to the person whose aggregates they are. The textual tradition itself offers limited help in this regard precisely because it reports that the Buddha often refused to answer metaphysical questions[4] because he did not see them as practically important, or ultimately answerable, or as conducive to edification. In fact, the Buddha famously insisted that anyone who declared that he would not practice or pursue the moral or ethical life (i.e., the Middle Way) with the Buddha until he had answered his metaphysical questions about such things as the eternality and infinity of the physical world, the nature of the soul, the nature of the body, and the soul–body relationship, and questions about the life and existence of the Buddha after his death, would certainly die without the Buddha having explained them. He likened such a person to a man struck by a poisoned arrow.

> Suppose, Malunkyaputta, a man were wounded by an arrow thickly smeared with poison, and his friends and companions, his kinsmen and relatives, brought a surgeon to treat him. The man would say: "I will not let the surgeon pull out this arrow until I know whether the man who wounded me was a noble or a brahmin or a merchant or a worker." And he would say: "I will not let the surgeon pull out this arrow until I know the name and clan of the man who wounded me; ... until I know whether the man who wounded me was tall or short or of middle height; ... until I know whether the man who wounded me was dark or brown or golden-skinned; ... until I know whether the man who wounded me lives in such a village or town or city; ... until I know whether the bow that wounded me was a long bow or a crossbow; ... until I know whether the bowstring that wounded me was fibre or reed or sinew or hemp or bark; ... until I know whether the shaft that wounded me was wild or cultivated; ... until I know with what kind of feathers the shaft that wounded me was fitted – whether those of a vulture or a heron or a hawk or a peacock or a stork; ... until I know with what kind of sinew the shaft that wounded me was bound – whether that of an ox or a buffalo or a deer or a monkey; ... until I know what kind of arrow it was that wounded me – whether it was hoof-tipped or curved or barbed or calf-toothed or oleander."
>
> All this would still not be known to that man and meanwhile he would die. So too, Malunkyaputta, if anyone should say thus: "I will not lead the holy life

---

[4] See especially *Majjhima Nikaya, Culamalunkya Sutta, The Shorter Discourse to Malunkyaputta*, pp. 533–536.

under the Blessed One until the Blessed One declares to me: 'the world is eternal' ... or 'after death a Tathagata neither exists nor does not exist,'" that would still remain undeclared by the Tathagata and meanwhile that person would die.[5]

Given the history we are currently relating, this particular view of the Buddha's response to metaphysical and philosophical questions is just one among many possible interpretations of his considered position on these topics.

Despite, or perhaps because of, the Buddha's unwillingness to answer such questions in clear and unambiguous ways, his followers often found themselves at odds with one another over the correct Buddhist answers to such questions. In fact, one could profitably read the history of Buddhism after the "Councils" or "communal recitations" as both extended discussions on the fine points of Buddhist philosophy as well as prolonged debates about the nature of authentic Buddhist practice. The former flowed from and influenced the development of the *Abhidhamma Pitaka*, while the latter emerged from the missionary work of the followers of the Buddha as they took his ideas and teachings from India to the rest of Asia and beyond. I do not mean to suggest, however, that these should be seen or understood as distinct and unrelated events or happenings. On the contrary, they were two sides of the same Buddhist coin, or, better, in Buddhist terminology, they interdependently arose out of the complex social and human conditions in which both philosophical theory and moral practice are lived and pursued.

Different local traditions

From this point of view, it is easy to see the historical unfolding and development of the ideas and teachings of the Buddha as various local answers to philosophical and practical questions about both what the Buddha meant by what he was reported to have said and how he was to be authentically followed.

In India, for example, there were at least eighteen different *Abhidhamma* traditions whose major philosophical questions and concerns focused on clarifying and explaining the Buddha's ideas on the metaphysical nature of

[5] Ibid., pp. 534–535.

the world and the events and processes taking place in it, as well as the basic structures of consciousness and its processes of knowledge. At the same time that these traditions were being formed there were also Mahayana texts and *Sutras* that were being composed and circulated that offered competing and sometimes incompatible views of everything, from the kind of being the historical Buddha was to alternative practices for achieving enlightenment and *Nibbana*. According to Paul Williams,[6] this latter tradition of Buddhism, which began to take shape around the first century BCE, produced its own collection of writings that also claimed to be the words of the Buddha himself. However, he also claims that this literature was not produced by a single, unified group of Buddhists, but by monks living and practicing within the already existing traditions.

According to Williams, the subject matter of these texts focused on the supremacy of the Buddha as a role model and on his unique perception and understanding of things. As a whole, these texts and *Sutras* advocated the path of the *Bodhisattva*, the aspirant to full Buddhahood, as a nobler and higher path to be pursued than the "lesser" path of the *Arahant*. In fact, one of the principal concerns of these "greater" vehicle texts was their concern with the welfare of all beings, and not just a small, specific group of human beings.

Williams also speculates that these early Mahayana Buddhists may have thought of themselves as "a righteous bulwark"[7] against the moral and spiritual decline that was happening all around them in their monastic communities, and that was an important reason for convening later Councils and recitations. Despite the fact that some of the followers of this "higher" way may have thought of their texts and beliefs as superior to their "Hinayana" counterparts, Williams does not think that their public behavior or individual practice was notably different in any fundamental way from that of other members of the *Samgha*. However, what initially was a minority of practioners within Indian Buddhism, came to see themselves as followers of a "greater" or Mahayana way.

Among the subsequent followers of this "superior" Indian tradition are the Madhyamika or "Middle Way" school of Nagarjuna, the Yogacara school of Asanga and Vasubandhu, and those who accepted the *Tathagata-garbha* literature. Each of these groups of Buddhists was engaged in serious

---

[6] Williams (1989), especially chapter 1 and pp. 32–33.   [7] Ibid.

philosophical study and speculation about the proper understanding of the Buddha's account of the meaning and purpose of life as well as the fundamental nature of reality. Eventually, given these kinds of intellectual pursuits, some monasteries evolved into something like universities where monks and scholars could be trained in and study the philosophical systems that were being created to explain and understand the specific ideas and teachings of the Buddha.

At the same time that these events were taking place in the monastic community, lay Buddhists were pursuing their own means and methods for understanding the Buddha's message. Some turned to Tantric texts and practices as a way of enhancing and supplementing their religious beliefs and practices. This union of *Tantra* and Buddhism is what ultimately came to be called Vajrayana or Mantrayana Buddhism, and it was an important part of the Buddhism that made its way into Tibet, as we shall see in **Chapter 11**.

It should not be surprising given the dynamic history of the spread and development of Buddhism within India itself to imagine similar kinds of changes and development as it made its way in both directions across Asia. That is exactly what happened.

Different geographical answers

In China as well as in most other places where Buddhism went, one of the first problems to be overcome was difference in languages. The texts of Buddhism needed to be translated into Chinese and other languages, and in order to do this the meanings of terms in both the original texts as well as the target languages needed to be specified and defined. As we have already seen, there were significant disagreements among the immediate followers of the Buddha over not only what he said but also what he meant by what he said, and all of this was further complicated by the fact that the historical Buddha seems to have said so many different things to so many different people over the course of so many years in so many different locations. When we now add the linguistic difficulties encountered as Buddhism made its way throughout Asia, it seems only natural to wonder whether anything like the "original" (assuming there was such a thing) or early form or forms of Buddhism was preserved in its dissemination.

If we look at Buddhism in China, for example, we see that the Chinese themselves recognized at least ten different schools or traditions of thought. Many of these forms of Chinese Buddhism can be traced back to their Indian sources, which should not be surprising. However, almost half of the Chinese forms of Buddhism – Tiantai, Huayan, Chan, and Pure Land – are considered part of a uniquely Chinese conception or interpretation of Buddhism. Moreover, all of this is true without any consideration of the various forms of Folk Buddhism that developed both in India and throughout Asia alongside the more scholarly and "respected" forms of professional monastic Buddhism.

In Korea and Japan as well, we see the same kinds of problems and developments. In each of these countries there were initially five or six recognized schools of Buddhism, some of whose roots could be traced all the way back to India, but others whose sources could be found in the intervening and uniquely Chinese experience and understanding of Buddhism. In Japan, for example, scholars typically distinguish between forms of Buddhism that are specifically Indian in inspiration and those that are peculiarly Japanese in their thinking. Among the latter we find the Tendai and Shingon schools, as well as Japanese Pure Land, Zen, and Nichiren Buddhism.

One and many forms of Buddhism

What all of this seems to indicate is that there is no easy answer to our original chapter title question about whether there is one Buddhism or many forms of Buddhism. On the one hand, the answer appears to be that there are many unique forms of Buddhism. Indian Buddhism, which has its own variations, is not exactly the same as Chinese Buddhism, which is clearly different from Tibetan Buddhism as well as Japanese Buddhism. On the other hand, the answer also appears to be that there is just one form of Buddhism, at least with respect to its most basic ideas and fundamental teachings, i.e., the Middle Way, the Four Noble Truths, and the Eightfold Path.

This one form, however, seems to have taken on various local qualities and features as it adapted itself to different geographical, cultural, and historical settings. So in typical philosophical fashion our answer to the chapter title question about whether "Buddhism" refers to a single referent, i.e., a single philosophical system, or to a complex network of interrelated philosophies must be both "yes" and "no." On the one hand, it refers to the ideas and teachings of the historical Buddha, but on the other hand, his teachings and ideas were adapted to specifically different cultural situations and contexts, with the result that "Buddhism" now designates both a single philosophical system as well as a complex network of distinct but inter-related philosophies (to say nothing about its various "religious" forms, as well). That this is the best answer to our title question should become more clear after we look more carefully at the specific elements of some of the most basic ideas of the Buddha in **Part II**, and their subsequent historical and cultural adaptations in **Part III**.

Things to think about

1. What is your answer to the title question of this chapter?
2. What might the changes in the ideals indicate about the Buddhist under-standing of its own teachings and practices?
3. What basic teachings do all three forms of Buddhism accept and why?
4. How does the concept of *upaya* help explain the differences among the various texts of the three traditions?
5. How does the fact that the Buddha taught for forty-five years to various kinds of audiences affect the form and content of his teachings?

Part II

Details of the *Dhamma*

The word *dhamma/dharma*, whose root "*dhr*" means "to bind," "to keep," or "to maintain," refers to a rather broad range of entities and relations. In fact, it seems to have the broadest field of semantic reference of any word in Pali (*dhamma*) or Sanskrit (*dharma*). On the one hand, *dhamma* is used to refer to both objects and their parts or elements (i.e., physical objects in the world around us). It also may refer to relations among objects, or more generally to any object of reference in thought or speech – in the same way that "thing" is used in ordinary English. On the other hand, *dhamma* may be understood to include "social morality" or the "moral law" as that which holds or binds people together. In this sense, *dhamma* refers to the underlying pattern or order of the cosmos and also to the pattern and order realized in the social and ethical rules and laws of human beings. Understood in this way, *dhamma* includes the ideas of virtue, duty, or proper moral and ethical conduct. Finally, as a technical term, *Dhamma* also means the specific teachings of the Buddha. As such, Buddhism is concerned with experiencing, discovering, understanding, practicing, and realizing the *Dhamma*.

Chapters 5 through **8** consider the basic teachings of the Buddha in more detail as well as their historical developments. **Chapter 5** begins with two stories relating to the scope of the Buddha's teachings as well as his general attitude toward philosophical views. It rehearses the religious and philosophical background against which the Buddha's ideas on *kamma*, *samsara*, and rebirth were formulated. It then considers the Buddha's conception of *kamma*, the evidence for and against it, and the notions of *samsara* and rebirth, and the logical relationships among these ideas. It also argues that the Buddha's ideas about *kamma*, *samsara*, and rebirth should be understood within the broader context of the Buddha's meditative practices and his most basic insight that who we are and what we think exists is a function of our mind, its cognitive or intellectual powers, and the actions that we will or intend. Readers will be encouraged to consider for themselves: 1. the evidence for and against the ideas of *kamma*, *samsara*, and rebirth; 2. the relationship of these ideas to the broader context of the Buddha's meditative practices; and 3. the logical relationships among these ideas as well as their connections to other related philosophical concepts.

Chapter 6 considers what is perhaps the single most important metaphysical notion of Buddhism – *paticca-samuppada*, which is variously translated as "dependent origination," "co-dependent origination," "conditioned arising," "conditioned co-production," "dependent arising," and "interdependent arising." These translations are simply ways of expressing the insight of the Buddha into the fundamental interconnectedness of all beings. According to this teaching of the Buddha, whatever happens or comes to be is a result of prior causes and conditions. **Chapter 6** considers six distinct conceptions of it, its relationships to the corresponding ideas of *kamma*, *samsara*, and rebirth, the conception of the self, and the realization of *Nibbana*, and the evidence for this fundamental idea.

Anicca/impermanence is one of the "Three Marks" (in addition to *dukkha* and *anatta*) or universal features of all existence. It captures the idea that everything that comes into existence is always already on the way out of existence. Given the preceding discussion of interdependent arising, **Chapter 7** is concerned with the logical relationships among interdependent arising, impermanence, emptiness, *anatta*, *dukkha*, *kamma*, rebirth, mindfulness, *moksa*, and *Nibbana*. It also introduces the *Abhidhamma* accounts of these terms and briefly considers the Mahayana developments of them.

Moksa and *Nibbana*/*Nirvana* are the Indian and Buddhist terms for freedom or release from the limitations of *samsara* and the ultimate goal of the Buddhist way of life. **Chapter 8** is concerned with both the prospects of release from the continuously revolving Wheel of Life, with its attendant fires/poisons of ignorance, greed, and hatred, and the basic features of the state of this "liberation/extinction." It considers the evidence for the Buddha's understanding and analysis of ordinary experience as fundamentally misconstrued because of the negative effects of ignorance and craving which lead to the suffering of further birth and death. It also considers the merits of the Buddha's epistemological and moral claims that meditation and mindfulness are conducive to the fully enlightened state in which no *kamma* is generated and one lives as a liberated *Arahant*.

5   *Kamma, Samsara,* and rebirth

Key teachings and terms

Jhana/Dhyana: Pali and Sanskrit terms for deep meditative state or intellectual state of absorption involving direct awareness and insight into reality and experience. The Buddhist tradition identifies four to eight distinct stages or levels of meditative absorption.

Kamma/Karma: Literally "action" or "deed," this term refers to the fact that actions, intentions, volitions, and, in general, states of mind have or produce consequences. The basic Buddhist account of it is that appropriate and inappropriate, wholesome and unwholesome mental tendencies or habits lead to actions that ultimately produce fruits or consequences.

Rebirth: Ancient Indian idea that one is reborn after death. It is usually connected to the idea of *kamma.* According to Buddhist cosmology there are six realms of rebirth: the realm of the gods or *devas,* the realm of the demi-gods, the human realm, the animal realm, the realm of the hungry ghosts, and the realm of hell. All six realms are thought to be real, but some forms of Mahayana Buddhism claim that they are best thought of as states of mind.

Rta: Indian term for the underlying structure and fundamental normative rhythm that organizes the energy and existence of all beings in the universe. It also refers to the law-like regularity and harmony of both the moral and physical spheres of the universe.

Samsara: Literally "wandering on" or "flowing on" this term conveys the idea of "aimless and directionless wandering" and refers to the ongoing and seemingly endless cyclical process of birth, life, death, and rebirth. In a more general way, it refers to the conditioned world of this life as it is experienced and caused by one's *kamma* with its concomitant *dukkha.*

Two stories

In order to help frame the discussion of the details of the Buddha's *Dhamma* that we will be considering in the next four chapters, I want to begin with two stories that reveal the Buddha's beliefs about the scope of his own teachings as well as his attitude toward philosophical views in general.

The Buddhist scriptures abound with stories, parables, and images that are meant to instruct, admonish, inspire, inform, and encourage their readers. Many of these rather ordinary images and tales cover the same ground as the Buddha's more technical teachings, and often they approach the same topics and ideas but from different points of view. Two of the more famous stories involve blind men and an elephant, and the Buddha and a handful of simsapa leaves.

According to the first story, once while the Buddha was living in Jeta's Grove in Savatthi, there were also a number of other ascetics, Brahmins, and wanderers from various sects living in the same area. Each group held various ideas, beliefs, and opinions, and each taught their own views. They were, as one can imagine, quarrelsome, disputatious, wrangling, and they argued with each other, saying things like, "The *Dhamma* is like this, the *Dhamma* is *not* like that! The *Dhamma* is *not* like this, the *Dhamma* is like that!"

A group of the Buddha's followers returning from alms seeking observed these activities and reported them to the Buddha, who said,

> Monks, wanderers of other sects are blind and sightless. They do not know what is beneficial and harmful. They do not know what is the *Dhamma* and what is not the *Dhamma*, and thus they are so quarrelsome and disputatious.
>
> Formerly, monks, there was a king in Savatthi who addressed a man and asked him to round up all the persons in the city who were blind from birth. When the man had done so, the king asked the man to show the blind men an elephant. To some of the blind men he presented the head of the elephant, to some the ear, to others a tusk, the trunk, the body, a foot, the hindquarters, the tail, or the tuft at the end of the tail. And to each one he said, "This is an elephant."
>
> When he reported to the king what he had done, the king went to the blind men and asked them, "Tell me, blind men, what is an elephant like?"
>
> Those who had been shown the head of the elephant replied, "An elephant, your majesty, is just like a water jar." Those who had been shown the ear

replied, "An elephant is just like a winnowing basket." Those who had been shown the tusk replied, "An elephant is just like a plowshare." Those who had been shown the trunk replied, "An elephant is just like a plow pole." Those who had been shown the body replied, "An elephant is just like a storeroom." And each of the others likewise described the elephant in terms of the part they had been shown.

Then, saying, "An elephant is like this, an elephant is *not* like that! An elephant is *not* like this, an elephant *is* like that!" they fought each other with their fists. And the king was delighted. Even so, monks, are the wanderers of other sects blind and sightless, and thus they become quarrelsome, disputatious, and wrangling, wounding each other with verbal darts.[1]

In the second story, while the Buddha was staying in Kosambi in a grove of simsapa trees, he collected a few leaves in his hand and addressed the monks thus:

What do you think, monks, which is more numerous: these few leaves that I have taken up in my hand or those in the grove overhead?

"Venerable sir, the leaves that the Blessed One has taken up in his hand are few, but those in the grove overhead are numerous."

So too, monks, the things I have directly known but have not taught you are numerous, while the things I have taught you are few. And why, monks, have I not taught those many things? Because they are without benefit, irrelevant to the fundamentals of the spiritual life, and do not lead to disenchantment, to dispassion, to cessation, to peace, to direct knowledge, to enlightenment, to *Nibbana.* Therefore I have not taught them.

And what, monks, have I taught? I have taught: "This is suffering"; I have taught: "This is the cessation of suffering"; I have taught: "This is the way leading to the cessation of suffering." And why, monks, have I taught this? Because this is beneficial, relevant to the fundamentals of the spiritual life, and leads to disenchantment, to dispassion, to cessation, to peace, to direct knowledge, to enlightenment, to *Nibbana.* Therefore I have taught this.[2]

I want to suggest that these stories give us two important insights into the Buddha's understanding of the limits of his own teachings as well as his thoughts about one's commitments to one's own views. The story of the Buddha and the simsapa leaves clearly indicates that although he knows many things, he actually teaches just a few of them, i.e., the Four Noble

---

[1] See Bhikkhu Bodhi (2005), pp. 214–215.   [2] Ibid., p. 360.

Truths, because these (alone?) lead to enlightenment and *Nibbana*. This is not to deny that there are other teachings that are interesting and important and even logically connected to the Four Noble Truths, but they seem, like the questions in the story of the man struck by the poisoned arrow, to be irrelevant to what is really at stake, namely, dealing with the practical problem at hand – liberation from the conditions of *samsara*. In short, the point seems to be that the Buddha taught only what really mattered.

The story of the blind men and the elephant, on the other hand, clearly indicates that attachment to views, any views, even those of the Buddha, can cause biased and distorted interpretations of the way things really are. The Buddha recognized that those who tenaciously cling to their own limited, and sometimes dogmatic, views of things often come into conflict with those who have a different view of things. In fact, the Buddha seems to be indicating his own recognition that views of any kind tend to give rise to conflicts and disputes precisely because by their very nature they are, like the individual blind men in the story, limited in their scope or field of vision. What this means, is that one must be consciously and continuously aware of the dangers of dogmatically clinging to any view, even the Buddha's view. This is an important, if often overlooked, point to keep in mind as we begin to consider some of the most basic ideas and teachings of the Buddha.

Contemporary cultural beliefs

As we saw in **Chapter 2**, the basic elements of the teachings of the Buddha can be traced to ideas whose roots can be found in the pre-Vedic and Vedic visions of things. From the pre-Vedic vision he inherited basic ideas about the possibility of rebirth, the value of ascetic practices, and the importance of meditation. The Vedic vision, on the other hand, provided the immediate intellectual context in which and against which the Buddha and his contemporaries formulated their own post-Vedic accounts of things.

The precise historical origins of the Indian ideas of *kamma*, *samsara*, and rebirth are less than clear. They appear to be part of what we have called the pre-Vedic vision of the Dasyus, but this is merely speculation without textual support and it is based on limited archaeological evidence that is anything but certain. When we turn to the Vedic vision, the *Vedas* themselves do not seem to recognize, or at best only anticipate, what would become something like the ordinary Indian understanding of these three distinct yet related concepts. Even the *Upanishads*, which contain scattered references[3] to these ideas, do not contain anything like a complete or systematic account of any of them.

Given what we know about the history and development of Indian thought, it is not difficult to imagine that there were a number of different and competing ideas in ancient India about what happens after death, and how that is or may be related to what one does while one is alive. As I indicated when presenting the pre-Vedic vision, it is easy to see how ancient Indians might arrive at the ideas of *kamma*, *samsara*, and rebirth.

Recall that we pointed out that once someone's basic biological needs for food, clothing, and shelter and one's practical environmental concerns about life and safety have been met, it is natural to suppose that they might turn their attention to deeper "metaphysical" questions about the point and purpose of living and dying since these are the basic facts of every human life. We also noted that it is rather obvious that many things in the world are beyond human control, and it is often difficult, if not impossible, to know or predict future events and outcomes, such as the weather and seasons and natural disasters or even human actions. Nevertheless, it is also quite clear that many of these very same forces and things in nature, including human beings, seem to follow patterns, even predictable cyclical patterns, in their actions. It is not difficult to imagine ancient Indians being puzzled with questions about what the source or sources of this apparent order and patterns are. Furthermore, it is easy to imagine them wondering if

---

[3] For example, *Katha Upanishad* says, "He, however, who has not understanding, who is unmindful and ever impure, reaches not the goal, but goes on to rebirth"; *Chandogya Upanishad* says, "those who are of pleasant conduct here – the prospect is, indeed, that they will enter a pleasant womb, either the womb of a Brahmin, or the womb of a ksatriya, or the womb of a vaisya. But those who are of stinking conduct here – the prospect is, indeed, that they will enter a stinking womb, either the womb of a dog, or the womb of a swine, or the womb of an outcast" ; and *Brhadaranyaka Upanishad* says, "What they said was *kamma*. What they praised was *kamma*. Verily, one becomes good by good action, bad by bad action" and "According as one acts, according as one conducts himself, so does he become. The doer of good becomes good. The doer of evil becomes evil. One becomes virtuous by virtuous action, bad by bad action." And "Where one's mind is attached – the inner self goes thereto with action, being attached to it alone. Obtaining the end of his action, whatever he does in this world, he comes again from that world to this world of action." In Radhakrishnan and Moore (1957), pp. 46, 66–67, 83, 87.

the order itself is real or merely apparent. Finally, one could quite naturally imagine them asking themselves if things are not in their control, then must there be some thing or things that does or do control or explain the pattern and order.

"Dasyu beliefs"

I have suggested that the ancient Dasyu way of understanding and dealing with these ordinary questions and problems of life was to recognize some superhuman or divine sources of power behind or in the forces and things in nature. They seem also to have recognized that nature itself or the cosmos conceived of as a whole exercised a kind of control over human affairs.

Like all humans, the Dasyus seem to have realized that we have the power simultaneously to work with and/or against nature and its forces and power. They recognized the immutable and inexorable truth that humans are born, live, and die, but they also appear to have held the view, based on their burial practices, that death was not the end of life. It is not known whether they clearly distinguished between rebirth in a different world (in some other location), or simply rebirth in this world at some future time. Whether they had considered some kind of causal (i.e., karmic) explanation of either possible rebirth scenario is also unclear as well.

As we have seen, traditionally, there have been two kinds of cases for believing that there is some kind of existence after death. The first kind of "religious" case is anchored in some type of revelation from a god or gods about the, or an afterlife. In this scenario someone claims to have heard or received a message about what awaits or happens to those who die and others choose to believe both the message and the person who has received the revelation.

The second kind of "philosophical" or "scientific" case is justified by observations about the way things seem to happen in nature and by logical inferences to the best explanation as a way to make sense out of the data of experience. In this kind of case, one recognizes through observation that things and events in nature appear to follow regular and orderly patterns or cycles. The sun rises and sets, the moon waxes and wanes, the tides rise and fall, and the seasons come and go in relative order and stability. In addition to these obvious facts, plants and crops seem to follow seasonal and annual patterns of growth, maturation, fruition, and death. In the cases of perennial flowers and plants, the "same" plants and flowers appear to return year after year after year. A similar kind of thing also seems to be true of animals and human beings and their offspring. How can such likenesses be rationally explained?

One possible explanation is to claim that the similarities and patterns or cycles that we experience in our interactions with nature and other human beings are best explained by appealing to the idea that it is literally the same, exact individual who has been born, lived, died and then been reborn all over again. This kind of inference is justified as being the best explanation for the puzzling and sometimes-overwhelming experience of observing someone who not only looks, and acts, but also speaks and sounds like another deceased human being. In other words, the simple fact that two temporally separated individuals look and act in ways that are for all intents and purposes completely or nearly completely indistinguishable from one another can most easily and rationally be explained by appealing to the idea of an enduring or perdurable self that passes from life to death to life again.

A second possible explanation, that may or may not be separable from the metaphysical commitments of the first, is to reason from observed effects to unobserved causes. This explanation begins with the fact that it is clear and evident to the senses that human beings, and all living things for that matter, are born and eventually die. The previously noted cyclical nature of phenomena as well as questions about where the new born come from (assuming they cannot come from nothing) would seem to entail that the living come from the dead in ways that are related to how the dead come from the living. If that is true, then the previously living must not only continue to exist in a "world" after death, but they must die again in that "world" in order to be born again into this world. This conclusion, however, would seem to entail two unfortunate consequences: first, the cycle of birth–life–death–rebirth itself appears to be unending, and second, there is the continuing and ongoing problem of dying over and over and over again. One obvious and pressing question is whether there is any way out of this cycle. A second, complementary question is whether there is any way to escape the problem of re-dying. The answers to these and other related questions are exactly what classical Indian philosophy and religion were concerned with.

It should be noted in passing, however, that none of this is meant to suggest that either of these explanations or anything like these lines of reasoning were actually formulated by any ancient Indians, including the Dasyus, but merely to show that something like the ordinary, common-sense conceptions of *kamma*, *samsara*, and rebirth are not logically inconsistent or incoherent.

Vedic beliefs

If we turn our attention to the Vedic vision of things, it is clear that the same kind of plurality of views about *kamma*, *samsara*, and rebirth exist. As we have seen, the Vedic vision includes the texts of the *Vedas* and the *Upanishads*, which are not always in agreement about the meaning and purpose of life or the fundamental nature of reality. As the table in **Chapter 2** indicated, what we for the sake of simplicity are calling the "Vedic vision" is actually at least two distinct and competing visions.

On the one hand, the *Vedas* themselves talk about the life of humans after death as involving both human and animal rebirth. They also, not surprisingly, talk about the karmic significance and importance of rituals properly performed by the Brahmins and their effects on both one's earthly existence as well as one's existence after death. Finally, the *Vedas* talk about the ideas of cosmic balance or harmony, and even the idea of cosmic justice with the concept of *rta*. Each of these ideas seems to anticipate at least some aspect of a more fully developed idea of *kamma*.

The *Upanishads*, on the other hand, especially as quoted in note 3 above, represent an even closer approximation to more fully developed ideas of *kamma*, *samsara*, and rebirth. Each of the quoted *Upanishads* clearly contains ideas directly related to questions about life after death, rebirth, *kamma*, and *samsara*. In fact, other passages in the *Upanishads* also talk about the causal powers of actions and their effects on both things in this life as well as life after death. Unlike the *Vedas*, the *Upanishads* focus not only on the value and significance of ritual actions, but also on the entire sphere of human actions beyond the practice of rituals.

Nevertheless, despite these extensions of the ideas of *kamma*, *samsara*, and rebirth, the *Upanishads* as a whole are unfortunately less than clear about many of the specific details and particular mechanisms of how each of these ideas works in reality. For example, they lack a clear account of the ontology of the human agent, the psychological forces at work within the agent who acts, the specific mechanisms of causal consequences, the range of rebirth possibilities, and the causal effects and contributions of external, environmental factors, such as the gods and chance, luck, fortune, or fate.

We should also keep in mind that while these views were being formulated and defended, competing and contradictory views about the impossibility of life after death, as well as the causal determinism of all actions, were being developed and defended by materialist and fatalist thinkers like the Carvakas and Gosala and the Ajivakas. It was in the midst of these vigorous ongoing philosophical disputes and disagreements that Siddhattha Gotama worked out his unique account and defense of his ideas about *kamma*, *samsara*, and rebirth.

The Buddha's view

When we turn our attention to the ideas and teachings of the Buddha, it is quite clear from the earliest textual traditions that the historical Buddha not only accepted the ideas of *kamma*, *samsara*, and rebirth, but that his enlightenment experience under the *Bodhi* tree involved a profound and direct experiential insight into the truths of all three ideas.

According to the early Buddhist tradition, on the night of his enlightenment, Siddhattha passed through four levels of meditation or concentration (*jhanas/dhyanas*) and his "mind was thus concentrated, purified, bright, unblemished, rid of imperfection, malleable, wieldy, steady, and attained to imperturbability."[4]

On the first level of meditation he was able to concentrate his mind and be free from sensual pleasure and impure thoughts, but his mind still engaged in discursive rational thinking. On the second *jhana* level he was able to transcend discursive thinking and attain a deeper and more unified state of mental peace, calm, and tranquillity. On the third level of meditation he was able to overcome his internal emotional states and thereby achieve a balanced and clear mind. Finally, on the fourth level of meditation, he achieved a complete experience of mindful equanimity and intellectual clarity that allowed him to have a penetrating insight into the ultimate truth about the fundamental nature of reality and existence.

Having ascended to these intellectual and meditative heights, the *Sutras* claim that Siddhattha literally awakened (i.e., became "the Buddha") to the

---

[4] *Majjhima Nikaya*, p. 341.

truths about rebirth, *kamma*, *samsara*, interdependent arising, and the Four Noble Truths in the three watches of the night. During the first watch (i.e., evening, around 6–10 p.m.) he saw all of his previous lives. During the second watch (i.e., midnight, or 10–2 a.m.) he saw the rebirth of other beings according to their *kamma*, and with a "divine eye"[5] he saw and understood how beings pass away and reappear according to their actions. Finally, during the third watch (i.e., early morning, around 2–6 a.m.) he not only destroyed all mental and emotional impurities, taints, defilements, desires, false views, and ignorance, but he also realized the interdependent arising of all beings and all existence as well as the Four Noble Truths. In fact, the Buddha is said to have claimed,

> When I knew and saw thus, my mind was liberated from the taint of sensual desire, from the taint of being, and from the taint of ignorance. When it was liberated, there came the knowledge: "It is liberated." I directly knew: "Birth is destroyed, the holy life has been lived, what had to be done has been done, there is no more coming to any state of being."[6]

What is particularly important about this passage with respect to the Buddha's teaching on *kamma*, *samsara*, and rebirth is both its context and its content. With respect to its content, it is quite clear that the Buddha claims that he "directly knew," i.e., had immediate cognitive experience, that any form of birth, or more exactly rebirth, that might have happened as a result of his past actions was now eliminated as a consequence of his subsequent practice and enlightenment. He had not only eliminated all intellectual and emotional defects and impediments, but he had also realized and understood the Four Noble Truths and consequently achieved what he had set out to achieve when he renounced his wife, son, and family, his friends, his possessions, and his very way of life in search of an answer to his questions about the meaning and purpose of life. There was, in short, "no more coming to any state of being" for one who had done what had to be done.

With respect to its context, there is no doubt that the Buddha's enlightenment and subsequent realization of *Nibbana* was a direct result of his intellectual activities and meditative practices. Every account of his enlightenment that I am aware of relates with more or less detail the intellectual

---

[5] Ibid., p. 341 and p. 106.   [6] Ibid., p. 106.

and meditative steps by which he finally came to be aware and awakened to the truth about reality. In fact, even the brief sketch of his life in **Chapter 1** indicated that it was his intellectual activities, rather than his ascetic bodily practices, that ultimately paved the way for his insight into reality and his realization of *Nibbana*. I cannot stress this last point enough.

While it is certainly true, especially on the Buddha's own account of interdependent arising, that every "thing" causally contributes to the ongoing existence of every other "thing," and so every moment in one's life contributes to its unfolding, nevertheless, it is possible to distinguish primary and secondary causal factors that contribute in different ways to the story of one's life. According to this understanding of things, then, although the Buddha did engage in serious ascetic practices, it was not these bodily practices *per se* that directly, immediately, and ultimately produced his enlightenment. Rather it was his intellectual and meditative practices that finally awakened him to the truth about the way things are.

We should also keep in mind, however, that it was not just any kind of meditation that occasioned the Buddha's enlightenment. Recall that shortly after Siddhattha had renounced his former materialistic and hedonistic way of life, he sought the advice and assistance of teachers who could train him in spiritual practices that might help him realize his goal. At first, he had sought the help and advice of two yoga masters, Alara Kalama and then Uddaka Ramaputra, both of whom taught and practiced different systems of meditation and mental concentration. Studying under Alara Kalama he quickly mastered his teachings and achieved the meditational state referred to as "the sphere of nothingness." According to this form of yogic practice, Siddhattha was able to achieve a meditative state of concentration in which his mind was able to transcend every distinct mental object of thought and rest in nothingness. Although this practice produced a heightened state of inner mental calmness, it did not, unfortunately, satisfy him. In fact, he said, "This *Dhamma* does not lead to disenchantment, to dispassion, to cessation, to peace, to direct knowledge, to enlightenment, to *Nibbana*, but only to reappearance in the base of nothingness."[7] As a result, Siddhattha left Alara Kalama despite Alara's offer to make him co-teacher of his community of followers.

His second teacher, Uddaka Ramaputra, taught a different form of yogic practice that resulted in the state of concentration known as

---

[7] Ibid., p. 258.

"neither-perception-nor-non-perception." This state went beyond the meditative level of "the sphere of nothingness" and produced an experience of minimal consciousness. Again, Siddhattha quickly mastered both the teaching and the practice taught by Uddaka. Although this meditative practice also produced a calm and still mind, Siddhattha rejected it for the same reasons that he had rejected his first teacher's method, because it did not produce the goal he was so eagerly seeking, i.e., enlightenment and the realization of the end of suffering. Once again, Siddhattha left.

It is important to keep in mind, however, that even though Siddhattha rejected both the offer to lead each teacher's group as well as their specific forms of yogic practice, he later incorporated both meditative states he had achieved into his own meditational scheme, as steps or stages of calming and stilling the mind in preparation for the liberating insight of enlightenment that he himself eventually achieved. Again, the context of the Buddha's claims is crucially important here, because it provides the background against which his teachings must be understood.

Recall for a moment that having been unsuccessful in his search for answers to life's problems and questions on either extreme of the pleasure and pain spectrum, Siddhattha decided to sit down and reflect quietly, with neither psychic nor physical rigors, on the common human plight. As Michael Carrithers claimed, "This led to the second great change in his life, for out of this reflection in tranquility arose at last awakening and release. He had 'done what was to be done,' he had solved the enigma of suffering."[8] The context is clearly Siddhattha's search for enlightenment, and the specific practice he is engaged in is intellectual meditation and reflection in tranquillity – not ascetic physical or psychic practices. This seems to indicate quite clearly that his insights and teachings about *kamma*, *samsara*, and rebirth must be understood as arising out of his direct, personal meditative experiences while in the pursuit of enlightenment and the realization of *Nibbana*. They were clearly not ideas and experiences that arose in the course of either his life of princely pleasures or his life of ascetic practices. They were, in fact, realized only in the midst of his "Middle Way" pursuit of the purpose and meaning of life and the fundamental nature of reality.

Given this context, the truth of the content of the Buddha's teachings on *kamma*, *samsara*, and rebirth, as well as the truth of his claims about the

---

[8] Carrithers (1983), p. 3.

removal of intellectual and emotional defects or taints, interdependent arising, and even the Four Noble Truths themselves, appear to depend directly and immediately on the state of the cognitive, intellectual, and meditative powers of those who are investigating and studying these ideas. In other words, one can really understand and grasp the ultimate truth and meaning of these ideas only after one has engaged in the appropriate kinds of meditative practices.

As we have seen, the Buddhist tradition claims that on the night of his enlightenment, Siddhattha passed through four levels of meditation or concentration and that as a result of this meditative practice his "mind was thus concentrated, purified, bright, unblemished, rid of imperfection, malleable, wieldy, steady, and attained to imperturbability." His insights into his own rebirths, as well as the rebirths of others according to their *kamma*, were only achieved after he had passed through the four levels of meditation described above. In fact, his insights into the destruction of the intellectual and emotional defects of the mind, the fact of interdependent arising, and finally the Four Noble Truths did not occur until the final watch of the night. Then, and only then, did the Buddha declare, "When I knew and saw thus, my mind was liberated from the taint of sensual desire, from the taint of being, and from the taint of ignorance." Then, and only then, was Siddhattha truly "the Buddha," because then, and only then, was he awakened to the truth about reality, liberated from wrong views, and free, at last, to realize *Nibbana*.

Given this reading of his enlightenment experience, I think it should begin to be clear why I claimed in **Chapter 2** that the single most important or most basic insight of the Buddha is the claim that who we are and what we think exists is a function of our mind and its cognitive or intellectual powers.

Recall that I proposed an analogy to help understand what I think the Buddha meant. I said that if I understand him correctly, what I take the Buddha to be claiming is that in the same way that I can maintain, shape, and transform my physical body through a proper diet and a serious weight-training program, I can also maintain, shape, transform, and indeed, strengthen, improve, and perfect my mind by meditative practices and exercises. It is precisely this insight and power, as we have seen, that the Buddha himself personally experienced and diligently practiced while under the *Bodhi* tree. Moreover, it was the Buddha's experiences with his

first teachers, Alara Kalama and Uddaka Ramaputta, and their yogic meditative practices, that formed the foundation of both his own understanding
of the value of meditative practices, and ultimately his "awakening" to the
truths about reality.

If this interpretation of the Buddha's awakening and his claims is correct,
then it is easy to see what he said about *kamma*, *samsara*, and rebirth. It is also
easier to understand why he said what he did about each of them.

In the case of rebirth, it is clear from what the Buddhist tradition records
that on the night of his enlightenment the Buddha directed his mind to
knowledge of the recollection of past lives.

> I recollected my manifold past lives, that is, one birth, two births, three
> births, four births, five births, ten births, twenty births, thirty births, forty
> births, fifty births, a hundred births, a thousand births, a hundred thousand
> births, many aeons of world-contraction, many aeons of world expansion,
> many aeons of world contraction and world expansion: "There I was so
> named, of such a clan, with such an appearance, such was my nutriment,
> such was my experience of pleasure and pain, such my life-term; and passing
> away from there, I reappeared elsewhere; and there too I was named, of such
> a clan, with such an appearance, such was my nutriment, such was my
> experience of pleasure and pain, such my life-term; and passing away from
> there, I reappeared here." Thus with their aspects and particulars I recol-
> lected my manifold past lives.[9]

There can be little doubt that the Buddha claimed to possess the intellectual power to recall his past lives as a result of his meditative practices.

In the case of *kamma* and *samsara*, it is also clear that the *Sutras* claim that
on the night of his enlightenment the Buddha directed his purified mind to
knowledge of the passing away and reappearance of beings.

> With the divine eye, which is purified and surpasses the human, I saw beings
> passing away and reappearing, inferior and superior, fair and ugly, fortunate
> and unfortunate. I understood how beings pass on according to their actions
> thus: "These worthy beings who were ill conducted in body, speech and
> mind, revilers of noble ones, wrong in their views, giving effect to wrong
> view in their actions, on the dissolution of the body, after death, have
> reappeared in a state of deprivation, in a bad destination, in perdition, even
> in hell; but these worthy beings who were well conducted in body, speech,

---

[9] *Majjhima Nikaya*, p. 105 and p. 341.

and mind, not revilers of noble ones, right in their views, giving effect to right view in their actions, on the dissolution of the body, after death, have reappeared in a good destination, in perdition, even in the heavenly world." Thus with the divine eye, which is purified and surpasses the human, I saw beings passing away and reappearing, inferior and superior, fair and ugly, fortunate and unfortunate, and I understood how beings pass on according to their actions.[10]

This passage confirms that as a result of his meditative practices the Buddha acquired the "divine eye" necessary to see both the passing away and reappearance of beings in various states based on the nature of their actions. Although it is less than clear about the specifics of *kamma,* it cannot be denied that the Buddha clearly recognized with his "divine eye" our bondage to the apparently unending cycle or rounds of rebirths that is known as *samsara* – the Pali word for "wandering or flowing on" or "aimless and directionless wandering." In fact, the Buddha says, "Monks, this *samsara* is without discoverable beginning. A first point is not discerned of beings roaming and wandering on hindered by ignorance and fettered by craving."[11]

Despite the fact that *samsara* is without any discoverable beginning, we know that the Buddha claimed to have discovered liberation from it and realized not only the knowledge of this liberation but also directly knew that rebirth was destroyed and that there was no more coming to any state of being for himself. In this respect, *Nibbana* is for the Buddha, at least, the resolution or end of *samsara,* and it is also the point of liberation or *moksa* sought for by most Indian thinkers. We shall have the opportunity to consider the relations among these three ideas in more detail in **Chapter 8**.

If we return now to the idea of *kamma,* it should not be surprising that there are other passages in the *Sutras* where the Buddha provides more of the details of his understanding of *kamma* and its relationship to *samsara* and rebirth.

First of all, it is important to keep in mind the Indian religious and philosophical context within which Siddhattha formulated his understanding of *kamma.* As we have seen, both the pre-Vedic and Vedic visions included some notion that the world and cosmos as well as the natural events and human actions taking place in them appear to follow consistent,

---

[10] Ibid., p. 106 and p. 341.   [11] *Samyutta Nikaya,* p. 957.

recurring, and even predictable patterns or cycles. The sun rises and sets, the moon waxes and wanes, the tides rise and fall, the seasons and their effects come and go in relative order and stability, and people tend, for the most part, to act in line with their established characters. Many of these patterns and cycles of activity exhibit law-like regularity and most do not appear to be dependent in any important sense on location or environment. As a result, some of the central questions for ancient Indian thinkers were whether the apparent patterns and cycles happened as a result of natural forces only, or whether they were caused by unseen supernatural forces (i.e., gods), or perhaps by some kind of combination of both.

By the time of the historical Buddha, it is clear that there were at least three or four distinct conceptions of how to explain the cycles and patterns of the natural and human orders. The first explanation rests on the recognition of a fundamental normative rhythm that structures the energy and existence of all beings. This is what is meant by the term *rta*.[12] The second explanation rests on the notion of duty or obligation in response to the normative nature of reality. According to this Vedic understanding of reality, all beings have a *dhamma* – a set of duties or obligations with respect to what must be done in order to maintain themselves and the order of existence – as a direct result of their participation in the ultimate reality. The *dhamma* of each being is then realized in its *kamma* or actions and the consequent effects that follow from its actions. For the Brahmins, as we have seen, the most important karmic actions were those associated with ritual practices that they believed helped to maintain the order of the universe by uniting the human and divine spheres of being. The third explanation extends the idea of *kamma* from the realm of rituals to all human actions. This post-Vedic understanding of human actions is what various thinkers living before, during, and after the life of Siddhattha Gotama were engaged in formulating and defending. Siddhattha too formulated his own account, which we shall turn to shortly. Finally, a fourth, materialistic explanation of the cycle and patterns of the natural and human orders claimed that the material forces and conditions at work in the universe completely causally determined all beings, actions, and events. According to this explanation, every event that occurs *must* happen in exactly the way that it does. All outcomes or effects are the result of fate

---

[12] Koller (2006), pp. 52–53.

and all are causally necessitated and determined. There is no freedom, indeterminacy, or free will. The Buddha, of course, rejected this account because of the meditative insights he realized on the night of his enlightenment.

As we have seen, the Buddhist tradition maintains that the truth of existence, or the Buddha's *Dhamma,* was realized as a series of insights into rebirth, *kamma, samsara,* interdependent arising, and the Four Noble Truths. Various *Sutras* offer different accounts of each of these ideas and their relationships.

In some texts, for example, we discover that *kamma* is part of a broader conception of how the universe as a whole (including the realms of rebirth) operates and the role of morality within that operation. Other texts focus on the specific ethical dimensions and implications of human actions. For example, the Buddha famously claims, "It is 'intention/volition' that I call *kamma*; having willed or formed the intention, one performs acts by body, speech, and mind."[13] According to this text, *kamma* includes actions of thought, word, or deed that originate from the exercise of intention, volition, or conscious choice. In other words, for the Buddha, *kamma* includes the idea that actions freely chosen and directly intended will lead necessarily to causal consequences in either the mind alone, or in the mind, the body, and the world together.

The inevitability of the causal connection between intention, action, and consequence in the Buddha's account of *kamma* is no more clearly seen than when he asserts that, "beings are owners of their actions, heirs of their actions; they originate from their actions, are bound to their actions, have their actions as their refuge. It is action that distinguishes beings as inferior and superior."[14] According to this quote, not only do we originate, own, and inherit the consequences of our actions, but they also bind us with their moral qualities. In short, we are as we do; we are good or superior because of our good actions and bad or inferior because of our bad actions. But what, we might ask, makes our actions good or bad?

That the Buddha thinks we are as we do or that we are the results of our actions should not be surprising because he actually claims that there are four distinct kinds of *kamma.*

---

[13] *Anguttara Nikaya,* III, 415 as translated by Gethin (1998), p. 120 and Bodhi (2005), p. 146.
[14] *Majjhima Nikaya,* p. 1053 and p. 1057.

There are, O monks, these four kinds of *kamma* declared by me after I had realized them for myself by direct knowledge. What four?

There is dark *kamma* with dark results; there is bright *kamma* with bright results; there is *kamma* that is dark and bright with dark and bright results; there is *kamma* that is neither dark nor bright, with neither dark not bright results, which leads to the destruction of *kamma*.[15]

According to the Buddhist tradition,[16] "dark" and "bright" *kamma* are related to "bad" or unwholesome actions and "good" or wholesome actions respectively. *Kamma* that is both "dark and bright" refers to bad and good actions done alternately by the same person, and *kamma* that is "neither dark nor bright" refers to the kind of action that is done with neither good nor bad intentions or volitions (i.e., is morally neutral or indifferent). It is commonly thought that this fourth kind of *kamma* is the type of action done by an enlightened being like the Buddha, who has transcended the limitations of the world of *kamma*, *samsara*, and rebirth through his insight into the ultimate truth about reality.

In addition to these four kinds of *kamma*, the Buddhist tradition also reports[17] that the teachings of the Buddha could be organized by grouping his teachings in numerical order from one to ten. For example, the Buddha taught one thing, that all beings are maintained by conditions. He also taught two things, namely, ignorance and craving for existence. Under the number three, he is said to have taught three unwholesome roots of action: greed, hatred, and delusion. He also taught three wholesome roots of action: non-greed, non-hatred, and non-delusion; three kinds of right conduct: in body, speech, and thought; three kinds of craving, and three kinds of suffering. In addition to the four kinds of *kamma*, he also taught the four foundations of mindfulness, the four *jhanas*, and the Four Noble Truths, to name just a few. This numerical way of organizing and listing the teachings of the Buddha continues up to the number ten, when we are told that the Buddha recognized ten unwholesome courses of action: taking life, taking what is not given, sexual misconduct, lying speech, slander, rude speech, idle chatter, greed, malevolence, and wrong view.

What is particularly interesting about this way of arranging the teachings of the Buddha, especially with respect to his teaching on *kamma*, is that it

[15] *Anguttara Nikaya* 4: 232 as translated by Bodhi (2005), p. 155.   [16] Bodhi (2005), p. 147.
[17] *Digha Nikaya, Sangiti Sutta: The Chanting Together*, pp. 479–510.

seems to have inspired the Buddhist tradition to organize his ideas about the mind, *kamma*, *samsara*, and rebirth in a more systematic and coherent way.

Following Rupert Gethin's[18] account, I want to suggest that the Buddha's claims about *kamma* (as well as *samsara* and rebirth) can most easily be understood when they are seen as being directly related to the claim that who we are and what we think exists is a function of our mind, its cognitive or intellectual powers, and the actions that we will or intend.

According to Gethin, "The key to understanding the Buddhist cosmological scheme lies in the principle of the *equivalence of cosmology and psychology*."[19] What he means by this is that the various realms of existence[20] are correlated and, in fact, causally determined by states of mind, which are, as we have seen, the ultimate sources of karmic action. This idea can be more clearly understood, when we recall that the Buddha thinks that will or intention just *is kamma* because actions of the body, speech, and mind, or thoughts, words, and deeds arise out of or are causally driven by conscious acts of intending or willing, or more generally, states of mind.

The same idea is reinforced when we consider the ten unwholesome courses of action and the three unwholesome roots of action. The ten courses of action are traditionally divided into three kinds of bodily deeds (taking life, taking what is not given, and sexual misconduct), four kinds of speech actions (lying speech, slander, rude speech, and idle chatter), and three kinds of mental actions (greed, malevolence, and wrong view). The three unwholesome roots of action, as we have indicated, are greed, hatred, and delusion. When we put these together with the Buddha's ideas about the nature of *kamma*, it should be clear that what he seems to be claiming is that the mental or psychological states of greed, hatred, and delusion are causally responsible for the ten unwholesome courses of action, which are themselves, in turn, responsible for the kind of life one lives and the kind of rebirth one reaps. Without going into any more of the details about the nature and the kinds of realms where one might be reborn, which incidentally the Buddha claimed to have directly experienced, the connections among *kamma*, *samsara*, and rebirth now appear to be complete.

---

[18] Gethin (1998), pp. 119–126.   [19] Ibid., p. 119, his emphasis.

[20] According to Buddhist cosmology there are six realms of rebirth: the realm of the gods or devas, the realm of the demi-gods, the human realm, the animal realm, the realm of the hungry ghosts, and the realm of hell. All six realms are thought to be real, but some forms of Mahayana Buddhism claim that they are best thought of as states of mind.

If my reading of the Buddha's teachings on *kamma*, *samsara*, and rebirth is correct, then I think we have good reasons for believing my earlier claim that the single most important or most basic insight of the Buddha is the notion that who we are and what we think exists is a function of our mind and its cognitive or intellectual powers. In fact, the interrelated ideas of *kamma*, *samsara*, and rebirth not only support this claim but also extend its implications into the realm of human actions, because, if the Buddha is right, what we do is a function of what we think and will and intend, and what we think, will, and intend leads to actions and consequences whose ultimate results determine the kind of life we live in this world as well as our rebirth in the next.

Whether or not any or all of this is true, of course, depends to some extent on how it is understood and taken. The early Buddhist tradition claims that Buddha himself said that on the night of his enlightenment he had a direct meditative experience of all of the elements of *kamma*, *samsara*, and rebirth. So as far as the Buddha is concerned these things are true because he saw them himself. The tradition also teaches, however, that the Buddha said that the same type of experience is possible for anyone who decides to test his claims and follow his path for him or herself. To that extent, at least, the opportunity for seeing and believing is available for anyone who decides to accept the Buddha's offer and follow his "Middle Way."

For those who refuse to accept the Buddha's offer, however, what should be abundantly clear, at this point, is that the Buddha's ideas and teachings about *kamma*, *samsara*, and rebirth are directly related to other important ideas that are logically connected to them, namely, the interdependent arising of phenomena, the impermanence of all things, a conception of the person or self who makes and experiences his or her own *kamma*, and the prospects of release from the rounds of rebirth and the cycle of *samsara* as well as the realization of *Nibbana*.

We shall have the opportunity to investigate and reflect on these and other related ideas when we consider the Buddha's specific ideas and teachings on each of these in **Chapters 6–8**.

Things to think about

1. What is the philosophical significance of ritual actions? Why do humans engage in ritual actions? What evidence is there that ritual actions are causally effective?

2. What was the connection between intellectual activities and ascetic practices in the Buddha's awakening and realization of *Nibbana*?
3. How and why would intellectual and meditative practices be causes of awakening?
4. How are intentions and actions related to *kamma*? Is all *kamma* bad according to the Buddha? Why or why not?
5. How are the Buddha's teachings on *kamma, samsara,* and rebirth related to his most basic philosophical insight?

6   Interdependent arising

Key terms and teachings

Dhammas/Dharmas: Pali and Sanskrit terms meaning "to support" or "to keep or maintain," in the *Abhidhamma* texts they refer to the individual elements or factors, both physical and psychological, that are causally responsible for the physical world and our experience of it. In a certain sense, they are the component "parts" from which all of reality originates.

Madhyamaka: Indian Mahayana Buddhist school, whose name means roughly, "middle way," traditionally thought to have been founded by Nagarjuna. Its central metaphysical claims focused on the idea of "emptiness" or *sunnatta/sunyata.*

Paticca-Samuppada/pratitya-samutpada: Variously translated as, "depen dent arising," "dependent origination," "conditioned co-production," "co-dependent origination," "inter-dependent-origination," or "inter dependent arising," all of these refer to the Buddha's account of causality. In short, this cluster of terms refers to the law-governed dynamics of change in which the events or happenings in the world and the mind are causally conditioned by and dependent on other processes, events, or happenings.

Sabhava/Svabhava: Pali and Sanskrit terms meaning "own-being," "self-being," substantial "self-existence," or "intrinsic nature," it is that by which phenomena or the *dhammas* are thought to exist independently of one another.

Yogacara: Indian Mahayana Buddhist school, whose name means, "Practice of yoga," and also known as the *Vijnanavada* or "Way of Consciousness" school, it focused on the nature and activities of consciousness in understanding reality.

The Buddha on causation

Although the account of the Buddha's teachings on *kamma*, *samsara*, and rebirth given in **Chapter 5** provides a basic outline of his understanding of these important and interrelated ideas, it is less than clear about some of the specifics of the crucial philosophical elements of *kamma* – i.e., the ontology of the human agent, the psychological forces and causes at work within the agent who acts, the specific mechanisms of causal consequences in this life, past lives, and future lives as well, and the causal effects and contributions of external, environmental factors and other causal agents. Whether and how these specifics can be known, of course, is an indispensable part of any philosophical view of the world. In fact, one of the most important, if disputed, metaphysical ideas in the history of philosophy throughout the world is the idea of causes – their natures, their powers, their connections to effects, and how all of this is or can be known by us.

In this chapter we will be examining what many consider the single most important metaphysical notion of Buddhism, its account of causes and causation and the interconnectedness of all beings, known as *paticca-samuppada*.

As we saw in **Chapter 5**, the Buddhist tradition maintains that on the night of his enlightenment, while in a deep meditative state Gotama Buddha realized that whatever happens or comes to be either in the mind or in the world is a result of prior causes and conditions. The particulars of his experience and his explanation of his insight are recorded in various ways in different *Sutras*. In this chapter we will examine some of these *Sutras*. We shall also consider six distinct conceptions of causation, its relationships to the corresponding ideas of *kamma*, *samsara*, and rebirth from **Chapter 5**, the conception of the self and the realization of *Nibbana* in **Chapters 7** and **8**, and the evidence for this most fundamental philosophical idea.

A general formulation

One of the easiest ways to understand the Buddha's teaching on interdependent arising is to begin with his most general formulation of it, and then to see how he applied it to particular cases or situations.

The *Nidanavagga*, or the *Book of Causation*, in Part II of the *Samyutta Nikaya* contains at least half a dozen instances of the most general formulation of the teaching on *paticca-samuppada*:

> Thus when this exists, that comes to be; with the arising of this, that arises. When this does not exist, that does not come to be; with the cessation of this, that ceases.[1]

The Buddhist tradition has generally interpreted the Buddha's teaching on interdependent arising in two ways. First, it is considered to be an account of causation or the process by which "things" come to be, exist, and change. Second, it is a claim about the ongoing ontological status of all beings, all phenomena, and all "things" that exist, whether these "things" and phenomena are beings of the mind or beings of the world.

With respect to the first interpretation, the quote clearly indicates that the coming to be of any being is a function of its causes and conditions. Thus, for example, we see that the existence of smoke ordinarily depends for its existence on the existence of fire. The arising of fire brings about the arising of smoke, and the cessation of fire brings about the cessation of smoke. In other words, fire causes smoke, and smoke is caused by fire. If we remove the cause, i.e., the fire, then we remove the effect, i.e., the smoke. The same is true in many other cases as well.

For example, suppose while playing billiards I strike the cue ball and cause it directly to hit the eight ball into the side pocket. Our common-sense understanding of the movement of the eight ball (i.e., the effect) includes the idea that it was caused by the movement of the cue ball (i.e., the cause), which was itself caused to move by me. In simple terms, the movement of the cue ball is the cause of the movement of the eight ball, the effect, and if I never strike the cue ball, then the eight ball will not move (assuming, of course, that no other forces act on the balls or the pool table).

Things are, however, slightly more complicated than either this or the previous example of causation would seem to imply. In fact, there are at least four distinct, yet related ways to understand both the general formulation of the teaching on *paticca-samuppada* and its application to each of these examples of causation: a common-sense view, a scientific view, a philosophical view, and the Buddha's view. Let us look at each more carefully.

---

[1] *Samyutta Nikaya*, pp. 533–620.

Four views of the general formulation

The first way to understand *paticca-samuppada* mirrors our common-sense understanding of causation, and distinguishes two classes of distinct but related kinds of things or beings. The first class of things, called "causes," is responsible for the coming to be of the second class, called "effects." According to this common-sense account, it is fire that is the cause of smoke, and the cue ball that causes the eight ball to go into the side pocket in the game of billiards.

This ordinary way of understanding causal events in the world rests on the rather obvious but simplistic distinction of causes and effects, where the former are typically thought to exist prior to the latter, and where the former are either sufficient, or necessary and sufficient, to explain the production of the latter.

A second, more sophisticated way to understand *paticca-samuppada* goes beyond our simple, common-sense view and is like our ordinary scientific account of causation. According to this understanding, we again distinguish two classes of distinct but related kinds of beings, i.e., causes and effects, but we also recognize a larger class of beings called "conditions." This third class of beings includes all of those beings recognized by common sense as "causes," but it also contains other beings, called "conditions," which may or may not be necessary to bring about the effect of a cause properly speaking.

For example, in the case of fire and smoke, a little bit of reflection quickly reveals that there must be other kinds of things in addition to the fire in order for there to be smoke that is produced. These other things include appropriate atmospheric conditions and pressure, a fuel source, such as oxygen or other gases that permit burning, a fire starter, such as a match or spark, and obviously, something that burns, like leaves, or firewood. In the billiards case, one clearly needs pool balls that can survive the impact of collisions, a level playing surface, a reliable cue stick, no external interference, etc.

One difference between this scientific understanding and the prior common-sense understanding is the richer and more complex account of both causes and conditions, usually by the application of the scientific method in order to isolate the proper causal agents, and the explicit recognition of a larger set of causal factors that are necessary to explain how the effects are produced by their appropriate causes.

The basic difference between this second view and a third, abstract "philosophical" account is that the latter goes beyond the empirical data and tries to clarify the conceptual relationships among the terms of causal explanations and the classes of beings involved in the causal process. Numerous Western philosophers[2] have formulated and defended many different and competing accounts of the elements involved in this conception of causation. Without going into all of the details of these controversial and rival approaches, we can simply recognize that philosophers have tended to introduce ever more complex, complicated, and sophisticated explanations of the nature of causation, and the relationships that exist or are thought to exist among causes, conditions, and effects, and both their logical and metaphysical necessity and sufficiency.

For example, one purely philosophical account might begin by distinguishing a class of things called "conditions" from a class of different but related things called "effects." Then, with respect to the class of "conditions" and its relationship to the class of "effects" it could distinguish conditions that are necessary and non-necessary, sufficient and non-sufficient to bring about effects. In other words, it might distinguish "causes" strictly or properly speaking from mere "conditions." The former would be commonly, though not uncontroversially, thought to be either sufficient to bring about their effects or both necessary and sufficient to bring about their effects, while the latter would be either necessary or non-necessary but usually never sufficient to bring about an effect.

A fourth way to understand causation is the Buddha's own account of *paticca-samuppada*. Before considering the traditional Theravada or Mainstream Buddhist understanding of this teaching, we should first note that there are other non-Mainstream or Mahayana understandings of *paticca-samuppada*, the most famous of which involves Nagarjuna's reasoned equivocation of *paticca-samuppada* and "emptiness" or *sunyata*. A second important and influential Mahayana interpretation was proposed by the Yogacara school, whose members were also known as followers of the *Vijnanavada* or "Way of consciousness." We shall consider both of these interpretations shortly, but first we shall examine the traditional Mainstream explanation.

---

[2] For example, Aristotle, Thomas Aquinas, William of Ockham, Thomas Hobbes, John Locke, Gottfried Wilhelm Leibniz, David Hume, Immanuel Kant, Alfred North Whitehead, and Curt Ducasse, to name just a few.

The Mainstream interpretation

According to the traditional Theravada understanding of *paticca-samuppada*, there are not strictly speaking any individual beings or classes of beings that are called "causes" that are ultimately metaphysically or really distinct from other individual beings or classes of beings that are recognized as "effects." The reason for this is that the "this" and the "that" of the Buddha's formulation are merely ordinary, conventional ways of referring to different "things" or "beings" that are actually not really metaphysically separate and distinct "beings" or "things."

The Mainstream Buddhist understanding of *paticca-samuppada* is that what the Buddha realized on the night of his enlightenment was the intellectual insight that all conventionally designated individual "things" are in reality not metaphysically independent or self-contained, subsistent "beings," but processes or happenings, and that these events or processes are themselves causally connected to literally every other process that is simultaneously happening at any given moment in the flux and flow of all events and processes.

According to this understanding of causation or causal processes, in order to really understand our fire and smoke example or our billiard ball example, we must recognize or see that there are *not* two metaphysically distinct kinds of beings called a "cause" and an "effect" (i.e., fire and smoke, and a cue ball and the eight ball), but that there are causally interrelated or "dependently arising" processes, events, or happenings conventionally designated as "fire" and "smoke" or "cue ball" and "eight ball." There are not separate, metaphysically distinct "things" or "beings" that actually exist independently and in isolation from one another. Instead, what really exists is a giant net or complex causal network of constantly changing and causally interacting happenings or events or processes. Our common-sense view and even our scientific and philosophical understandings of what we conventionally designate as "things" as well as their causal relationships are not only oversimplifications of this true picture of reality, but they are actually falsifications of the way things really are because of our ignorance in not seeing reality as it really is.

In other words, the basic difference between ordinary, unenlightened folks and the Buddha is that he awakened to the truth about reality on the night of his enlightenment, and as a result of a meditative insight finally grasped the conditioned arising of reality – that things are not things but happenings. In fact, the Mainstream tradition claims that this part of his enlightenment experience is the most fundamental insight that he realized, and his chief disciple Sariputta confirmed this view, when he maintained, "One who sees *paticca-samuppada* sees the *Dhamma*; one who sees the *Dhamma* sees *paticca-samuppada*."[3]

Before we turn our attention to Nagarjuna's explanation and the Yogacara interpretation of the Buddha's teaching on interdependent arising, it may be helpful to pause for a moment to specify the basic elements of the traditional Theravada understanding of *paticca-samuppada*. There appear to be at least half a dozen basic features of this account.

Basic features of *paticca-samuppada*

First, the early Buddhist tradition claims that the Buddha himself directly realized the truth of the teaching of interdependent arising when he awakened to it on the night of his enlightenment. The *Sutras* are quite clear about this. They also report the Buddha's recognition of the profundity and difficulty of seeing and understanding the truth of *paticca-samuppada*.

> This Dhamma that I have attained is profound, hard to see and hard to understand, peaceful and sublime, unattainable by mere reasoning, subtle, to be experienced by the wise. But this generation delights in worldliness (i.e., sense pleasures and the thoughts of craving associated with them), takes delight in worldliness, rejoices in worldliness. It is hard for such a generation to see this truth, namely, specific conditionality, or interdependent arising. And it is hard to see this truth, namely, the stilling of all formations, the relinquishing of all acquisitions, the destruction of craving, dispassion, cessation, Nibbana.[4]

Second, and more specifically, what he saw or realized was, despite our conventional naming practices to the contrary, that there are not strictly speaking any metaphysically distinct and independently existing "things" as such. All conventionally designated "things" are impermanent because they are constantly changing, and as a result they lack an enduring self or a fixed essence or *svabhava*.

---

[3] *Majjhima Nikaya*, p. 283.   [4] Ibid., p. 260.

It is impossible, it cannot happen that a person possessing right view could treat any formation as permanent – there is no such possibility.[5]

Bhikkhhus, material form is impermanent, feeling is impermanent, perception is impermanent, formations are impermanent, consciousness is impermanent. Bhikkhus, material form is not self, feeling is not self, perception is not self, formations are not self, consciousness is not self. All formations are impermanent; all things are not self.[6]

Third, in other words, "things" understood as "beings" with fixed or unchanging essences do not exist. This is traditionally referred to as the Buddha's teaching on "no-enduring-self" that we shall examine in more detail in **Chapter 7**.

Fourth, what does exist exists as processes or events or happenings that are themselves the results of causal interactions that have interdependently given rise to them.

Fifth, all of these events or processes or happenings occur in a complex, causal network of interdependent arising.

Sixth, the teaching on interdependent arising as an essential part of the *Dhamma* as a whole is not only profound, hard to see and understand, but also unattainable by mere reasoning, subtle, and to be experienced by the wise only. In short, it is not something that is evident, and it is clearly not apparent to an ordinary person who is hindered by ignorance, craving, and habitual thinking.

This Mainstream understanding of interdependent arising was, however, subsequently challenged by two distinct and influential schools of Mahayana Buddhist thought, the Madhyamaka and the Yogacara, both of which offer a fundamental reinterpretation or revision of the traditional Theravada view of *paticca-samuppada*.

The Madhyamaka interpretation

According to the Madhyamaka interpretation of interdependent arising, especially as formulated by its most famous spokesman, Nagarjuna, *pratitya-samutpada* is understood to be equivalent to the metaphysical doctrine known as "*sunyata*" or "emptiness." Nagarjuna argued that the doctrine of *pratitya-samutpada* could only make sense or be logically coherent if *all*

---

[5] Ibid., p. 928.   [6] Ibid., p. 322.

beings and, in fact, *all* phenomena lacked a fixed self-essence or permanent enduring self. In short, everything is empty of anything. His support for this claim was that any kind of fixed self-essence or other relatively unchanging mode of existence in any "thing" or "being" would necessarily prevent and make it impossible for it to come to be and pass away in the manner the Buddha had claimed. In other words, for Nagarjuna, *all* "things" and "beings" must be understood as processes, events, or happenings that are quite literally empty of any and all fixed self-essences.

The Yogacara interpretation

The Yogacara interpretation of interdependent arising, on the other hand, which was formulated by Asanga and Vasubandhu, was, as its name indicates, derived from meditative practices and cognitive experiences. It also saw itself as correcting the epistemological problems involved in the Madhyamaka position on causation. According to the Yogacara view, *pratitya-samutpada* was directly related to two important philosophical topics: the nature of experience and the nature of the mind.

Yogacara thinkers claimed that the Madhyamaka equating of interdependent arising and emptiness was incorrect, because for them, real emptiness was derived from the direct realization by one's natural or original state of mind of the non-existence or emptiness of both the perceiving subject and the perceived objects. In other words, *pratitya-samutpada* is an epistemic rather than a metaphysical insight into the interdependent arising of experience, which is initially and ignorantly conceived of dualistically in terms of independent subjects and independent objects. Properly understood, however, by those who are enlightened, *pratitya-samutpada* refers to the realization of the fundamental unity of all phenomena as empty and as interdependently arising out of the activity of the mind.

Given this brief account of the basic difference between the Madhyamaka and Yogacara interpretations of *pratitya-samutpada*, there should be little doubt about my previous claim that the Buddhist tradition has generally interpreted the historical Buddha's teaching on interdependent arising in two distinct ways.

First, it is considered to be an account of causation or how "things" come to be, exist, and change. Second, it is a claim about the ongoing ontological status of all beings, all phenomena, and all "things" that exist, whether these "things" and phenomena are beings of the mind or beings of the world. In fact, both of these ways of interpreting *paticca-samuppada* are also evident in its more specific applications to human existence and the elements or "*dhammas*" of human existence and all other beings. We shall consider the application of interdependent arising to human existence first, and then the *Abhidhamma* accounts of things.

Paticca-samuppada and human existence

In order to understand the application of the general principle of interdependent arising to human existence and the moral sphere we should recall that the First Noble Truth has traditionally been understood to involve important metaphysical and epistemological claims about both the nature of the human person and our knowledge of the ontology of ourselves and other "things" in the world as well. The Buddha said,

> Now this, bhikkhus, is the noble truth of suffering: Birth is suffering; aging is suffering; illness is suffering; death is suffering; sorrow and lamentation, pain, grief and despair are suffering; union with what is displeasing is suffering; separation from what is pleasing is suffering; not to get what one wants is suffering; in brief, the five aggregates subject to clinging are suffering.

In light of the Buddha's general teaching on *paticca-samuppada*, it should not be difficult to see that each element of suffering or *dukkha* specified in the First Noble Truth is actually a process or event and not a "thing" with a fixed, unchanging essence. In fact, little reflection is required to see that being born, aging, being sick, dying, experiencing pain and despair, as well as suffering in general are all dynamic happenings or events. Not only are they designated linguistically as gerunds (i.e., verbal nouns), but they also are typically experienced as fleeting and transitory states that come to be and pass away without enduring. "The five aggregates of attachment," on the other hand, appears to refer to some one "thing" or collection of "things" that is or are not a process, event, or happening.

However, given the account of interdependent arising that we have been examining in this chapter, it should be clear that what the Buddha meant by "the five aggregates of attachment" is that the human person, just like the "objects" of experience, is and therefore should be seen and understood as a collection or aggregate of processes or events – as *anatta*, and not as possessing a fixed or unchanging substantial self. We shall be examining the particular metaphysical features of this account of the human person in more detail in **Chapter 7**, but in the meantime I briefly want to rehearse the Buddha's understanding of "the five aggregates" in order to provide the context for his application of *paticca-samuppada* to the human person and the sphere of morality.

As previously noted, the Buddhist tradition identified the following five processes, aggregates, or bundles as constitutive of our true "selves": *Rupa* – material shape/form; *Vedana* – feeling/sensation; *Sanna/Samjna* – cognition; *Sankhara/Samskara* – dispositional attitudes; and *Vinnana/Vijnana* – consciousness. Given the general principle of interdependent arising that we have been considering, this would seem to indicate that the Buddha thought that each of these "elements" or "parts" of the "self" is actually just a fleeting pattern that arises within the ongoing and perpetually changing context of process interactions. This is, in fact, exactly what we see when we turn to his comments about *paticca-samuppada* in the case of human existence. The Buddha said,

> And what, monks, is interdependent arising? With ignorance as condition, volitional formations come to be; with volitional formations as condition, consciousness; with consciousness as condition, name and form; with name and form as condition, the six sense bases; with the six sense bases as condition, contact; with contact as condition, feeling; with feeling as condition, craving; with craving as condition, clinging; with clinging as condition, existence; with existence as condition, birth; with birth as condition, aging-and-death, sorrow, lamentation, pain, dejection, and despair come to be. Such is the origin of this whole mass of suffering. This, monks, is called interdependent arising.
>
> But with the remainderless fading away and cessation of ignorance comes cessation of volitional formations; with the cessation of volitional formations, cessation of consciousness; with the cessation of consciousness, cessation of name and form; with the cessation of name and form, cessation of the six sense bases; with the cessation of the six sense bases, cessation of contact; with the cessation of contact, cessation of feeling; with the cessation of feeling, cessation of craving; with the cessation of craving, cessation of clinging; with the cessation of clinging, cessation of the existence; with the cessation of the existence, cessation of birth; with the cessation of birth,

aging-and-death, sorrow, lamentation, pain, dejection, and despair cease.
Such is the cessation of this whole mass of suffering."[7]

The first thing to notice about this account of interdependent arising is
that it involves the causes and conditions that interdependently give rise to
the human person and his or her experience of *dukkha*.

The Buddha clearly distinguishes twelve distinct elements, components,
or factors that causally contribute to the arising and ceasing of suffering:
ignorance (*avijja/avidya*), volitional formations (*sankhara/samskara*), consciousness (*vinnana/vijnana*), name and form (*nama-rupa*), the six sense
bases (*salayatana/sad-ayatana*), contact (*phassa/sparsa*), feeling (*vedana*),
craving (*tanha/trsna*), clinging (*upadana*), existence or becoming (*bhava*),
birth (*jati*), and old age and death (*jaramarana*). Five of the twelve (i.e.,
volitional formations, consciousness, form, feeling, and the six sense
bases of perceptual experience) directly correspond to the "five aggregates"
or *skandhas* previously identified as the basic elements or processes that
interdependently give rise to the human person. In addition to these five
foundational processes, the remaining factors (i.e., ignorance, contact, craving, clinging or grasping, existence, birth, old age and death) all appear to be
specific properties, accidental features, or moral qualities of the more basic
five *skandhas*.

A second thing to notice about this account of causation is that it is clearly
connected to his teachings on *kamma*, *samsara*, and rebirth, as well as the
possibility of eliminating the whole mass of suffering and realizing *Nibbana*.

In fact, shortly after specifying the twelve elements of interdependent
arising in the human person the Buddha again asks,

> And what, monks, is interdependent arising? With birth as condition, aging
> and death come to be: whether there is an arising of Tathagatas or no arising
> of Tathagatas, that element still persists, the stableness of the Dhamma,
> the fixed course of the Dhamma, specific conditionality. A Tathagata awakens
> to this and breaks through to it. Having done so, he explains it, teaches it,
> proclaims it, establishes it, discloses it, analyzes it, elucidates it. And he says:
> "See! With birth as condition, monks, aging and death."[8]

He repeats this same set of claims with respect to each of the other twelve
elements and then concludes, "Thus, monks, the actuality, the inerrancy,

---

[7] *Samyutta Nikaya*, pp. 533–534.   [8] Ibid., p. 551.

the invariability, the specific conditionality in this: this is called interdependent arising."[9]

These additional comments seem to highlight three more important features of the teaching on interdependent arising. First, the Buddha "awakened" to it as part of his enlightenment experience. Second, the ordering of the causes and conditions as specified by him is not random or chaotic, but purposive and invariable. Third, those who have seen (in the sense of understood) *paticca-samuppada* have the power to teach and explain it. In other words, ordinary, ignorant, and unenlightened people cannot and do not see interdependent arising, even though it is a basic unchanging feature of the fundamental nature of reality.

A sixth feature of this account of interdependent arising is that it involves causes and conditions that are part of *both* the origination and cessation of the "whole mass of suffering" that characterizes human existence. This is an important feature of his account because when it is joined with the previous feature noting the invariability of the process (both forward and backward or in origin and cessation), it opens up the real possibility for believing that one can, through one's own actions, work to eliminate the causal powers and conditions that bind one to the cycle of rebirth or *samsara* and ultimately achieve *Nibbana*. This is presumably exactly what the Buddha himself realized on the night of his enlightenment.

We should also keep in mind, however, that the Buddha claimed that his teaching is "profound, hard to see and hard to understand." It should not be surprising then to learn that the Buddhist tradition recognized both the complexity and complicated nature of the Buddha's account of interdependent arising when it compiled his teachings on it. There are at least a half dozen distinct problems or difficulties that one encounters in the numerous versions of the teachings as they are preserved in the Mainstream texts.

Some conceptual difficulties

First, even the most casual survey of the Pali *Suttas* reveals that there are variations in the list of elements involved in the process of interdependent arising. Second, some *Sutta* lists of the elements omit some of the factors involved in interdependent arising. Third, some of the lists change the order

---

[9] Ibid.

of the elements involved in the process. Fourth, sometimes the lists begin with ignorance and proceed to old age and death, and sometimes they begin with old age and death and end with ignorance. Fifth, some *Suttas* actually begin in the middle of the traditional pattern and then work their way toward ignorance or toward old age and death. Sixth, and most surprisingly, aside from the lists themselves, there are actually no specific directions or formal explanations about how one is to understand the elements and their interrelations.

One cannot help but wonder whether it was these very facts that led later Madhyamaka Buddhists such as Nagarjuna and Yogacara Buddhists such as Asanga and Vasubandhu to formulate their own understanding and interpretation of the Buddha's teaching on *paticca-samuppada*. Perhaps it was these very same difficulties that inspired Vasubandhu[10] and Buddhaghosa[11] to formulate their own "multiple lifetimes" explanations of the teachings on interdependent arising.

According to these latter interpretations of the teaching on *pratitya-samutpada*, one should understand the ordinary account of interdependent arising as involving causal factors that are operative from one's past life or lives, in one's present life, and also into one's future life or lives. In other words, it is because of what one has thought, said, and done in one's past lives, that one is currently experiencing the karmic consequences in this life. And it is because of one's thoughts, words, and deeds in this life that one is currently or will shortly experience their karmic consequences either in this life or the life or lives to come. Whatever the ultimate truth of either of these historical developments in Buddhism may be, things were even more complicated by the additional philosophical reflections on the Buddha's teachings that are contained in the Buddhist *Abhidhamma* texts.

The *Abhidhamma* view

The terms "*Abhidhamma*"/"*Abhidharma*" are the Pali and Sanskrit words meaning roughly "higher" *Dhamma* or teaching. In the Buddhist tradition they refer to both the texts of the third part of the "three baskets" – the *Tipitaka* – the third part of the Mainstream Buddhist canon, and the philosophical methods for understanding the content of the teachings of the Buddha. In general, the *Abhidhamma* texts are engaged in two distinct but

---

[10] See his *Visuddhimagga*.   [11] See his *Abhidhammakosa*.

related activities. First, they try to give a complete, exhaustive, and detailed account of the fundamental nature of reality by analyzing its structures, both physical and psychological, into their most basic elements or constituents, called "*dhammas/dharmas*." Second, they try to adjudicate disagreements that arise as a consequence of their first activity.

Without going into either the specific details of the different *Abhidhamma* analyses of *paticca-samuppada*, or the various disputes involved in the different philosophical attempts to explain both what the Buddha meant by each element of the teaching on interdependent arising as well as how to understand the teaching as a whole, it should be noted that both the Theravada and Sarvastivada *Abhidhamma* traditions claim that the teaching applies to all levels or kinds of beings or things in reality. On the one hand, as we have seen, it is an account of causation or how things or beings come to be, exist, and change. On the other hand, it is also an account of the metaphysical or ontological status of all beings, all phenomena, and all "things" that exist, whether these "things" and phenomena are beings of the mind or beings of the world.

According to the *Abhidhamma* tradition, *paticca-samuppada* explains how ordinary "things" like rocks, plants, trees, animals, and human beings come to be, exist, and undergo changes through the causal interactions of *dhammas*. It also explains how "things," or more precisely processes, like human actions happen as a result of the interplay of *dhammas*. In the sphere of morality and human actions, for example, it clarifies the process by which "I" or my "five aggregates" respond to developing situations in the world by considering various potential courses of action and then deciding what "I" will do based on my thoughts, wants, and desires and past experiences as well. Finally, the teaching on interdependent arising applies to each moment of consciousness itself, i.e., the fundamental processes of consciousness and its *dhammas* that give rise to the thoughts, beliefs, and ideas that undergird and causally contribute to my ongoing experiences in the world, my conduct, and my future plans and intentions.

What is particularly interesting and important about this last feature of the *Abhidhamma* understanding of *paticca-samuppada* is that it highlights the role that the mind or consciousness and its *dhammas* play in both our thoughts about the world and ourselves, and our actions as well.

Recall that in **Chapter 2**, I claimed that the single most important or most basic insight of the historical Buddha is the idea or claim that who we are and what we think exists is a function of our mind and its cognitive powers. In other words, it is our mind and our uses of it that causally determine both what we are and how we see and understand our self, the world, and other things. This appears to be directly supported by the third feature of the *Abhidhamma* account of interdependent arising, because it not only explains how ordinary objects of experience come into being, but it also explains how our mind and consciousness arises and how it is causally related to the objects of experience and even the experience itself. In fact, the *Abhidhamma* explanation of *paticca-samuppada*, especially with respect to its analysis of consciousness and its *dhammas*, emphasizes the dynamic and processional nature of all of reality, despite its apparent stability.

According to *Abhidhamma* understanding, the dynamic causal interactions among both the *dhammas* and the twelve elements or conditions that interdependently give rise to the human person and his or her experience of *dukkha*, occur simultaneously and quite literally in the moment, and from each moment to the succeeding moment. They do not happen successively (because all are causally efficacious at once) or as extended over time (because that would entail a fixed, intrinsic nature enduring through time) with each element making its unique causal contribution at the appropriate time and place in the causal sequence, but literally all together at the same time and all at once.

Such an understanding of interdependent arising clearly highlights the Buddha's enlightenment insight into the fundamentally dynamic and causally interconnected nature of reality and our experience of it. It also reinforces the Buddha's claim that his *Dhamma* is the "Middle Way" between the metaphysical extremes of eternalism (i.e., the claim that the person and reality each subsist with an unchanging, intrinsic nature) and annihilationism (i.e., the claim that there is no real causal connection between events or the moments in a process).

In addition to these features, the *Abhidhamma* interpretation of the Buddha's teaching on *paticca-samuppada* focuses attention on both the mind and its connection to the entire causal network of relationships and conditions that give rise to our ongoing experience of reality. Its account of reality and causal relationships helps one realize that "things," or more exactly processes, are so structured that even small changes in their "initial" or local conditions can have enormous effects and consequences down the line or throughout the causal network.

In this respect, the *Abhidhamma* understanding of causation ought to remind us of contemporary quantum theory, and the "butterfly effect" of chaos theory. In the former, atomic events with varying degrees of random-ness in them nevertheless combine in large numbers to produce overall patterns of great reliability. The patterns, as is obvious from sense experi-ence, exist. The only question is whether they are caused by the mind, by matter, or by some combination of both. In the latter, as John Polkinghorne[12] reports, scientists have come to realize that the world is composed of a series of interrelated systems or processes that are so exquisitely sensitive to cir-cumstance that the smallest disturbance can produce large and ever-growing changes in their behavior. This fact about reality was discovered (or recon-firmed, if the Buddha was right) by Edward Lorenz while trying to model the behavior of the earth's weather systems. What he "discovered," and the Buddha had presumably already awakened to on the night of his enlight-enment, was that the smallest variations in the input to his equations (i.e., their "initial" conditions) produced exponentially large deviations in the behavior of his solutions (i.e., the outcomes or effects of the causes). This phenomenon is now known as the "butterfly effect"; for the Buddha it was known as *paticca-samuppada* or interdependent arising.

Both of these examples from twentieth-century science seem to confirm, or at least count as pieces of evidence in support of, the Buddha's enlight-enment insight that the real and apparent metaphysical structure of reality is actually the outcome of just a particular configuration of causal factors and conditions that are always already dynamically interacting with one another. The problem, according to the Buddha and the Buddhist tradition, is that most of us are completely unaware of this fact because of the debilitating effects of ignorance and craving. We are, in short, simply unawakened and therefore unable to see the ultimate truth about the way things really are. There is, however, hope for correcting this situation, at least if one thinks the Buddha is right about causation. Why should one think he is correct?

A philosophical assessment

Aside from the testimony of the Buddhist tradition, as well as the claims of the Buddha himself, there are at least eight philosophical reasons to think that the Buddha is right about *paticca-samuppada*.

---

[12] Polkinghorne (1995), p. 79.

First, the most general formulation of the teaching not only seems to be intuitively correct, it also is minimally consistent with ordinary experience, if not absolutely confirmed by it. At any rate, it is clearly not contrary to experience, even if the conventional practice of naming "things" tends to conceal the truth of the way they really are.

Second, it seems clear that our common-sense understanding of causation is a colossal oversimplification of the way things really are. This fact is easily and readily confirmed by watching television weather channels and the causal power of weather systems.

Third, even though our scientific and philosophical accounts of causation are more sophisticated than our common-sense view of things, the Newtonian scientific account of a basic physics class is still a huge oversimplification of things – especially in view of quantum theory. Moreover, the history of Western philosophical accounts of causation is simply too full of controversy for one to reasonably think that any one understanding of it is completely correct.

Fourth, despite the controversy surrounding the various interpretations of the Buddha's account of *paticca-samuppada*, it is not only consistent with some of the more sophisticated science of the twentieth century, but it is also a "middle way" between the general causal accounts of random chaos on one extreme and complete mechanical determinism on the other.

Fifth, at the same time, at the level of the human person and human action, his account of *paticca-samuppada* is a "middle way" between absolute freedom and complete free will and no-choice hard determinism – a seemingly intransigent controversy in Western philosophy.

Sixth, the Buddha's account of causation is broad enough to include crucial roles for many commonly recognized important subjects, including: the mind, freedom, nature, nurture, habituation, wisdom, ignorance, and a purpose and goal for life. What human beings experience, according to the Buddha's account of our situation, is conditioned, though not completely determined, choices that are always open, at least to a certain extent, to change and revision. This understanding of reality has the advantage of making our spiritual practices meaningful precisely because it is anchored in a vision of causality that recognizes that causes and conditions can really be influenced and changed.

Seventh, the vision of the Buddha is broad enough to recognize that things can be otherwise than they are, but also that they are the way they are because of prior causes and karmic conditions. One of the most basic insights of the Buddha's account of causation is that appropriate kinds of actions can change the way things are, and the way things are is a function of the way we see and make them.

Such a vision is also decidedly optimistic about the present and the future, especially with respect to *dukkha*, which provides an eighth reason for accepting his account of *paticca-samuppada*. In fact, on the very practical level, his account of causation entails that *dukkha* can be overcome, because if we eliminate its causes and conditions we also can eliminate their effects. Finally, if we eliminate the conditions of *dukkha*, not only can we eliminate *dukkha*, but we also can realize *Nibbana*.

There surely are other reasons why one might think the Buddha's account of interdependent arising is correct. There are also reasonable and formidable objections that one might raise against his account as well. I leave these to the reader to formulate as part of your own assessment of the Buddha's teachings. In the meantime, it is important to keep in mind that whatever the ultimate outcome of this assessment may be, there is little doubt that it must include an evaluation of his account of the logical and metaphysical consequences of *paticca-samuppada*, namely, impermanence, emptiness, and no-enduring-self, and its potential practical consequences as well, namely, *moksa* and *Nibbana*. We shall consider each of these ideas in more detail in **Chapter 7** and **Chapter 8**.

Things to think about

1. Why is an account of causation so important for philosophy?
2. How would you explain the most general formulation of the Buddha's teaching on interdependent arising? How are the traditional interpretations of *paticca-samuppada* related and different?
3. In what ways is the *Abhidhamma* understanding of *paticca-samuppada* different from the Theravada, Madhyamaka, and Yogacara interpretations?
4. How does interdependent arising apply to questions about free will and determinism?
5. What are the strengths and weaknesses of the Buddha's account of *paticca-samuppada*?

7 Impermanence, no-enduring-self, and emptiness

Key terms and teachings

Anatta/Anatman: Literally "no-self," this term refers to the denial of a fixed, permanent, unchanging self or soul (*atta/atman*), and is, in addition to *dukkha* and *anicca*, one of the Three Marks of existence. On a more general level, it refers to the Buddha's denial of any fixed or permanent substantial nature in any object or phenomenon. According to the Buddha, everything lacks inherent existence, because all things arise in dependence on impermanent causes and conditions.

Anicca/Anitya: Terms for the first of the "Three Marks" of existence according to the teachings of the historical Buddha, they mean "impermanence." Impermanence refers to the coming to be, and passing away of all conditioned phenomena, whether physical or psychological, that interdependently arises.

Puggalavadins/Pudgalavadins: Pali and Sanskrit terms for "Personalists," or those who think the **puggala/pudgala** or "person" exists as a subsistent entity.

Sarvastivadins: Sanskrit term for those who think that "everything exists" in the past, present, and future simultaneously.

Sautrantikas: Sanskrit term for those who reject the authority of the *Abhidhamma Pitaka* and instead are "followers of the *Suttas.*"

Sunnatta/Sunyata: Pali and Sanskrit terms meaning "emptiness" or "nothingness," these terms usually refer to the Mahayana interpretations of interdependent arising and the original state of mind, even though there is good evidence for an early Mainstream Buddhist understanding that involves the metaphysical structure of the human person. The Madhyamaka and Yogacara schools of Mahayana Buddhism each offers its own, unique account and defense of emptiness.

Which came first?

One of the easiest ways to think about the cluster of terms to be considered in this chapter is to ask oneself how they are related to the idea of *paticca-samuppada*. For example, are "things" impermanent/*anicca* because they arise interdependently, or do they arise interdependently because they are impermanent? Are the "objects" of ordinary experience both thought to be and actually characterized as possessing no-enduring-self/*anatta* because they arise interdependently, or are they interdependently arisen because they lack an enduring-self? Finally, are "beings" empty/*sunnatta* because they arise interdependently, or do they arise interdependently because they are empty?

This way of thinking about the key terms in this chapter should remind those familiar with the writings of Plato and his accounts of the activities of Socrates of the scene in the *Euthyphro*[1] when Socrates inquired with respect to piety and its relationship to the gods about whether the gods loved things because they were pious things, or whether pious things were pious because they were loved by the gods. According to Socrates, the latter scenario made things accidentally dependent on the, sometimes capricious, whim and will of the gods, while the former scenario clearly implied that there are things (i.e., forms or unchanging, eternal patterns or essences of things) beyond the power and control of the gods.

The answers to questions like Socrates' raise important philosophical issues, including metaphysical questions about the way things are or how they exist, and epistemological questions about whether and how we can actually know what we claim to know about the way things are. The same can be said about our questions about *anicca*, *anatta*, and *sunnatta* and their relationships to *paticca-samuppada*. In fact, I think it is possible to distinguish at least three distinct "Buddhist" answers to our original questions: first, there is the answer attributed by his immediate followers to the historical Buddha; second, there are the more fully developed philosophical and psychological *Abhidhamma* answers of the early Buddhist tradition; and third, there are the Mahayana answers.

The purpose of this chapter is, therefore, to investigate the Buddha's original understanding, the *Abhidhamma* details, and the Mahayana developments of each of these terms and their accounts of their relationships to

---

[1] *Euthyphro*, 10a.

other terms we have already considered (i.e., *kamma*, *samsara*, rebirth, and interdependent arising) as well as their connections to terms we have not yet considered (i.e., *moksa* and *Nibbana*). For the sake of ease as well as logical dependence we will begin with their relationships to interdependent arising and then consider their relationships to *kamma*, *samsara* and rebirth. We will end the chapter by considering their relationships to *moksa* and *Nibbana*, the subjects of the next chapter.

The Buddha on impermanence

One of the most direct ways to approach the Buddha's understanding of impermanence is to start with his account of what is traditionally referred to as the teaching on the "Three Marks" of existence. Two of the more famous versions of the teaching are found in the *Anguttara Nikaya* and the *Dhammapada*. According to the latter text, the Buddha claimed,

> When you see with discernment/wisdom, "All compounded things are *anicca/*impermanent," "All compounded things are *dukkha*," and "All things/states are *anatta*/without self or no-enduring-self," ... This is the path to purity.[2]

In the former text, the Buddha said,

> Whether *Tathagatas* arise in the world or not, it still remains a fact, a firm and necessary condition of existence, that all formations are impermanent ... that all formations are subject to suffering ... that all things are non-self.
>
> A *Tathagata* fully awakens to this fact and penetrates it. Having fully awakened to it and penetrated it, he announces it, teaches it, makes it known, presents it, discloses it, analyzes it and explains it: that all formations are impermanent, that all formations are subject to suffering, that all things are non-self.[3]

There are at least a half dozen particularly striking features of these quotes. First, in order to be seen or understood, the "Three Marks" require wisdom or discernment; one must be intellectually or cognitively awakened to them – they are not and cannot be grasped by ordinary humans who are ignorant. We shall return to this point below.

Second, the first two marks or signs of existence (i.e., impermanence and *dukkha*) are true of all conditioned or interdependently arisen beings and

---

[2] *Dhammapada*, 277–279.   [3] *Anguttara Nikaya*, p. 77.

phenomena. Whatever comes to be and passes away through the process of *paticca-samuppada* is necessarily impermanent and unsatisfactory.

Third, the remaining Mark or characteristic is traditionally understood to include not only all conditioned things, but also the unconditioned (i.e., *Nibbana*) as well. For those who are awake and see things as they really are, there is simply nothing that has a self or an enduring nature or essence.

Fourth, the vision of these "Marks" or features of existence arises on the path away from craving, hatred, and delusion, and is seen by those whose ignorance has been overcome by wisdom and insight into the way things really are.

Fifth, regardless of whether the historical Buddha or any other enlightened beings, for that matter, sees them, the "Three Marks" are "necessary conditions" of all existence. This point would seem to entail that it is not possible, either logically or metaphysically, for any being or thing to exist permanently, without *dukkha*, and by itself. If that is true, there are at least three questions that should come to mind. First, why is it true? Second, are there any logical or metaphysical relationships between or among the "Three Marks?" Third, why are the "Marks" related in that way or ways?

Sixth, the, or a Buddha is, as such, awakened to the truth of these Marks or characteristics and penetrates them, teaches them, makes them known, and explains them to those who are ignorant and unawakened to them.

In addition to these remarks, according to the *Mahasudassana Sutta* of the *Digha Nikaya*, the Buddha tells his disciple Ananda, "conditioned states are impermanent, they are unstable, they can bring us no comfort, and such being the case, we should not rejoice in conditioned states, we should cease to take an interest in them, and be liberated from them."[4] In fact, shortly after informing Ananda that he will not be reborn again he adds, "Impermanent are compounded things, prone to rise and fall, having risen, they're destroyed, their passing truest bliss."[5]

These quotes clearly highlight the metaphysical relationship between "conditioned states" and "compounded things" (i.e., beings that arise interdependently or through the process of *paticca-samuppada*) and impermanence. They also, however, go beyond the purely metaphysical nature of the relationship and offer practical or moral advice about how one is to act in response to these kinds of beings. The Buddha clearly encourages and

---

[4] *Digha Nikaya*, p. 290.   [5] Ibid.

instructs Ananda in the appropriate attitude and courses of actions toward conditioned, impermanent things. He is not to rejoice in them, he is not to be interested in them, and finally, he is to be liberated from them. Why, one might reasonably ask, should Ananda or anyone else believe what the Buddha teaches and do as he says?

One answer to this question is rather obvious – because the Buddha said so. He is a teacher and he speaks with the authority of one who has seen the way things really are and he has, so to speak, "been there and done that." A second, more nuanced response is because one believes or thinks or knows that the Buddha is correct about conditioned, compounded, and impermanent things. But why should one think the Buddha is correct? What kind of argument, defense, or justification could one give to support one's claims?

I want to suggest that if you stop and think about the concepts involved in the teaching on the "Three Marks" as well as his claims about interdependent arising, then one can construct a persuasive line of reasoning in support of accepting both the Buddha's claims about impermanence and his advice about how to act with respect to conditioned states and compounded things.

Interdependent arising, again

Recall for a moment that the Buddha's teaching on *paticca-samuppada* is ultimately justified according to the Buddhist tradition by his insight on the night of his enlightenment. As we saw in **Chapter 6**, the Mainstream Buddhist understanding of *paticca-samuppada* insists that Sakyamuni Buddha literally awakened and saw the way things really are or realized the truth about reality on the night of his enlightenment, and as a result of this meditative insight finally grasped the truth about the fundamental nature of reality.

What the Buddha understood or realized was, despite our conventional naming practices and ordinary unenlightened thinking to the contrary, that there are not strictly speaking any metaphysically distinct and independently existing beings as such. All conventionally designated "things" or "beings" are impermanent because the network of causes and conditions that give rise to them is constantly changing, and as a result they lack an enduring self or a fixed essence (i.e., they are *anatta* and lack *svabhava* – intrinsic nature or self-existence). In fact, almost immediately after claiming that it cannot happen that a person possessing right view could treat any interdependently arisen thing as permanent, the Buddha adds, "It is impossible, it cannot happen that a person possessing right view could treat any thing as self – there is no such possibility."[6] This seems to indicate rather clearly that there is an important and intimate connection and relationship between the individual characteristics of the "Three Marks" and *paticca-samuppada*.

There are at least two ways to think about these connections and relationships. First, we could begin with the "Three Marks" and ask about their interrelationships, and then consider how they are connected to the teaching on interdependent arising. For example, one could ask: Are things impermanent because they are *dukkha* and *anatta*, or *anatta* and *dukkha*? Is there a particular order among the terms, or not, and does that order matter, especially with respect to the coming to be, passing away, and interrelationships of the "Marks," or not? Are things *anatta* because of *dukkha* and impermanence, or impermanence and *dukkha*? Are they *dukkha* because they are impermanent and *anatta*, or *anatta* and impermanent?

One could imagine lots of answers to these questions. For example, one might think that the most obvious answer is that things are *dukkha* (D), because they are *anatta* (A) and impermanent (I). Understood in one way, this means that since "things" are impermanent, they are *anatta*, and being *anatta* they give rise to *dukkha*, which is the experience of unenlightened and unawakened people who do not see things as they really are (i.e., $I => A => D$). However, understood in another way, this might mean that the experience of *dukkha* is the product of the conjunction of impermanence and *anatta* (i.e., $I + A => D$). But one could also imagine someone thinking that things are impermanent because they lack a self and are *dukkha*. In other words, it is possible to think that people who, accidentally, though correctly realize that things are *anatta*, might also join their experience of *dukkha* with this insight to conclude that impermanence arises because things lack enduring selves and are *dukkha* (i.e., $A + D => I$). One could also imagine another situation in which someone thinks that things are *anatta*, because they are impermanent and *dukkha*. In other words, the experiences of impermanence and dissatisfaction, whether jointly (i.e., $I + D => A$) or successively (i.e., $I => D => A$), give rise to the experience of *dukkha*.

---

[6] *Majjhima Nikaya*, p. 928.

There are obviously other possible scenarios, different lines of causal interactions, and other ways of thinking about impermanence, *dukkha*, and *anatta* that one could imagine as answers to the previous questions, but the point of this exercise is not only to think more carefully and more deeply about the teaching on the "Three Marks," but also to highlight the inter-dependent nature of the relationships among these characteristic features of existence. This is, after all, precisely what the Buddha himself did on the night of his enlightenment, and it is exactly what he taught with respect to *paticca-samuppada*.

A second way to think about the relationships between the teaching on the "Three Marks" and *paticca-samuppada* is to start with the latter and consider its relationship to the features or "Marks" of existence.

As we saw in the previous chapter, the teaching on interdependent arising is fundamentally a claim about the law-governed dynamics of change in which the events, processes, or happenings in both the world and the mind are causally conditioned by and dependent on other events, processes, or happenings. In other words, "things," which are ordinarily conceived of as "beings" with fixed or unchanging essences or natures do not actually exist in that way, and whatever exists, exists as events, processes, or happenings, that are themselves the ongoing results of causal interactions that are interdependently giving rise to them.

If we apply this understanding of *paticca-samuppada* to the individual characteristics of the "Three Marks," two distinct consequences may be inferred. First, it would seem to follow that each "Mark" or characteristic of existence is in actuality an event, process, or happening – and not a "thing" as "things" are conventionally understood. Second, it would also follow that each "Mark" of existence owes its reality to a complex network of causes and conditions from which each interdependently arises and to which each and all are causally interconnected.

It is important to realize, however, that these consequences, which follow logically from the Buddha's account of interdependent arising, are unfortunately not obviously consistent with either our ordinary experiences of the world (i.e., recall our fire and smoke example or the billiard balls scenario) or our usual way of conceiving or conventionally designating what we understand to be happening around us and/or even in our own thoughts and minds. Hence the multiplicity of possible scenarios considered above, and the historical Buddha's insistence that we need to wake up to the truth about reality. Yet this situation, contrary to experience as it may be, should not be surprising. The Buddhist tradition has always maintained that ignorance, and, consequently, not seeing things as they really are, are two basic problems for all unenlightened human beings. The truth of the matter is that only those who are truly enlightened and awakened, who see with insight, discernment, and wisdom, who diligently follow the Buddha's pure path, can see and know that all compounded things and formations arise interdependently and are ultimately impermanent.

If we turn our attention to the Buddha's conception of the second "Mark" of existence, *dukkha*, both what he thinks and why he thinks it should already be somewhat clear from his account of *dukkha* in the Four Noble Truths. It will also lead us directly into a consideration of the third "Mark" of existence, *anatta*.

The Buddha on *dukkha* and *anatta*

In **Chapter 3** we learned that on the night of his enlightenment experience the Buddha underwent a radical re-visioning of life and his understanding of it. We also learned that his basic teachings involve a new philosophical outlook, *dassana*, or "truth" – a new way of seeing and understanding the world and its metaphysical structure. This radically new way of knowing and being in the world was set forth in his First Sermon and succinctly summarized in what is commonly referred to as the Four Noble Truths.

According to the Buddha, the path to liberation from *kamma*, *samsara*, and rebirth begins with a reorientation in one's knowledge, understanding, and causal interactions with the world. The first step on this path to liberation begins, quite literally, with an insight into, and subsequent recognition and acceptance of, the First Noble Truth, namely, that everything involves *dukkha*. The remaining Noble Truths simply specify the origin, causes and conditions, and means by which one can overcome and stop *dukkha*.

According to the Buddha, the most basic source of *dukkha* is "the five aggregates of attachment." In other words, the root cause of *dukkha* is craving and desiring that arises interdependently within and from the five aggregates that compose us, as a direct and immediate consequence of the wrong ideas or views that we habitually form of our "selves" and other "things." Our fundamental mistake is actually twofold: first, we think that we are or possess a fixed, substantial or essential self – an immaterial being (i.e., *atman*), which transmigrated from past lives into this life, and will continue to exist into the next life as well; and second, we think that all other "things" possess an intrinsic nature or self-being (i.e., *svabhava*) by which they maintain their unchanging identity and enduring existence, and that pursuing and possessing them will somehow make us happy or satisfied. The Buddha, however, claims that both of these thoughts are wrong.

The former is wrong because he refused to posit the existence of an entity whose very being was not verifiable by direct experience. As we have seen, he had personally engaged in the kinds of introspective meditative experience that presumably could and would have confirmed the continuing and ongoing existence of his own *atman*, but he had failed after many attempts to discover any fixed inner essence of himself. At least initially, he and his followers denied the existence of enduring selves underlying the ever-changing flux of daily experience, precisely because there simply was no empirical evidence of abiding selves. Instead, the Buddha taught *anatta* or the no-enduring-self view of the human person and all beings – the third "Mark" of existence.

He also claimed, according to the *Khandhasamyutta*, that if there were a self, then it would never be subject to affliction and it would be completely subject to our control. But we all know from experience that both consequents are false, so there is no enduring self. In the same *Sutta*, the Buddha also offered a fittingness argument against any impermanent and changing "thing" being regarded as "This is mine, this I am, this is myself." His basic line of reasoning was that if all impermanent things cause suffering and constantly change, it is not appropriate that they be thought of as "self" – at least as "self" was commonly understood by his fellow Indians. According to the Buddha, all of the aggregates that constitute my ongoing existence obviously satisfy the antecedent, so all of them are "This is not mine, this I am not, this is not myself."[7]

At the same time, as we have seen, the Buddha rejected the existence of *atman* as logically necessary to explain the Indian teachings on *kamma*, *samsara*, and rebirth. As we noted in **Chapter 5**, the Buddha admits that there is an ongoing series or cycle of rebirths that does in fact occur, but there is no fixed and unchanging self, soul, or *atman* that undergoes the transmigration. The causal and karmic explanation of this is, of course,

---

[7] *Samyutta Nikaya*, pp. 901–902.

paticca-samuppada, which, if correct, explains why the latter idea is wrong, and why no conditioned state or compounded thing can ever make us happy or satisfied.

Interdependent teachings

We have seen that the Mainstream Buddhist understanding of *paticca-samuppada* is that what the Buddha realized on the night of his enlightenment was the intellectual insight that all conventionally designated individual "things" are in reality not metaphysically independent or self-contained, subsistent "beings," but processes or happenings, and that these events and processes are themselves causally connected to literally all other processes and events that are simultaneously happening at any given moment in the flux and flow of a complex network of interconnected events and processes. I now want to suggest that this particular teaching sits at the intersection of some of the most basic and important of the Buddha's teachings, i.e., the Four Noble Truths, the "Three Marks," *kamma*, *samsara*, and rebirth. I also want to claim that it provides clear answers to our previous questions about why it is not possible for any being to exist permanently, without *dukkha*, and by itself, the nature of the relationships among the "Marks" of existence, why the "Marks" are related in those ways, and why anyone should believe and follow the Buddha's advice about one's attitude and actions toward conditioned states and compounded things.

The short answers are: first, because of our ignorance we falsely believe that both our "selves" and "things" are independently existing "beings" and that if we possess some or all of them they will satisfy us and make us happy. Second, actually, all "beings" and "things" are interdependently arisen from other processes in a complex network of interrelated causes and conditions. Third, the same dependently originated relationships apply to the "Three Marks." Fourth, the same causal and karmic forces that lead to *samsara* and rebirth also make all beings impermanent, *dukkha*, and *anatta*.

The ideas and claims expressed in these answers also provide answers to the original questions at the beginning of the chapter. It now should be clear that for the Buddha, all "things" are impermanent, *anatta*, and empty precisely because they do not exist the way we commonly and habitually think they do, and they exist the way they actually do because they arise interdependently.

Abhidhamma details

The *Abhidhamma*[8] accounts of impermanence, *anatta*, and emptiness, as well as its answers to the original questions of the chapter are somewhat more complex and complicated than the Buddha's initial explanations and answers, even though they claim to be authentically Buddhist.

According to this understanding of "things," impermanence is a feature of all "things" because all "things" come into being, and pass away as a result of interdependent arising. In short, "things" are as they are and what they are as a result of causes and conditions, which are processes or events or happenings. Since the causes and conditions themselves are always engaged in the process of changing, the "things" which originate with or from them are constantly changing as well. However, the "things" themselves are more metaphysically complicated than they first appear to be in the Buddha's sermons or to our senses.

The *Abhidhamma* view is that "things" are actually composed of constituent "parts" or "elements," and these "parts" are themselves composed of *dhammas*. In other words, ordinary "things" are not only composite beings, but they are actually double-composite beings.

For example, recall that we have seen that the Buddha taught that the human person is actually composed of five "aggregates" or heaps, i.e., material shape or form, feelings or sensations, cognitions, dispositional attitudes, and consciousness. According to the *Abhidhamma* understanding of the process of change and interdependent arising, the aggregates themselves that constitute the human person require a principle to explain how each of them comes into being, appears to endure, and then undergoes the process of decay, and finally passes away. The justification for this is that each aggregate appears to have some semblance of ongoing or continuing existence, despite the fact that the "things" they compose are always changing. In fact, my introspective experience of my own consciousness and conscious states seems to reveal that they are not only mine, but also that they continue to be mine over the course of time. Some principle or starting point of explanation is, therefore, required, according to *Abhidhamma* thinkers, to explain this situation. In short, some more basic element of

---

[8] There are two canonical *Abhidhamma* collections – the *Theravada* and *Sarvastivada* – and numerous "Higher Dharma" manuals. For the sake of ease and clarity I shall be speaking in general terms about the various *Abhidhamma* accounts, unless otherwise indicated.

existence, in addition to the aggregates, is necessary to explain these facts. For *Abhidhamma* thinkers, the fundamental building blocks of both my experience and reality as well are called *dhammas*. These *dhammas* are the basic metaphysical elements of physical and mental existence.

According to the *Abhidhamma* view of things, the *dhammas* themselves are not, strictly speaking, "things" or substantial beings, but they are merely metaphysical parts and principles of explanation of the process of change or interdependent arising. Their existence, which is not and cannot be directly confirmed by sense experience, is, nevertheless, necessary to explain the parts, steps, or stages in the process of change or becoming, as well as our way of understanding or making sense out of changing events and situations. They are, in short, the basic material constituents of the physical objects in the world around us, like quarks, gluons, and meons in contemporary science, and the fundamental elements of our mental life (i.e., our mind or consciousness and its mental states) as well.

In simple terms, the *dhammas* are the ultimate metaphysical parts of "things" such as human beings, animals, plants, and rocks. They are the most basic metaphysical building blocks or happenings that are causally responsible for the coming to be, the ongoing duration, and subsequent decay, and passing away of the "things" or processes of which they are "parts." They also are the ultimate principles of explanation and final sources of epistemic justification with respect to how we know "things" and the changes that they are undergoing. The problem, however, is that the Buddha and his followers deny that our ordinary, unenlightened and ignorant mental states are sufficient to see "things" as they really are, and, in fact, they insist that our deluded mental conditions are among the most basic causes of *dukkha* and ignorance.

According to the early Buddhist tradition, the ignorance and craving of an unenlightened mind prevent us from knowing things as they really are, and that is why it maintains that for the Buddha the path to liberation from *kamma*, *samsara*, and rebirth, and ultimately enlightenment itself, begins with a reorientation in one's knowledge, understanding, and causal interactions with the world. In short, unless and until one changes one's mind and one's attitudes towards "things" – both how we view them and how we respond to them – or in other words, unless and until one awakens to the truth about the way "things" really are, one will continue to fail to see and understand (i.e., will remain ignorant of) the single most important or most basic insight of the historical Buddha, that it is our mind and our uses of it that determine how we see and understand our self, the world, and all "things." Enlightenment is possible, according to the Buddha and his early followers, but only with the cessation of ignorance, craving, and habitual wrong thinking. If we fail to eliminate the causes and conditions that interdependently give rise to ignorance and craving, we shall unfortunately never know "things" as they truly are, and we shall never attain *Nibbana*.

The Puggalavadins

At the same time that these *Abhidhamma* teachings on the mind and its relationship to reality were being gathered and compiled, there were also followers of the Buddha who clearly maintained that even if "things" other than human beings are impermanent processes or events, there nevertheless must be some kind of source of metaphysical unity and permanence, or at least quasi-permanence, for humans, in order to explain our ongoing experience of ourselves as a unified, conscious knower, as well as our *kamma* and its consequences. These Buddhists, called Puggalavadins, or "Personalists," claimed that the *Abhidhamma* analysis of the human person into impersonal mental and physical *dhammas* not only failed to account for his or her personhood or humanity, but it also ignored the reality of the experience of a unified self. In other words, the reductive analysis of the human person to *dhammas* omitted both the whole from which its parts were separated (i.e., the "person") and its formal operative unity as well. The same reductive analysis of the human person also failed to explain satisfactorily how *kamma* and its causal effects and continuity across multiple lives operated and could be meaningfully understood.

According to these thinkers, the *puggala/pudgala* or "person" was just as real as the five aggregates from which it arose, even though they insisted, somewhat paradoxically, that the "person" as such was neither identical to the five aggregates nor different from them. This rather puzzling account seems to suggest a view of the person and personal identity in which the former dynamically emerges into a quasi-enduring state out of the complex interactions of the aggregates, while the latter is merely a conventional conceptual distinction that is not anchored in any real ontological differences among the person and their physical and mental components. Such a view clearly has the advantage of recognizing the ongoing process of change and impermanence in the human being. Its account of the person does not, however, unfortunately, seem to be consistent with the early Buddhist teaching on *anatta*. Perhaps for this reason, as Peter Harvey[9] points out, almost all other Buddhist schools criticized followers of the doctrine of "personhood."

The Sarvastivadins

Other Buddhists, known as Sarvastivadins, offered their own accounts of the causal interactions of the *dhammas*, and they also tried to explain how we are able to see, perceive, and know both the events that arise from the *dhammas* as well as the *dhammas* themselves.

As previously noted, the *Abhidhamma* texts tried to explain how the *dhammas* are the most basic metaphysical building blocks or happenings that are causally responsible for the origin, the ongoing duration, and subsequent decay, and passing away of the "things" or processes of which they are parts. One of the most basic problems involved in this explanation is identifying exactly how many parts, steps, stages, or moments there are in the ongoing process of change itself. Theravada thinkers claimed that only three stages or moments exist: arising, enduring, and passing away. Sarvastivada thinkers, however, disagreed and identified four distinct moments: arising, enduring, decaying, and passing away.

Without going into the specific details of this particular dispute, what is important to realize is that the followers of the Buddha were forced to work out very specific answers to some rather complex and complicated philosophical questions about the details of his teachings. In this case, the Theravada and Sarvastivada thinkers were left trying to explain how the various *dhammas* were causally connected in order to explain both the apparent continuing existence of "things" as well as the existence of human agents who know both themselves and these interdependently arisen "things."

According to the Sarvastivadins, the *dhammas* must be said to exist at all times – in the past, at the present, and in the future – at once, in order to explain how memory and knowledge of past things works, as well as how past *kamma* causally affects and influences the present and future, how the

---

[9] Harvey (1990), p. 85.

present interdependently arises and currently exists, and also how future events arise and can be known. They supported these views by claiming that each *dhamma* possessed its own intrinsic nature, self-existence or *svabhava*. In other words, they made the *dhammas* themselves into metaphysically distinct, independent beings, in the same way that the Puggalavadins reified the person. As a result of this conception of the *dhammas*, they were able to explain how the *dhammas* could endure through time and continue to exist in the past, present, and future simultaneously.

The Sautrantikas

Still other Buddhists, called Sautrantikas or "followers of the *Suttas*," vigorously disagreed with these ideas and maintained that only the present actually exists, and that neither the past nor the future exist, even though the past exercises a causal influence on both the present and future through a kind of "karmic momentum" from past actions. They also zealously criticized the reification of the *dhammas* as not only contrary to the ideas of impermanence and interdependent arising, but also as clearly contrary to the Buddha's original teaching on *anatta*. On their view, one could conceptually distinguish the *dhammas* from the "things" they composed, but because no "thing" is or can exist independently from any other (because of the teaching on interdependent arising), all such accounts of the *dhammas* are merely conventional, instrumental explanations that do not actually get at the ultimate nature of things. This last point, in particular, helped prepare the way for the later Madhyamaka teaching on "Two Truths" that we shall consider shortly.

At this point it should be clear that there is not a single, unified, and uncomplicated *Abhidhamma* answer to any of the original questions of this chapter, or anything like a simple, commonly accepted explanation of impermanence, *anatta*, and emptiness. Yet this situation should not be all that surprising given the complexity of the issues involved, the apparent ambiguity of some of the Buddha's own teachings, as well as their obvious lack of philosophical and psychological detail. Each and every one of these facts contributed in its own way to the ongoing study, investigation, and development of numerous Buddhist accounts of the fundamental nature of reality. This development is especially clear in the Mahayana answers to our original questions and their accounts of impermanence, *anatta*, and especially emptiness. Before considering their answers, however, we must first consider the Buddha's account of emptiness.

The Buddha on emptiness

The observant reader will not have failed to realize that we have not actually considered either the Buddha's or the *Abhidhamma* accounts of emptiness *per se*. There are three reasons for this: first, according to the Mainstream Buddhist tradition and its *Suttas*, the historical Buddha simply did not have much to say about emptiness, at least in comparison to other important ideas; second, the *Abhidhamma* accounts are simply too complex and complicated for an introductory text and audience; and third, as a result of historical circumstances, emptiness has come to be associated, almost exclusively, with Mahayana Buddhism, and especially with the *Prajnaparamita* or *Perfection of Wisdom Sutras*, the *Diamond Sutra*, and the *Heart Sutra*.

If we consider what the Mainstream *Suttas* say the Buddha himself taught, as opposed to what some of his disciples said about emptiness, his focus appears to be twofold: first, with respect to metaphysics and the nature of the world, and second, with respect to epistemology and the practice of meditation. With respect to the first, the Buddha responds to his disciple Ananda's question, "In what way is it said, 'Empty is the world'?"

> It is, Ananda, because it is empty of self and of what belongs to self that it is said, "Empty is the world." And what is empty of self and of what belongs to self? The eye, Ananda, is empty of self and what belongs to self. Forms are empty of self and of what belongs to self. Eye-consciousness is empty of self and of what belongs to self ... Whatever feeling arises with mind-contact as condition – whether pleasant or painful or neither-painful-nor-pleasant – that too is empty of self and of what belongs to self.
>
> It is, Ananda, because it is empty of self and of what belongs to self that it is said, "Empty is the world."[10]

It is clear from the texts surrounding this response, which are concerned with questions about what is subject to disintegration, impermanence, and Ananda's request for a "Cliff Notes" version of the *Dhamma*, that the Buddha sees a connection, a clearly interdependently arisen connection, among the

---

[10] *Samyutta Nikaya*, pp. 1163–1164.

concepts of disintegration, impermanence, emptiness, lack of self, revulsion toward the five aggregates, dispassion, liberation, knowledge, and the realization of *Nibbana*. In fact, in response to Ananda's request for a teaching of the *Dhamma* in brief, the Buddha proposes to teach the way that is suitable for uprooting all conceivings,

> For, bhikkhus, whatever one conceives, whatever one conceives in, whatever one conceives from, whatever one conceives as "mine" – that is otherwise. The world, becoming otherwise, attached to becoming, seeks delight only in becoming.
>
> Whatever, bhikkhus, is the extent of the aggregates, the elements, and the sense base, he does not conceive that, does not conceive in that, does not conceive from that, does not conceive, "That is mine."
>
> Since he does not conceive anything thus, he does not cling to anything in the world. Not clinging, he is not agitated. Being unagitated, he personally attains Nibbana. He understands: "Destroyed is birth, the holy life has been lived, what had to be done has been done, there is no more for this state of being."
>
> This, bhikkhus, is the way that is suitable for uprooting all conceivings.[11]

And he continues,

> What do you think, bhikkhus, is the eye (and all of the remaining aggregates considered individually), permanent or impermanent? – "Impermanent, venerable sir." – "Is what is impermanent suffering or happiness?" – "Suffering, venerable sir." – "Is what is impermanent, suffering, and subject to change fit to be regarded thus: 'This is mine, this I am, this is my self'?" – "No, venerable sir." ...
>
> Seeing thus, bhikkhus, the instructed noble disciple experiences revulsion towards the eye (and all of the remaining aggregates considered individually) ... as condition – whether pleasant, or painful or neither-painful-nor-pleasant ... Experiencing revulsion, he becomes dispassionate. Through dispassion [his mind] is liberated. When it is liberated there comes the knowledge: "It's liberated." He understands: "Destroyed is birth, the holy life has been lived, what had to be done has been done, there is no more for this state of being."
>
> This, bhikkhus, is the way that is suitable for uprooting all conceivings.[12]

---

[11] Ibid., pp. 1145–1146.
[12] Ibid. and for similar remarks see *Majjhima Nikaya*, pp. 231–233.

In the light of these teachings, there can be little doubt that the Buddha sees both metaphysical (i.e., with respect to the ontology of the person and material "things") and epistemological (i.e., with respect to how we conceive and understand our selves and "things") connections among this network of interrelated terms, ideas, and beings that lead ultimately to the penetrating insight of liberating knowledge, the cessation of this current state of being, and the final realization of *Nibbana*.

With respect to epistemology and meditation, the *Culasunnata Sutta* and the *Mahasunnata Sutta* or the *Shorter and Greater Discourses on Voidness*, the Buddha explains to Ananda what he means by "abiding in voidness." In the *Shorter Discourse* he outlines the numerous stages and mental states (i.e., from ordinary sensation and perception through the four *jhanas* and ultimately to the formless state of mind) through which one passes in meditative practice as one considers the various kinds of "things" and "objects" of thought that constitute the distinct realms of the Buddha's cosmology (i.e., the world of the five senses, the world of pure forms, and the formless world, which includes infinite space, infinite consciousness, the base of nothingness, and the base of neither-perception-nor-non-perception). According to the Buddha, these meditative stages culminate in the "signless (i.e., devoid of any sign of permanence) concentration of the mind" known as insight. At this stage, the Buddha claims the meditator realizes that,

> "This signless concentration of mind is conditioned and volitionally produced. But whatever is conditioned and provisionally produced is impermanent, subject to cessation." When he knows and sees thus, his mind is liberated from the taint of sensual desire, from the taint of being, and from the taint of ignorance. When it is liberated he come to the knowledge: "It is liberated." He understands: "Birth is destroyed, the holy life has been lived, what had to be done has been done, there is no more coming to any state of being."[13]

It seems clear from this quote that the Buddha teaches that there is a direct, interdependently arisen causal relationship among the meditative practices of abiding in voidness, the insight into the way "things" are, the liberation of the mind from the three taints, the knowledge of this liberation, the cessation of *samsara* and rebirth, and the ultimate realization of *Nibbana*.

---

[13] *Majjhima Nikaya*, p. 969.

In the *Greater Discourse on Voidness*, within the context of the consideration of a question about whether monks who delight in the company of others will ever obtain the bliss of renunciation, the bliss of seclusion, the bliss of peace, and the bliss of enlightenment, the Buddha again describes the process by which one may enter and abide in voidness. According to his teaching, one should steady his mind internally, quiet it, bring it to single-ness, concentrate it, and thereby enter upon, abide in, and proceed through the four *jhanas*. The result is that one acquires confidence, steadiness, and full awareness of the truth about voidness and the fundamental nature of reality.

The Buddha (and Thich Nhat Hanh as we shall see) also maintains that this state of concentrated mind and awareness can be extended to ordinary activities such as walking, standing, sitting, lying down, talking, and even thinking itself. Eventually, through the practice of mindfulness and one's own efforts one can abandon attachment to sensual desires as well as clinging to the five aggregates. In fact, the Buddha insists,

> When he abides contemplating rise and fall in these five aggregates affected by clinging, the conceit "I am" based on these five aggregates affected by clinging is abandoned in him. When that is so, the bhikkhu understands: "The conceit 'I am' based on these five aggregates affected by clinging is abandoned in me."[14]

At the end of the *Sutta*, the Buddha advises Ananda that the real reason for seeking the company of a teacher like the Buddha is to avoid his own undoing by being "struck down by evil unwholesome states that defile, bring renewal of being, give trouble, ripen in suffering, and lead to future birth, aging, and death."[15] The way to avoid these results is to seek the company of the Teacher who will instruct one in effacement, the mind's release, complete disenchantment, dispassion, cessation, peace, direct knowledge, enlightenment, and *Nibbana*. On the more practical level this means following his advice about wanting little, being content, secluded, and aloof from society, as well as arousing one's energy, virtue, concentra-tion, wisdom, deliverance, knowledge and vision of deliverance, in order to achieve one's final goal: liberation and *Nibbana*.

---

[14] Ibid., p. 975.   [15] Ibid., p. 976.

The Buddha offers the same kind of meditative and practical advice to his own son in the *Maharahulalovada Sutta* or *The Greater Discourse of Advice to Rahula*. In response to Rahula's question about how mindfulness of breathing can be developed and cultivated in order to produce great benefits, the Buddha initially urges him to consider the basic material elements of his body and all physical "things" (i.e., the earth element, water element, fire element, air element, and space element), and realize that "This is not mine, this I am not, this is not myself."[16] He then urges him to develop meditation on what is traditionally referred to as the "four divine abodes or abidings" – loving-kindness, compassion, altruistic joy, and equanimity, and also on foulness, in order to abandon lust, craving, and greed. Finally, the Buddha instructs Rahula to "develop meditation on the perception of impermanence; for when you develop meditation on the perception of impermanence, the conceit 'I am' will be abandoned."[17]

The Buddha's pedagogical strategy in each of these contexts seems to be remarkably consistent. Start with empirical data and ideas derived from direct unenlightened experience about the presumed physical and metaphysical structure of "things," consider the ontology of the human person and the five aggregates, abide in voidness or emptiness, ascend through the four meditative *jhanas* while purifying the mind of distorting elements in order to see "things" as they really are, achieve insight into impermanence and *anatta*, and finally realize enlightenment, liberation, and *Nibbana*.

Although followers of the Buddha might reasonably disagree about which, if any, of these steps, stages, or moments in the process toward the realization of *Nibbana* is the most important or most critical, i.e., meditation itself, impermanence, emptiness, *anatta*, interdependent arising, liberation from *samsara* and rebirth, and even *Nibbana*, there can be little disagreement about the interconnectedness of these ideas – it is simply impossible to think coherently, correctly, and completely about any one of them in isolation or without reference to the others. This is especially true if you consider the particular images the Buddha uses to illustrate his teachings.

For example, consider a lump of foam, a water bubble, a mirage, a magical illusion, smoke, a dream, a circle formed by twirling a firebrand, a flash of lightning, or the moon's reflection on water. At first glance, each of these "things" has the appearance of being a discrete individual object, existing

---

[16] Ibid., pp. 527–530.   [17] Ibid., p. 531.

independently and on its own. Yet gradually, over the course of time, experience and careful reflection teach us that they are actually fleeting, impermanent, and lacking self-existence. Eventually, if we are disciplined enough to investigate them, we come to realize two things about them: first, their apparent existence has more to do with our way of seeing and thinking about them than their actual existence, and second, their actual existence depends on many causes and conditions that interdependently give rise to them.

As Bhikkhu Bodhi[18] notes, many of these images were later taken up by Buddhist thinkers, especially the Madhyamakas, who highlighted the earlier Mainstream notion that our conceptions of the world and our own existence are largely distorted by the process of ordinary, unenlightened cognition. In other words, the unenlightened way we habitually see and think about ordinary "things" has a profound and distorting effect on the way we think they are. Our task, according to the Buddha, is to see "things" as they really are – interdependently arisen, impermanent, *anatta*, and empty.

The same is true of the five aggregates, the human person, and other apparently enduring things, like rocks and mountains. Each of them is, in an important and fundamental way, just like the preceding examples, "void, hollow, insubstantial"[19] and lacking in substance. The problem in a nutshell is that when they are seen with and through a mind that is habitually ignorant and unenlightened, they appear in ways that deviate from their true forms. Instead of being seen as impermanent, *anatta*, and empty, they appear as fixed substances with intrinsic natures and self-existences. According to the Buddha and his followers it is our mis-seeing and misunderstanding of them as they actually are, that subsequently leads to craving, desiring, and the entire network of interdependently arising consequences of the teaching on *paticca-samuppada*.

Once again, we are back to the central thesis of this book, namely, that the Buddha's most basic insight is about the mind and its operation – that it is our mind and our uses of it that determine how we see and understand our self, the world, and all "things." In fact, if this insight is correct, then the answer to our original questions appears to be: "It depends on how you think about things." And those who think correctly about things know that they arise interdependently.

---

[18] Bodhi (2000), p. 1086.   [19] *Samyutta Nikaya*, p. 951.

Mahayana developments

Given the diversity of *Abhidhamma* answers to the original questions of this chapter as well as their different accounts of impermanence, and *anatta*, it should not be surprising that there is a spectrum of Mahayana answers and accounts of the same. It also should not be surprising that many of the Mahayana developments help support and clarify the Buddha's most basic insight. At this point in our discussion of the "Details of the *Dhamma*" we shall only briefly highlight the Mahayana teachings on emptiness, the Madhyamaka teaching on "Two Truths," the Yogacara focus on the mind, and the Vajrayana teachings on consciousness and Buddha-nature.

With respect to the Mahayana teaching on emptiness, it is customary to distinguish two main views, the Madhyamaka and the Yogacara. According to the Madhyamaka view, especially as it was articulated by Nagarjuna, emptiness is literally equivalent to interdependent arising, because it refers to the fact that nothing can or does exist in isolation from its causes and conditions. As a result, every "thing" is empty of an intrinsic nature and own-being. In fact, failure to realize this "ultimate truth" about all "things" leads to the creation of mental formations that not only cause *dukkha* but also are sources of *samsara*. These same negative mental formations are the sources of our ordinary, unenlightened experience of the world and they are the sources of our "conventional truth" about "things" (i.e., that they are independently existing substances with intrinsic natures). The basic difference between these "Two Truths" (i.e., ultimate and conventional) is that the former is only seen in the wisdom of the enlightened person, while the latter is the result of ordinary mental defilements and conventional, unenlightened thinking. According to Nagarjuna, the correct realization of the "ultimate truth," however, eliminates negative mental formations and *dukkha*, and subsequently paves the way for the attainment of *Nibbana*.

According to the Yogacara view, on the other hand, emptiness refers to the original or natural state of the mind in which there is no dualistic distinction between the knower and the known or the perceiving subject and the perceived object. On this view of "things," it is the mind or consciousness and its operations that serve as the foundation for the interdependent arising of both our "selves" and the "things" we experience. Unenlightened beings falsely believe that there is a real metaphysical distinction between themselves as knowers and the objects of their knowledge. They also mistakenly believe that both subjects and objects possess their own intrinsic natures or independent self-existences. Their failure to see "things" as they really are – as interdependently arisen from the mind and consciousness – is what causes their experiences of *dukkha*, *samsara*, and rebirth. Enlightened or awakened beings, on the other hand, through rigorous meditative practices, have stilled their minds, eliminated mental defilements, and achieved insight into the true nature of mind and conditioned consciousness. The result of this insight is release from *samsara* and the realization of *Nibbana*.

Finally, Vajrayana Buddhists adopted Tantric texts and practices involving rituals and meditative techniques in order to enhance their efforts for liberation from the cycle of rebirth and the achievement of *Nibbana*. Following the Yogacara view of things, they engaged in meditative practices that sought to remove the ignorance and mental defilements that interfere with the realization of our innate and intrinsic Buddha-nature. Without going into the details of this important idea, which we shall be considering more carefully in **Chapter 11**, Vajrayana Buddhists claimed that through a series of meditative practices, including visualization techniques and various forms of yoga, one eventually realizes both the fundamental unity of all things in their common Buddha-nature or Buddha-essence and their ultimate emptiness of self-being.

According to Vajrayana Buddhists, practitioners of the highest forms of yoga gain insight into the subtlest levels of consciousness where one realizes the profound "emptiness" and unity of all "things" in their transcendent Buddha-nature. The ultimate goal of this form of Buddhist practice is to help its followers to reorient their mental faculties not only to see "things" as they really are, but also to realize this truth in practice in compassionate living, in the release from *samara*, and the ultimate attainment of *Nibbana*.

We shall leave the remaining features of the Mahayana developments for **Part III**. In the meantime, it should be clear that there are various Mahayana answers to our original questions in this chapter. In fact, I invite the reader to formulate your own answers to them as you make your way through the last four chapters of the book. I also want to point out that the Mahayana responses contain an important practical dimension because they are directed at actually living the answers and thereby achieving release from *samsara* and the attainment of *Nibbana*. It is to a more detailed account of these practical consequences of Buddhist practice that we turn in **Chapter 8**.

Things to think about

1. How are the "Three Marks" related to one another for their existences and how are they related to the Buddha's teaching on interdependent arising?
2. Why do the *Abhidhamma* texts posit the existence of *dhammas*? Is their argument convincing?
3. Which account of the *dhammas* seems best to you and why? Is the account of the *dhammas* consistent with the teaching on emptiness? Why or why not?
4. What role does meditation play in realizing or understanding emptiness?
5. How does mindfulness help one transcend conventional truth and see the ultimate truth?

8   *Moksa* and *Nibbana*

Key terms and teachings

Asavas/Asravas: Pali and Sanskrit terms usually translated as "outflows," that refer to the defilements or impurities that cause repeated rebirths. In the Pali texts there are three or four impurities: sense desires, the desire for continuing existence, wrong views, and ignorance.

Samyojana: Pali and Sanskrit term meaning "binding" or "fetter." The Buddhist tradition recognizes ten fetters that bind one to *samsara*: belief that there is an enduring individual self, unjustified doubt with respect to the Buddha and his teachings, excessive concern with rituals and monastic and ethical rules, sensuous desire, lust or craving, hatred, ill will or aversion, craving for the Form realm, craving for the Formless realm, excessive self-love, being restless or agitated, and ignorance. The first five are known as the "lower fetters" (that bind one to the Desire Realm) and the last five are known as the "higher fetters" (that bind one to the Form and Formless Realms).

Upaya: Sanskrit term for "skillful means" or "skill-in-means." Although generally associated with the Mahayana tradition and the perfections of a *Bodhisattva*, it also refers to the Buddha's ability to suit his teachings to the capacity of his disciples and his audiences in order to bring them to enlightenment.

Intellectual roots and ultimate goals

It is both fitting and appropriate as we complete **Part II** on the "Details of the *Dhamma*" to consider the two terms (i.e., *moksa* and *Nibbana*) that simultaneously point backward to the Indian roots and context of Buddhism and forward to the ultimate goals of Hindu and Buddhist practices. Such a consideration has the advantages of reinforcing the roles of the religious, intellectual, and cultural contexts in and from which the teachings of the historical Buddha were formulated, as well as highlighting the distinctiveness of his teachings.

Moksa and *Nibbana* not only refer to the highest goods and final ends of Hindu and Buddhist practices, but they also presuppose knowledge of other important ideas (i.e., *dukkha*, *tanha*, *paticca-samuppada*, *kamma*, *samsara*, rebirth, impermanence, emptiness, *anatta*, ignorance, and enlightenment) in order to be properly understood. Given our previous treatment of these related ideas in the preceding chapters of **Part II**, in this chapter we will begin with the general Indian notion of *moksa* as release from *samsara*, and then distinguish the Buddha's teachings on *Nibbana* from it. Our goal is to complete our presentation of the "Details of the *Dhamma*" and anticipate the conditions for the "Development of the *Dhamma/Dharma*" in **Part III**.

The Indian conception of *moksa*

Although there are differences in details among the classical *dassanas* of Indian philosophy and religion with respect to their understandings of the meaning and purpose of life, the fundamental nature of reality, and their accounts of *moksa*, there is at least some general agreement, even among the heterodox systems of the Jains and Buddhists, about the prospects for achieving freedom from the cycle of birth, life, death, and rebirth. As a consequence, at a certain level of generality, the basic features of what we might for the sake of ease call "the Indian conception of *moksa*" are rather clear.

First, *moksa* is the ultimate aim or goal in life. All other aims and goals (i.e., duty or obligation, material goods and possessions, sexual desires and pleasures, reputation, etc.), whenever and however they are pursued, are merely temporary and transitory, and they are finally replaced by the goal of destroying the bondage of *samsara*.

Second, in order to overcome one's bondage to *samsara*, one must engage in practices, whether physical or mental or both, that will eliminate the causes and conditions of one's bondage to the cycle of birth, life, death, and rebirth.

Third, whatever the specific means for eliminating the causes and conditions of bondage may be (i.e., acquiring knowledge, or engaging in religious rituals, or performing moral actions, or practicing meditation or any combination of these), the results of the practices must include wisdom (instead of ignorance) about the meaning and purpose of life, generosity or non-attachment (instead of greed or craving) with respect to the various kinds of goods in life, love or compassion (instead of hatred) for those who share one's condition, the elimination of *kamma* (however it is conceived) and the actions that bind one to the cycle, and finally overcoming repeated deaths and rebirths and realizing ultimate liberation from *samsara*. The enduring result of all of these practices, at least for the majority of the orthodox *dassanas*, will be union with the ultimate source of reality and lasting bliss and happiness.

Fourth, and last, *moksa* must be both logically and practically possible or else there would be no meaning and purpose in life and no reason to do anything at all.

At the same time, however, there are at least two basic disagreements among the *dassanas* and their accounts of *moksa*: first, there are metaphysical differences about the ontological status of the elements involved in *samsara*, and second, there are practical differences about the kinds of practices that are conducive to liberation from *samsara*. Without going into the specific details of these differences, it should be clear from the preceding chapters that the Buddha disagrees with both the ontological accounts and practical features of the orthodox *dassanas*. The ontological differences have been covered in his accounts of impermanence, *anatta*, emptiness, and *paticca-samuppada*, and the practical differences have been clarified in his teachings on the Four Noble Truths, the Eightfold Path, and his focus on the importance of meditative practices. In addition to these teachings, however, his particular contribution to Indian philosophical and religious ideas about *moksa* is his unique conception of *Nibbana* – especially its metaphysical, epistemological, and ethical dimensions. It is to his rather complex conception of *Nibbana* that we now turn our attention.

The question of *Nibbana*

Even the most casual survey of the *Suttas* reveals that the Buddha's teachings on *Nibbana* are anything but simple. Not only are there multiple etymologies of the term itself, there are also numerous views and interpretations about everything, from whether the historical Buddha actually gave a complete and coherent account of it, to claims about his refusal to answer specific questions about it and his insistence that it is simply better, all things considered, not to be too concerned with details of its nature and final realization. There are at least three general understandings (i.e., Mainstream, Mahayana, and even Western) of what the Buddha said and what he meant by "*Nibbana*," as well as numerous specific interpretations of the same. There are also at least two distinct kinds of *Nibbana* that the Buddhist tradition recognizes, and two kinds of *Nibbana* that the Buddha himself is said to have experienced during his life and after his death.

In addition to these facts, there are complex philosophical questions and issues surrounding the idea of *Nibbana*. There are metaphysical questions related to the ontology of those who achieve it, just what they achieve when they achieve it, and exactly what the essence of *Nibbana* is. Epistemologically, there are questions about whether and how it can be known, and whether and how it can be meaningfully spoken of and described. There are also epistemic issues related to the Buddha's clear refusal to answer specific questions directly related to *Nibbana*, as well as his use of numerous synonyms to explain what *Nibbana* is. Third, there are ethical and moral issues related to the kinds of practices that are necessary to achieve release from *samsara* and realize *Nibbana*.

And just when you think things could not possibly get any more complicated, there are the historical developments in the Buddhist tradition's understanding of *Nibbana* as Buddhism moved from India to other places in the world, in which there was both a downplaying of the significance of it, for example, in the Pure Land tradition, and a subsequent re-emphasis on its immediacy, for example, in the Chan and Zen traditions. Finally, and perhaps most frustratingly, there are the Western misconceptions and misunderstandings of both the term and its meaning and the Buddha's teachings about it that form the contemporary context in which most Western people simply have mistaken notions about *Nibbana* and the Buddha's account of it.

As a result, the remainder of this chapter will be dedicated to clarifying each of these considerations and situations. We shall begin with an account of the etymology of the term, and then consider the original teachings attributed to the Buddha. Second, we will examine the cluster of philosophical questions and issues related to the earliest accounts of it. Third, we will consider the Mahayana interpretations of the term and the Buddha's teachings. Fourth, and last, we will try to explain both how and why the Western conceptions of *Nibbana* came to be, and how they should be replaced by a correct understanding of the ultimate aim of all Buddhist practices.

The etymology of "*Nibbana*"

Contemporary scholars such as Damien Keown[1] and Bhikkhu Bodhi[2] point out that the word "*Nibbana*" has an ambiguous and interesting etymology. According to Keown, "the word nirvana is formed from the negative suffix [sic] *nir* and a Sanskrit root which may be either *va*, meaning to blow, or *vr*, meaning to cover. Both connote images of extinguishing a flame, in the first case by blowing it out and in the second by smothering it or starving it of fuel."[3] He then adds, "Of these two etymologies, early sources generally prefer the latter, suggesting that they understood nirvana as a gradual process, like cutting off the fuel to a fire and letting the embers die down, rather than a sudden or dramatic event."[4] Bhikkhu Bodhi, on the other hand, points out that even if we explain the philology of a term that does not settle the question of its interpretation. In fact, he insists that exactly what is to be made of the various explanations of *Nibbana* given in the *Nikayas* has been a subject of debate since the early days of Buddhism.[5]

Bodhi begins his account of the philology of "*Nibbana*" by noting that it is well known that its root means the extinction of a fire or a lamp. He also points out that in popular works on Buddhism, "*Nibbana*" plain and simple is often taken to signify *Nibbana* as experienced in life, while "*parinibbana*" refers to *Nibbana* attained at death. According to Bodhi, this is a misinterpretation, and he maintains, following E. J. Thomas in his *History of Buddhist Thought*, that the prefix *pari-* converts a verb from the expression of a *state* to the expression of the *achievement of an action*, so that the corresponding noun "*Nibbana*"/"*nirvana*" refers to the state of release, and "*parinibbana*"/ "*parinirvana*" refers to the attaining of that state. He claims, however, "the distinction does not really work very well for the verb, as we find both '*parinibbayati*' and '*nibbayati*' used to designate the act of attaining release, but it appears to be fairly tenable in regard to the nouns."[6] Then he

---

[1] Keown (2003), p. 195.   [2] Bodhi (2000), p. 49.   [3] Keown (2003), p. 195.   [4] Ibid.
[5] Bodhi (2000), p. 50.   [6] Ibid., p. 49.

immediately adds, parenthetically, that we nevertheless sometimes find "*Nibbana*" used to denote an *event*. He concludes that what all of this seems to indicate is that the various words related to and used in relation to "*Nibbana*"/"*nirvana*" and "*parinibbana*"/"*parinirvana*" "designate *both* the attaining of release during life through the experience of full enlightenment, and the attaining of final release from conditioned existence through the breakup of the physical body of death."[7]

Bodhi continues his account of the philology of "*Nibbana*" by noting that the past participle forms, "*nibbuta*" and "*parinibbuta*" are from a different verbal root from the nouns "*Nibbana*" and "*parinibbana*." The former is from *nir* + *vr*, while the latter is from *nir* + *va*. According to Bodhi, "The noun appropriate to the participles is *nibbuti*, which occasionally occurs in the texts as a synonym for *Nibbana* but with a function that is more evocative (of tranquility, complete rest, utter peace) than systematic."[8] After pointing out that it seems that no prefixed noun "*parinibbuti*" is attested to in Pali, he concludes,

> At an early time the two verb forms were conflated, so that the participle *parinibbuta* became the standard adjective used to denote one who has undergone *parinibbana*. Like the verb, the participle is used in apposition to both the living Buddha or arahant and the deceased one. Possibly, however, *parinibbuta* is used in relation to the living arahant only in verse, while in prose its technical use is confined to one who has expired. In sutta usage, even when the noun *parinibbana* denotes the passing away of an arahant (particularly of the Buddha), it does not mean "Nibbana after death." It is, rather, the *event* of passing away undergone by one who has already attained Nibbana during life.[9]

All of this clearly confirms my initial claim about the ambiguity of the etymology of "*Nibbana*." On the one hand, we have a word whose various linguistic forms (i.e., noun, verb, adjective, participle) are plausibly open to a number of different but related interpretations (i.e., thing, action, state, quality, process) and philosophical understandings. On the other hand, we have a word whose evocative meanings (peace, rest, tranquillity, cessation, security, and release) are so conceptually rich and complexly related both to the process itself and those who are undergoing or have undergone the process, that it is practically impossible to specify in any clear and

---

[7] Ibid.   [8] Ibid., pp. 49–50.   [9] Ibid.

consistent way all of the conceptual distinctions among them. So where does that leave us?

Perhaps the best strategy is to begin with the recognition that any discussion of *Nibbana* is always and necessarily provisional in nature, that is, it is subject to the conditions and limitations of the context in which it is being considered. Such a strategy has two distinct but related advantages. First, it clearly recognizes that in interpreting the Buddha's teachings we must be mindful of and sensitive to the circumstances in which they were presented and the persons to whom they were directed. This means being aware of what the Buddhist tradition refers to as the Buddha's practice of *upaya* or skillful means – suiting his teachings to the capacity of his disciples and his audiences in order to bring them to enlightenment and their ultimate goal.

Second, it also recognizes the reality of both the historical circumstances and local situations in which his teachings were spread beyond India that contributed to the subsequent and still ongoing re-evaluation and reinterpretation of this particular term as well as the whole of his teachings by the Buddhist tradition. This second advantage is particularly important because it allows us to recognize both the historical development of the Buddhist tradition (that we will be considering in more detail in **Part III**) and an increasingly more profound understanding of his teachings. It also helps explain why there are so many different, often compatible and sometimes incompatible, teachings on *Nibbana*.

The early conception of *Nibbana*

When we turn our attention to the original teachings attributed to the historical Buddha on the subject of *Nibbana*, what we find initially is an account of the ultimate good or goal of his teaching and practice. For example, in the *Mahaparinibbana Sutta* of the *Digha Nikaya* (a collection of the Long Discourses of the Buddha for a popular audience) we learn that it is what the Buddha came to know, taught, and where he has gone.

> Morality, samadhi, wisdom, and final release,
> These glorious things Gotama came to know.
> The Dhamma he'd discerned he taught his monks:
> He whose vision ended woe to Nibbana's gone.[10]

---

[10] *Digha Nikaya*, p. 254.

In the *Mahagovinda Sutta* we are told that the Buddha alone taught the actual path of practice leading to *Nibbana*.

> The Lord has well explained to his disciples the path (of actual practice, as opposed to the mere teaching about the Eightfold Path) leading to Nibbana, and they coalesce, Nibbana and the path of practice, just as the waters of the Ganges and the Yamúna coalesce and flow together. And we can find no proclaimer of the path leading to Nibbana ... other than the Lord.[11]

The *Agganna Sutta*[12] distinguishes, at least nominally, *Nibbana* from *Parinibbana* and reports that the Buddha taught that anyone in any class who is restrained in body, speech, and thought, and who has developed the seven factors or requisites of enlightenment (i.e., mindfulness, investigation of bodily and mental phenomena, energy, delight, tranquillity, concentration, and equanimity), will attain "final *Nibbana*" (which unfortunately is left undefined) in this very life. This teaching clearly indicates a direct connection between bodily and mental discipline, meditation, and the realization of *Nibbana*. In fact, it explicitly claims that anyone, regardless of their station in life, who engages in the appropriate kinds of practices, can achieve what the Buddha achieved. But what exactly did he (and might they) achieve?

The *Brahmajala Sutta* helps clarify this question by pointing out that some non-Buddhist ascetics held five different and wrong views about the possibility of realizing final *Nibbana* in this life. The first identified sensual enjoyment as the supreme *Nibbana*. The other four identified it with each of the four *jhanas*. The Buddha, however, claims that he teaches

> liberation-without-clinging attained after seeing the six bases of contacts (i.e., the five senses and mind) as they really are, namely, their arising and passing away (i.e., interdependent arising), the gratification and danger in them, and the escape from them ... And being stilled, quenched and cooled even in this very life, I proclaim the supreme *Nibbana* that is free from clinging.[13]

In other words, the Buddha does not teach that *Nibbana* is to be identified with any of the fivefold sense pleasures or any of the deep meditative states. But what exactly does he think it is?

---

[11] Ibid., p. 302.   [12] Ibid., p. 415.   [13] Thera and Bodhi (1999), p. 247.

Maurice Walshe[14] reports that when it comes to what we know about *Nibbana*, a witty scholar once said that all we have to go on is our own misconception of it, because until we have realized or experienced it ourselves we cannot know it as it really is. He immediately adds that if we cannot say much about what it *is*, we can at least say something about what it is *not*.

On the one hand, some scholars (especially early Western scholars, as we shall see below), following the etymology related to the blowing out or extinguishing of a fire or a lamp think that *Nibbana* implies total extinction or complete annihilation. On this view, one not only destroys the defilements associated with the mind and its unwholesome operations, but also literally one is extinguished from any and all forms of existence. Other scholars, on the other hand, point to texts where the Buddha seems to indicate that *Nibbana* is either a state of bliss or happiness (i.e., a subjective psychological state) or the highest state or form of reality itself (i.e., an objective metaphysical being). Unfortunately, these competing and obviously inconsistent views of *Nibbana* do not help us get any clearer about what the Buddha actually thought about it.

In order to help with this situation, Walshe advises us to consider the words of the Venerable Nyanatiloka in his *Buddhist Dictionary*:

> One cannot too often and too emphatically stress the fact that not only for the actual realization of the goal of Nibbana, but also for a theoretical understanding of it, it is an indispensable preliminary condition to grasp fully the truth of Anatta, the egolessness and insubstantiality of all forms of existence. Without such an understanding, one will necessarily misconceive Nibbana – according to one's either materialistic or metaphysical leanings – either as annihilation of an ego, or as an eternal state of existence into which an Ego or Self enters or with which it merges.[15]

A careful reading of Nyanatiloka's words, however, confirms that *Nibbana* is neither annihilation nor a state that one enters into or merges with. The result is that we are again no clearer about what the Buddha really thinks *Nibbana* is than when we started. Another possibility for answering our question is simply to look at more *Suttas*.

---

[14] Walshe (1995), p. 27.   [15] Ibid., p. 28.

Realizing *Nibbana*

As we saw in **Chapter 6**, the Buddha claims,

> This Dhamma that I have attained is profound, hard to see and hard to
> understand, peaceful and sublime, unattainable by mere reasoning, subtle,
> to be experienced by the wise. But this generation delights in worldliness
> (i.e., sense pleasures and the thoughts of craving associated with them), takes
> delight in worldliness, rejoices in worldliness. It is hard for such a generation
> to see this truth, namely, specific conditionality, or interdependent arising.
> And it is hard to see this truth, namely, the stilling of all formations, the
> relinquishing of all acquisitions, the destruction of craving, dispassion, ces-
> sation, Nibbana.[16]

According to this text, the *Dhamma*, and by extension, everything it
involves, including *Nibbana*, is beyond "mere reasoning" and "to be experienced by the wise." *Nibbana* is not something that can be attained by thinking about it, it must be "experienced" – "by the wise" – and what must be
experienced by the wise is the state when ignorance and all forms of
craving, wanting, and desiring have been eliminated, uprooted, and
destroyed.

Immediately before this teaching, the Buddha informs his monastic
followers about his enlightenment and the fundamental differences
between himself and *Nibbana*. According to the Buddha, he who was "subject to birth, aging, sickness, death, sorrow, and defilement" was "seeking
the unborn, unaging, unailing, deathless, sorrowless, undefiled, supreme
security from bondage, Nibbana."[17] On the night of his enlightenment he
achieved his goal and attained this "undefiled supreme security from bondage, Nibbana." He also gained the knowledge and vision of this fact when
he realized, "My deliverance is unshakeable; this is my last birth; now there
is no renewal of being."

Taken together these texts seem to offer a remarkably clear account of, if
not *Nibbana* itself, at least the kind of person one must be to realize it and the
steps necessary to achieve it. Whatever *Nibbana* ultimately is, those who live
in ignorance, greed, lust, and hate definitely do not perceive it. In fact, the
Buddha clearly teaches that it may be seen *only* by those who have destroyed
their mental defilements, relinquished all attachment to material things,

---

[16] *Majjhima Nikaya*, p. 260.   [17] Ibid., pp. 259–260.

and engaged in the appropriate kinds of concentration and meditation required to produce the intellectual vision of it. He also claims that one must understand the truth of interdependent arising *before* one can see the truth of *Nibbana*. In other words, these texts seem to indicate that in order to see and realize *Nibbana*, one must renounce one's former, ordinary, and unenlightened way of life, accept the Four Noble Truths, and be on the Eightfold Path, presumably as a monk, though as we saw in the *Agganna Sutta* above, that is not absolutely necessary.

Later in the same collection of *Suttas*, the Buddha explains to Ananda what the meditative path or way to abandoning the five lower fetters is.

> Here, with seclusion from the acquisitions, with the abandoning of unwholesome states, with the complete tranquilization of bodily inertia, quite secluded from sensual pleasures, secluded from unwholesome states, a *bhikkhu* enters upon and abides in the first *jhana*, which is accompanied by applied and sustained thought, with rapture and pleasure born of seclusion.
>
> Whatever exists therein of the five aggregates, he sees those states as impermanent, as suffering, as disease, as a tumor, as a barb, as a calamity, as an affliction, as alien, as disintegrating, as void, as *anatta*. He turns his mind away from those states and directs it towards the deathless element thus: "This is the peaceful, this is the sublime, that the stilling of all formations, the relinquishing of all attachments, the destruction of craving, dispassion, cessation, *Nibbana*."[18]

He then completes his account of the meditative practices that lead to the realization of *Nibbana* when he explains the path to abandoning the five higher fetters or the path to becoming an *Arahant*.

> Bhikkhus, a bhikkhu who is an arahant with taints destroyed, who has lived the holy life, done what had to be done, laid down the burden, reached his own goal, destroyed the fetters of being, and is completely liberated through final knowledge, directly knows ... Nibbana as Nibbana.[19]

What this text claims is that anyone who has destroyed the taints or *asavas* has removed the fundamental intellectual and affective obstacles, impurities, and defilements that are causally responsible for continuing rebirth in *samsara*. According to the early Buddhist tradition, the three taints are sense desires or general craving for pleasure, the desire for continuing existence, and holding

---

[18] Ibid., pp. 539–540.   [19] Ibid., pp. 87–88.

wrong views, which is sometimes distinguished from a fourth taint, namely, ignorance or failing to properly understand the Buddha's specific teachings on the Four Noble Truths, *kamma*, interdependent arising, and the Three Jewels or Three Refuges (i.e., the Buddha, the *Dhamma*, and the *Samgha*).

The *Arahant*, or "worthy one," is the follower of the Buddha who has achieved the goal of realizing *Nibbana* through the elimination of the taints and the destruction of the cognitive and emotional defilements that lead to continuing rebirth in *samsara*. In other words, the *Arahant*, who is typically, though not necessarily a monk, is someone who by accepting the Four Noble Truths and living the holy life of the Eightfold Path has awakened to the truth about the meaning and purpose of life and the fundamental nature of reality. He or she (though there is some dispute in the early Buddhist tradition about whether the laity (rarely) and/or women (very rarely) can be *Arahants*) has achieved enlightenment and realized *Nibbana* just like the Buddha. The only difference between the two according to the Mainstream Buddhist tradition is that the Buddha achieved enlightenment through his own efforts or by himself, while the "worthy one" does it by following the teachings of the Buddha.

Such a person has, as a result of moral living, meditative practice, and embracing the Buddha's wisdom, done what had to be done to guarantee that at death he or she would be released from *samsara* and not be reborn. Not only have they eliminated the intellectual, emotional, and moral impediments to release from the cycle of birth, life, death, and rebirth, but they also have removed the restrictions or what is traditionally referred to as the "fetters" or what binds one to *samsara*.

Not surprisingly, the *Alagaddupama Sutta* presents the goal of becoming an *Arahant* as a gradual process that involves three preliminary steps or stages (each with its own beginning and ultimate realization states): being a stream-enterer, a once-returner, and a non-returner.

Stream-enterers are of two kinds: some enter with wisdom or reason as their dominant faculty and others enter with faith as their dominant faculty. This type of follower of the Buddha has some knowledge and understanding of the Four Noble Truths and Eightfold Path as well as some intellectual grasp of *Nibbana*. They also have eliminated three fetters: they understand the Buddha's teaching on *anatta*, they do not doubt the Buddha or his teachings, and they realize that merely formal ritual and rule observation is not enough to guarantee enlightenment. The early Buddhist tradition claims that the Buddha said that the stream-enterer will reach final *Nibbana* in a maximum of seven more births, which all occur either in the human world or in one of the heavenly realms.

The once-returner, who will return to this world only one more time and then realize *Nibbana*, has completely removed the first three fetters and is now focused on eliminating sensual desire and hatred.

Non-returners completely eliminate the first five fetters and are said to be reborn in one of the celestial realms called the Pure Abodes (the highest levels of the Form realm) from which they will realize final *Nibbana* without ever returning to this world.

Finally, the *Arahant* removes the remaining five fetters, and provisionally realizes *Nibbana* in this life and upon bodily death achieves final *Nibbana*.

Nibbana and other teachings

This account of the ascent through the stages leading to final *Nibbana* should remind the reader of the steps or stages of the Eightfold Path. As we saw in **Chapter 3**, the Eightfold Path as traditionally presented was divided into three groupings: *sila* or morality (appropriate speech, action, and livelihood), *samadhi* or meditation (appropriate effort, mindfulness, and concentration), and *panna* or wisdom or insight (appropriate view or thought). We also noted there that even though the actual *Sutta* order of presentation of the groupings is moral excellence, concentration, and wisdom, most scholars do not think that there is any real significance to the ordering of either the elements of the Eightfold Path or its groupings. The reason for this is the rather obvious fact that each element is continuously and iteratively cultivating and reinforcing the other elements throughout one's practice. As Peter Feldmeier points out,

> Perhaps, however, the path can also be understood as all three purifications mutually developing with and reinforcing each other. Mental restraint is virtually impossible without the mental cultivation found in concentration, or more important, in insight practice. Further, as one comes to greater insight into the nature of the clinging mind, one becomes even more morally virtuous, rejecting subtler forms of greed and attachments. This freedom of mind allows for even deeper levels of concentration. In short, all three practices tend to mutually cultivate and support each other.[20]

[20] Feldmeier (2006), p. 66.

Bhikkhu Bodhi expresses the same idea:

Morality restrains the defilements in their coarsest form, their outflow in unwholesome actions; concentration removes their more refined manifestations in distractive and restless thoughts; wisdom eradicates their subtle, latent tendencies by penetrating with direct insight.[21]

Both of these comments highlight the clearly interdependent relationships that exist among the steps of the Eightfold Path, and it is not difficult to see these steps and stages as another example of the Buddha's teaching on *paticca-samuppada*. What is particularly significant about all of this, however, is that the Buddha has proposed a specific and manageable ethical plan for realizing *Nibbana*. In fact, the Buddha appears to have offered a multi-tiered and multi-faceted plan for the realization of ultimate liberation from *samsara*.

As we have seen, the first three Noble Truths are basically concerned with metaphysical and epistemological claims related to the realization of *Nibbana*. The First Noble Truth is concerned with the way things are in our "selves" and the world and how they ought to be seen. The second Noble Truth focuses on the cause of the First Truth. The Third Noble Truth specifies that the cause can be eliminated. The Fourth Noble Truth then offers the practical moral advice necessary to remove both *tanha* and *dukkha* and achieve the ultimate goal, *Nibbana*.

According to the Buddhist tradition, the Fourth Noble Truth's path to *Nibbana* begins with an initial acceptance of the Buddha and his teachings as provisionally true. In other words, one must first hear and then commit oneself to the Buddha and what he teaches as the starting point of the path. In order to begin the path or enter the stream, one must at least provisionally believe in *kamma*, *samsara*, rebirth, and one's responsibility for the consequences of one's actions and intentions. One must also be committed to the appropriateness of the Buddha's view. In short, one must take the Buddha at his word and then follow his advice.

Second, one's thoughts and emotions must be directed to the "Middle Way" between the extremes of sensuous pleasure and excessive mortification.

---

[21] Bodhi, ed. (2000), in his introduction to *The Vision of Dhamma*, p. xxi.

Third, one must employ appropriate forms of speech. One must avoid lying and all forms of harmful speech and instead speak, like the Buddha himself, with compassion and kindness toward all beings.

Fourth, one must always act in the appropriate or morally correct way, i.e., by cultivating wisdom and compassion.

Fifth, one ought to make one's living by morally praiseworthy means that do not cause harm and suffering for others.

Sixth, one must be fully committed to the effort involved in pursuing the path. One must be consciously and mindfully aware, at all times and in all places, of the thoughts and responses one is having to the way things are going both in our "selves" and in the world around us.

Seventh, one must be continuously cultivating the motivation and mental awareness required to practice the path in the appropriate way at all times.

Finally, one must foster the various levels of mental calmness and collectedness that are the fruits of appropriate mental concentration. This is precisely the path that the stream-enterer, once-returner, and non-returner are in the midst of undertaking and what the *Arahant* has already completed.

Kinds of *Nibbana*

The discussion of the steps or stages to becoming an *Arahant* also raises the question of just how many kinds of *Nibbana* the Buddha and the Buddhist tradition recognize. One of the easiest ways to answer this question is to start with the Four Noble Truths.

The Buddha himself said, "Monks, it is because of not understanding and not penetrating the Four Noble Truths that you and I have roamed and wandered through this long course of samsara."[22]

It seems rather clear from this quote that the Buddha thought that the most basic cause of rebirth is ignorance, or failing to understand and penetrate the Truths about *dukkha*, its orign, its cessation, and the Path for reorienting one's practices and life in order to achieve enlightenment, release from *samsara* and the realization of *Nibbana*. The appeal to ignorance as a cause of birth, life, death, and rebirth, as well as a cause of *dukkha* should also immediately remind the reader of its foundational role in his teaching on interdependent arising quoted in **Chapter 6**:

---

[22] *Samyutta Nikaya*, p. 1852.

And what, monks, is interdependent arising? With ignorance as condition, volitional formations come to be; with volitional formations as condition, consciousness; with consciousness as condition, name and form; with name and form as condition, the six sense bases; with the six sense bases as condition, contact; with contact as condition, feeling; with feeling as condition, craving; with craving as condition, clinging; with clinging as condition, existence; with existence as condition, birth; with birth as condition, aging-and-death, sorrow, lamentation, pain, dejection, and despair come to be. Such is the origin of this whole mass of suffering. This, monks, is called interdependent arising.

But with the remainderless fading away and cessation of ignorance comes cessation of volitional formations; with the cessation of volitional formation, cessation of consciousness ... Such is the cessation of this whole mass of suffering.

This text clearly indicates that ignorance – not seeing or failing to see things as they really are – is the root cause of the problem of the unenlightened human condition. In order to correct this problem, the Buddha suggests that we follow him on the Path that he walked. In order to follow him, one must have faith in the Buddha and his teachings, take him at his word and then decide to follow his advice. In other words, one must make an effort or exert oneself to believe the teacher and try to understand what is "actual, unerring, not otherwise,"[23] namely, the Four Noble Truths. In short, one must become a stream-enterer.

Once one has entered the stream or begun to make one's way on the Path, one must be fully committed to taking the steps necessary to remove the fetters, eliminate the craving that is the cause of *dukkha*, and thereby realize the cessation of *dukkha*, which is commonly known as *Nibbana*. According to the Buddha, only by working constantly, tirelessly, and relentlessly in the pursuit of the wisdom that will ultimately overcome one's ignorance can one realize the actual, unerring, unchanging truth about the fundamental nature of reality, the meaning and purpose of life, and finally achieve *Nibbana*.

The proof or justification of all of this is that the historical Buddha claimed that he had fully realized all of this during his final round of existence in *samsara* and that on the night of his enlightenment he had achieved *Nibbana*.

[23] Ibid., p. 1851.

Nibbana-in-Life and Final *Nibbana*

The early Buddhist tradition accepted the Buddha's word on this and referred to this as one kind of *Nibbana* – *Nibbana*-in-life or *Nibbana* with substrate or remainder. The Mainstream tradition distinguished this kind of *Nibbana* from a second kind that was only realized with death – Final *Nibbana* or *Parinibbana* – *Nibbana* without substrate or remainder. This second kind of *Nibbana*, which cannot be achieved in this present state of existence, is realized only with the death of the body or the dissolution of the five aggregates. This kind of *Nibbana* is what the Buddha realized at the moment of his physical death and it is also exactly the same kind of *Nibbana* that an *Arahant* will realize with his or her own bodily death. The former kind of *Nibbana*, on the other hand, is what the Buddha realized on the night of his enlightenment and what he continued to abide in and live by for the remaining years of his life. This same kind of *Nibbana*-in-life is what the *Arahant* achieves while still alive. Having realized this state, both the Buddha and the *Arahant* are fully awake to the fundamental truths about the nature of reality and the meaning and purpose of life. They have freed themselves from the ten fetters, overcome all attachments, eliminated ignorance, craving, and *kamma*, and released themselves from the cycle of birth, life, death, and rebirth. One obvious question, however, is what happens to "them" then?

The early Buddhist tradition claims that the historical Buddha simply refused to answer this question. In fact, it claims that this is just one of a number of questions that the Buddha refused to answer. In the *Culamalunkya Sutta* the Buddha deals with what are traditionally referred to as the ten "undetermined" or "unexplained" or "undeclared" questions. It says,

> Then, while the venerable Malunkyaputta was alone in meditation, the following thought arose in his mind:
> "These speculative views have been left undeclared by the Blessed One, set aside and rejected by him, namely: 'the world is eternal' and 'the world is not eternal'; 'the world is finite' and 'the world is infinite'; 'the soul is the same as the body' and 'the soul is one thing and the body another'; and 'after death a Tathagata exists' and 'after death a Tathagata does not exist' and 'after death a Tathagata both exists and does not exist' and 'after death a Tathagata neither exists nor does not exist.' The Blessed One does not declare these to me, and I do not approve of and accept the fact that he does not declare these

to me, so I shall go to the Blessed One and ask him the meaning of this. If he declares to me (the solutions to the logical disjuncts)...then I will lead the holy life; if he does not declare these to me, then I will abandon the training and return to the low life. ...

"If anyone should say thus: 'I will not lead the holy life under the Blessed One until the Blessed One declares to me (the solutions to the logical disjuncts) ... that would still remain undeclared by the Tathagata and meanwhile that person would die' (just like the person wounded by the poisoned arrow who wanted to know many things about the person who had wounded him before he let the doctor treat him)...

"Malunkyaputta, (even) if (or whether) there is (a solution to the disjuncts), the holy life cannot be lived ... there is birth, there is aging, there is death, there are sorrow, lamentation, pain, grief, and despair, the destruction of which I prescribe here and now. ...

"Why have I left that undeclared? Because it is unbeneficial, it does not belong to the fundamentals of the holy life, it does not lead to disenchantment, to dispassion, to cessation, to peace, to direct knowledge, to enlightenment, to Nibbana. That is why I have left it undeclared.

"And what have I declared? 'This is suffering' – I have declared. 'This is the origin of suffering' – I have declared. 'This is the cessation of suffering' – I have declared. 'This is the way leading to the cessation of suffering' – I have declared.

"Why have I declared that? Because it is beneficial, it belongs to the fundamentals of the holy life, it leads to disenchantment, to dispassion, to cessation, to peace, to direct knowledge, to enlightenment, to Nibbana. That is why I have declared it.

"Therefore, Malunkyaputta, remember what I have left undeclared as undeclared, and remember what I have declared as declared."[24]

The Buddhist tradition has offered at least half a dozen interpretations of why the Buddha refused to answer these questions. The first and most obvious interpretation is that the Buddha did not think that the answers to these kinds of questions were relevant to his teachings. In other words, knowing the answers to them was not going to help one achieve the goal of his path, namely, *Nibbana*.

A second, related interpretation is that the answers are not connected in any way to the Buddha's purpose, which is to help his followers achieve release from *samsara*.

---

[24] *Majjhima Nikaya*, pp. 533–536.

A third interpretation is that the Buddha simply did not know the answers to these questions, and that is why he refused to answer them.

A fourth interpretation is that he did in fact know the answers to the questions, but being a good teacher, he realized that Malunkyaputta and followers like him could not understand them or could not handle the answers to them. In other words, the Buddha realized that some of his followers simply lacked either the intellectual abilities or moral dispositions (or both) necessary to understand the answers to these kinds of questions and to deal with them in their lives and practices.

A fifth interpretation is that the Buddha simply refused to answer any kind of speculative or metaphysical questions. On this interpretation his entire life must be seen as an effort to solve a specific practical question about how to eliminate *dukkha* and achieve *Nibbana*, rather than a search for answers to profound, and ultimately theoretical, metaphysical questions.

A sixth, related interpretation is that the Buddha did not answer these questions because by their very natures as questions of a certain kind they are ultimately unanswerable. In other words, he did not declare answers to them because they are not answerable.

There are surely other possible interpretations of this teaching (i.e., with respect to the kinds of assumptions they presuppose about their terms, and the logical and real possibilities with respect to their answers), but I think it should be abundantly clear that regardless of whatever interpretation or interpretations are correct, there can be little doubt, at least with respect to Malunkyaputta, that the Buddha probably thought he was or would be attached to these answers or views, and that such an attitude was not only an impediment to his progress on the Path, but also an indication of his own craving for things that would only lead to more suffering and ultimately rebirth in *samsara*.

I also think it should be clear that the answer to our original question about what happens to the Buddha or an *Arahant* when they achieve Final *Nibbana* or *Parinibbana* is that the Buddha never said and it really does not matter. Everyone who has achieved either *Nibbana*-in-life or Final *Nibbana* has finally managed through his or her own efforts (or with the help of the Buddha's teachings) to overcome the fundamental and habitual ignorance that characterizes the unenlightened life of someone caught in *samsara*. They have quenched the fires of greed and hatred and acquired a new, enlightened understanding and achieved an unattached response to the world and its situations. They are quite literally beyond the conceptual categories that apply to any and all conditioned becoming, and so the Buddha cannot say whether they exist, do not exist, both exist and do not exist, or neither exist nor not exist.

Philosophical questions about *Nibbana*

Perhaps at this point in the chapter we are now in a position to answer the cluster of philosophical questions and issues related to the earliest accounts of *Nibbana*. I also think that the answers to these kinds of questions serve as an indicator of the lines of subsequent developments in the Buddhist tradition's understandings and teachings about *Nibbana*.

Recall that earlier in this chapter I claimed that there are important metaphysical questions related to the ontology of those who achieve *Nibbana*, just what they achieve when they achieve it, and exactly what the essence of *Nibbana* is. At the same time, there are interesting epistemological questions about whether and how *Nibbana* can be known, and whether and how it can be meaningfully spoken of and described. There are also epistemic issues related to the Buddha's clear refusal to answer specific questions directly related to *Nibbana*, as well as his use of numerous synonyms to explain what *Nibbana* is. Finally, there are ethical and moral issues related to the kinds of practices that are necessary to achieve release from *samsara* and the realization of *Nibbana*. These are obviously not the only kinds of philosophical questions that one might ask about *Nibbana*, but I think the answers to them will take us a long way in better understanding the Buddha's teaching on the ultimate goal of all Buddhist practices.

If we consider these questions in reverse order, it should be clear that the short answer to the ethical or moral question about the kinds of practices that are necessary to achieve release from *samsara* and the realization of *Nibbana* is by becoming a stream-enterer, following the Eightfold Path, and eventually becoming an *Arahant*.

With respect to the epistemological questions, we have already considered a number of possible interpretations related to the Buddha's apparent refusal to answer specific questions directly related to *Nibbana*. The second question, however, about his use of numerous synonyms to explain what *Nibbana* is, is a different matter.

Somewhat paradoxically, the Mainstream tradition reports both that "Nibbana is directly visible" and that the Buddha offered more than three-dozen synonyms for it.

In the *Anguttara Nikaya*, for example, the Buddha replies to the Brahmin Janussoni's question about the way *Nibbana* is directly visible, immediate, inviting one to come and see, worthy of application, to be personally experienced by the wise, as follows:

> When, Brahmin, a person is impassioned with lust ... depraved through hatred ... bewildered through delusion, overwhelmed and infatuated by delusion, then he plans for his own harm, for the harm of others, for the harm of both; and he experiences in his mind suffering and grief. But when lust, hatred and delusion have been abandoned, he neither plans for his own harm, nor for the harm of others, nor for the harm of both; and he does not experience in his mind suffering and grief. In this way, Brahmin, *Nibbana* is directly visible, immediate, inviting one to come and see, worthy of application, to be personally experienced by the wise.[25]

In the *Asankhatasamyutta* or the *Connected Discourses on the Unconditioned*, the Buddha explains both the unconditioned and the path leading to it. The former he describes as the destruction of lust, hatred, and delusion, and the latter he says involves "mindfulness directed to the body," "serenity and insight," "concentration," "the four establishments of mindfulness," "the four right strivings, "the four bases for spiritual power," "the five spiritual powers," "the seven factors of enlightenment," and "the Eightfold Path."[26] He then describes the unconditioned as

> "the uninclined ... the taintless ... the truth ... the far shore ... the subtle ... the very difficult to see ... the unaging ... the stable ... the undisintegrating ... the unmanifest ... the unproliferated ... the peaceful ... the deathless ... the sublime ... the auspicious ... the secure ... the destruction of craving ... the wonderful ... the amazing ... the unailing ... the unailing state ... Nibbana ... the unafflicted ... dispassion ... purity ... freedom ... non-attachmnent ... the island ... the shelter ... the asylum ... the refuge ... the destination and the path leading to the destination.[27]

---

[25] Thera and Bodhi (1999), p. 57.   [26] *Samyutta Nikaya*, pp. 1372–1374.
[27] Ibid., pp. 1378–1379.

Perhaps the most famous account of *Nibbana* in strictly metaphysical terms occurs in the *Udana* of the *Khuddaka Nikaya* (a collection of miscellaneous, popular texts that form the fifth division of the *Nikayas*), when the Buddha teaches,

> There is, monks, that base where there is neither earth, nor water, nor heat, nor air; neither the base of the infinity of space, nor the base of the infinity of consciousness, nor the base of nothingness, nor the base of neither-perception; neither this world nor another world; neither sun nor moon. Here, monks, I say there is no coming, no going, no standing still; no passing away and no being reborn. It is not established, not moving, without support. Just this is the end of suffering.[28]

And shortly thereafter, he adds,

> There is, monks, an unborn, unbecome, unmade, unconditioned. If, monks, there were no unborn, unbecome, unmade, unconditioned, no escape would be discerned from what is born, become, made, conditioned. But because there is an unborn, unbecome, unmade, unconditioned, therefore an escape is discerned from what is born, become, made, conditioned.[29]

In fact, the early tradition claims that the Buddha talked about *Nibbana* in so many different ways, that one cannot help but wonder why.

I think it is possible to distinguish no less than four distinct Mainstream ways of describing or characterizing just what *Nibbana* is (i.e., as a psychological state in which one has eliminated the defilements, as a psychological state in which one has eliminated *dukkha*, as a metaphysical state of either the Buddha or an *Arahant* after death, or as a metaphysical state beyond the ordinary realm of conditioned experience and existence), without even mentioning the various *Abhidhamma* interpretations of it. There are also at least three distinct Mahayana ways of characterizing just what *Nibbana* is

---

[28] Bodhi (2005), pp. 365–366

[29] Ibid., p. 366. This particular text raises the all-important question of just how one is to read and interpret the Buddha's teachings. On its surface, the teaching, if it is intended to be an argument, is clearly fallacious, because it seems to deny the antecedent in order to infer the negation of the consequent. There are, however, other ways to read this teaching – not as an argument, but as a series of claims about what the Buddha actually experienced on the night of his enlightenment, and what follows from those discernments. In other words, having discerned the escape, it must be true that there is an unconditioned, because if there were no unconditioned, then no escape could have been discerned.

(i.e., the Madhyamaka interpretation with respect to emptiness, the Yogacara interpretation with respect to non-duality or non-subject-object thinking, and the general Mahayana focus on *Nibbana* and its relation to the moral and ethical practices of a *Bodhisattva* as opposed to the *Arahant*), that we shall examine shortly.

Before considering these diverse characterizations, I want to insist that I do not think that any one description or group of interpretations does a better job clarifying or revealing the nature of *Nibbana*. Yet that should not be surprising given the Buddha's use of *upaya* or skillful means, and the Mahayana distinction between conventional truths and ultimate truths discussed in the last chapter.

According to the latter, all of the synonyms, terms, and interpretations of *Nibbana* are simply so many conventional ways of trying to express what cannot be said in words but only directly experienced. The ultimate truth about *Nibbana* is, as the Buddha himself said, beyond "mere reasoning" and "to be experienced by the wise" – as something beyond the phenomena of ordinary conditioned experience. In other words, *Nibbana* is not something that can be attained by thinking about it conceptually, it must be directly experienced – "by the wise" – when ignorance and all forms of craving, wanting, and desiring have been eliminated, uprooted, and destroyed.

With respect to the former, it should be clear from his answers to Malunkyaputta as well as his sayings in many other *Suttas* that the Buddha recognized that his teachings needed to be suited to their audiences. Like all good teachers, he recognized that different followers are at different points along the path or stream leading to the goal of release from *samsara* and the realization of *Nibbana*. One does not talk to graduate students in the same way one talks to grade school students. As a result, it is only natural that the Buddha would employ as many different terms and ways as possible to explain what *Nibbana* is in order to help his followers understand his teachings and avoid things that would not only lead to more suffering but also to rebirth in *samsara*.

The remaining epistemological questions about whether and how *Nibbana* can be known, and whether and how it can be meaningfully spoken about and described are rather easy to answer. The answers to the former question are that it can be known – "by the wise" – and also presumably to some degree at least by those who have decided to follow the Buddha and his Path or those who have entered the stream of his teachings. The answers to the latter questions are all of the various ways and means that the Buddha used to describe and explain his teachings on *Nibbana*.

Even without appealing to the Mahayana distinction between conventional and ultimate truths, and also recognizing the Buddha's insistence that *Nibbana* must be experienced and cannot be achieved by "mere reasoning," I think it is possible to get some sense, however imperfect, unclear, and limited it might be, of what the Buddha teaches about it. If that were not true, there would simply be no point to studying his teachings or following his Path.

Finally, the important metaphysical questions related to the ontology of those who achieve *Nibbana*, just what they achieve when they achieve it, and exactly what the essence of *Nibbana* is, should be able to be answered by the reader based on the account of *Nibbana* presented in this chapter as well as the accounts of the other key terms that we have considered as elements in the details of the Buddha's *Dhamma*.

Other interpretations of *Nibbana*

I want to conclude this chapter by saying something about the historical developments in the Buddhist tradition's understanding of *Nibbana*, and how and why it was initially misunderstood and misinterpreted by scholars in the West. These points should help pave the way for **Part III** – "Development of the *Dhamma/Dharma*."

As previously indicated, there are at least three fundamentally different Mahayana interpretations of the Buddha's teaching on *Nibbana*. On the one hand, there is the Madhyamaka interpretation, according to which it is understood to be the ultimate reality. On this interpretation *Nibbana* is the only being that is completely unconditioned, and in that respect it is *sunyata* or empty; all other things are conditioned and arise interdependently through their various causes and conditions. In our unenlightened or unawakened state we simply fail to see these conditioned beings as they really are, i.e., empty or *sunyata*, and instead we habitually and falsely view them as having fixed essences or natures. To be enlightened, however, is to see *Nibbana* as being equivalent to one's true nature, to one's Buddha-nature or Buddha-essence – what something really is.

On the other hand, there is the Yogacara interpretation, according to which to realize *Nibbana* fully is to understand that there is no real metaphysical difference between it and *samsara*. On this interpretation, to be awakened or enlightened is to see that there is no real basis for subject-object thinking or consciousness. As a result of seeing things as they really are one comes to realize that there is not even the slightest difference between *Nibbana* and *samsara*. In fact, they are simply two different ways of experiencing reality – either as enlightened or as an unenlightened being.

A third Mahayana interpretation involves seeing or conceiving *Nibbana* in relation to the practices of the *Bodhisattva*. According to this interpretation, which consciously critiques the *Arahant* as being selfishly concerned with their own enlightenment and release from *samsara*, the *Bodhisattva* vows to postpone their own achievement or realization of *Nibbana* until all other beings have realized it whether through their own efforts or with the help of a Buddha or *Bodhisattva*.

This third Mahayana interpretation is responsible for the gradual diminishing of the importance of *Nibbana* itself, and a refocusing of attention on the moral and ethical components of the teachings of the historical Buddha. This "more practical" understanding of the Buddha's teaching tends to focus on the life and actions of the historical Buddha following his enlightenment rather than on the specific concepts or ideas of his teachings. Its central focus is on the need to cultivate wisdom and compassion in order for one to realize enlightenment and *Nibbana*. This tendency to downplay the significance of *Nibbana* and focus instead on the actions appropriate to one who has wisdom and compassion was later adopted by Pure Land Buddhists who thought that the ultimate goal of Buddhism was so far beyond the ordinary person's ability to realize it, that the best they could hope for is to be reborn in a Pure Land and then work out their ultimate release from *samsara*. We shall examine the teachings of Pure Land Buddhism in more detail in **Chapter 10**.

I should also point out at the same time, however, that the tendency to downplay the significance of *Nibbana* and focus instead on the possibility and opportunities of the Pure Land(s), was balanced by the Chan and Zen tendencies to focus one's practice on the development of the insight that *Nibbana* can be seen in this life as saturating every element of *samsara*. We shall have the opportunity to investigate these ideas in more detail when we study Huineng's Buddhism in **Chapter 9**.

Finally, let me say a word about the Western tendency to misconstrue the Buddha's teachings on *Nibbana*. On the one hand, there was a tendency among some early scholars to equate *Nibbana* with the Western Christian notion of heaven. Although it is possible to see how this might have been done, at this point it should be clear that the Buddha never imagined it as anything like heaven – at least anything like the orthodox Christian understanding of it. In fact, the early Buddhist tradition is emphatic in its insistence that the Buddha taught that no god or gods could help one achieve or realize *Nibbana*. On the other hand, there has been a tendency among some other Western scholars to insist that the Buddha taught that the realization of *Nibbana* entailed complete annihilation of the self. Again, I think it is easy to see how one might interpret his teachings that way, especially if one tends to focus on just a limited number of texts and sayings and one reads them in certain idiosyncratic ways. I think that the broad and detailed account of his complex teachings on *Nibbana* in this chapter will help the reader see why these Western interpretations are incorrect, and how they can be replaced by a more accurate understanding of the ultimate aim of all Buddhist practices. I also hope that the richness of his account of this topic and the Buddhist traditions' different understandings of it will serve as an example of the various ways in which the teachings of the Buddha were interpreted and extended by his followers. It is to these "developments" of the *Dhamma* that we direct our attention in **Part III**.

Things to think about

1. What is the Indian conception of *moksa* and how is it related to the meaning and purpose of life? In what ways did the Buddha accept and reject this notion of *moksa*?
2. What specific philosophical problems are created by the etymology of "*Nibbana?*"
3. Why do you think that *Nibbana* must be "experienced" in order to be understood?
4. Why do you think the Buddha refused to answer questions about *Nibbana*?
5. Do you think the Mahayana ideal of the *Bodhisattva* diminishes the importance of *Nibbana* as a goal of Buddhist practice? How and why did this happen?

Part III

Development of the *Dhamma/Dharma*

Part III of this book is concerned with the historical and geographical unfolding and philosophical development of Buddhism. **Chapter 9** is concerned with the history and development of the Chinese appropriation of Buddhism. It considers Buddhism's conceptual relationship to the teachings of Confucius and Daoism and focuses on the particular texts and ideas of Bodhidharma and Huineng. It concludes with a brief discussion of the teachings of the highly influential *Lotus Sutra*.

Chapter 10 continues to trace the development of Buddhism as it was transmitted from China into Japan. Unlike **Chapter 9,** which was concerned with the development of the *Dharma* from the point of view of its teachers, this chapter considers the logical development of the teachings themselves. It begins by focusing on the philosophical roots of the Indian sources of Pure Land ideas, and argues that one of the central questions of Japanese Buddhism is the relationship between texts and doctrines and discipline and practice. It concludes with a consideration of the logic of some of the key ideas and teachings of Pure Land Buddhism in China and Japan.

Chapter 11 focuses on the Tibetan appropriation of Buddhism. It begins with a consideration of the sources of Tibetan Buddhism and distinguishes it from pre-Buddhist beliefs. It then traces the development of Tibetan Buddhism from its official recognition by its "*Dharma*" kings to the establishment of its most important schools. The chapter ends with a consideration of the various Tibetan interpretations of meditative practice and enlightenment and provides the context for the ideas and teachings of the Dalai Lama.

The final chapter of the book, **Chapter 12**, explores the teachings of two influential contemporary Buddhists: the Dalai Lama and Thich Nhat Hanh.

In this chapter we consider the Dalai Lama's recent work with the Mind & Life Institute and his most recent book, *The Universe in a Single Atom*. Thich Nhat Hanh, on the other hand, is concerned with presenting and defending "engaged Buddhism," and this chapter considers his claims about this kind of practice. The chapter concludes with the recognition and an argument that Buddhist metaphysical and epistemological ideas and teachings are ultimately directed to, confirmed by, and realized in the enlightened practices of its followers.

9 Bodhidharma's and Huineng's Buddhisms

Key terms and teachings

Dao: Chinese term for the "way"/"path" and source of all being.

Diamond Sutra: English name of the Mahayana *Vajracchedika-prajnaparamita Sutra.* It is concerned with the perfection of wisdom and the teaching on emptiness.

Gradual Enlightenment: In Chinese Buddhism this is the view of the "Northern School" that enlightenment is realized only gradually after many years of practice and meditation.

Koan: Zen term (from Chinese *kung-an*) literally meaning "public case." It refers to a question or puzzle that is meant to help practitioners overcome dualistic thinking and realize insight into reality.

Lankavatara Sutra: Collection of Mahayana teachings, especially of Yogacara Buddhism, focusing on the role of the mind, various forms of consciousness, emptiness, and *tathagata-garbha* (womb of the Buddha). It was very influential in the Chan and Zen traditions.

Lotus Sutra: English name for the *Saddhammapunarika Sutra* which expounds the idea that there is really only one true vehicle or *Ekayana*, and that the Buddha, out of compassion, continues to be present in the world to help those in need of his assistance.

Paramitas: Sanskrit term for "perfections" or "virtuous qualities" possessed by the Mahayana ideal of practice, the *bodhisattva*. These include: generosity or giving – *dana*, morality – *sila*, patience or forbearance – *khanti/ksanti*, effort or zealous striving – *viriya/virya*, meditation or focused mind – *jhana/dhyana* or *samadhi*, and wisdom or insight – *prajna*.

Platform Sutra: Chinese *sutra* containing the biography and teachings of Huineng, the sixth patriarch of the Chan school of Buddhism.

Paccekabuddha/Pratyekabuddha: Pali and Sanskrit for a "solitary" Buddha who does not teach the *Dhamma* to other beings.

> **Sudden Enlightenment:** In Chinese Buddhism this is the view of the "Southern School" that enlightenment is realized instantaneously in a single moment of insight.
> **Two Entrances and Four Practices:** One of a small number of works thought to contain the authentic teachings of Bodhidharma. This text is also known as the *Outline of Practice*.
> **Wu-wei:** Chinese for "no action." It refers to non-coercive, spontaneous action in accord with one's true nature.
> **Yana:** Sanskrit term for "vehicle." It refers to the various spiritual paths one follows. It is most commonly found conjoined with other terms to designate particular paths, i.e., Hinayana (Lesser vehicle), Mahayana (Greater vehicle), and Ekayana (One vehicle).

Buddhism in China

Aside from questions about the history and development of Buddhism in India, one of the most fascinating and interesting episodes in the rich and complex history of the spread and development of the teachings of the Buddha is the story of its dissemination and assimilation in China. Although a complete account of this tale is well beyond the scope of this text, I think it is possible to capture the basic features of this momentous event or series of events by focusing our attention on the ideas and teachings of Bodhidharma and Huineng, and a single *sutra*, the *Lotus Sutra*, as being illustrative of the development and eventual adoption and adaptation of Buddhism in China. As a result, the purpose of this chapter is to consider both the transmission and ultimate transformation of Buddhism as it moved from India into China. We shall accomplish this task in three ways.

First, we shall begin by considering the historical circumstances of the initial spread of Buddhism from India to China. In this regard we will consider its conceptual relationships to both the teachings of Confucius and the teachings of Daoism. Second, we shall examine the early developments in the Chinese appropriation of Buddhism. In this context, we will examine the teachings and ideas of Bodhidharma and Huineng. Finally, we will focus our attention on the specific teachings of the highly influential *Lotus Sutra*, as an example of the Mahayana emphases on the *Bodhisattva* path, the perfection of wisdom, Buddha-nature, skillful means, the ongoing efficacy of the Buddha beyond his *Parinirvana*, and the important distinction between a single vehicle and multiple vehicles or *yanas* for conveying the Buddha's teachings.

Historical background

Even the shortest version of the story of the spread of Buddhism from India to China must begin with King Asoka of India (third century BCE), one of the greatest early political patrons of Buddhism. After renouncing his early military activities, the king not only became a lay follower of the *Dharma*, but he also sent ambassadors and missionaries to other kingdoms to spread the teachings of the Buddha, and his sons and successors established monasteries and universities throughout their kingdom.

In addition to this missionary activity and political support, Buddhism also made its way into Central Asia along the Silk Road as merchants and traders carried its teachings and their goods from India into Central Asia and ultimately into China. It is generally accepted that there were actually two different routes of dissemination into China, a northern land route and a southern sea route. The northern route initially carried the teachings of the Buddha north and west from India (third to first centuries BCE) toward what is now Pakistan and Afghanistan. A couple of centuries later (first century BCE to first century CE) the *Dharma* was carried by merchants, traders, and missionary monks who followed the Silk Road east through Central Asia into China, and later still, it was spread from China into Korea (fourth to fifth century CE), and from Korea to Japan (sixth century CE). Finally, it spread from India and China into Tibet in the seventh century CE.

Like its northern counterpart, the southern route included a series of temporally distinct waves of transmission. Initially, the southern route carried the Buddha's teachings south through India into Sri Lanka and east into Myanmar (third century BCE). Later, it was carried south east, by sea, through Indonesia into Cambodia, Vietnam, and southern China (first to second century CE). Finally, it was spread again from southern India and Sri Lanka into Myanmar in the fifth and sixth centuries CE.

According to these chronologies of the routes, it is easy to see why some scholars suggest that there were actually simultaneous northern and southern transmissions of Buddhism into China. Whatever the actual historical facts of that situation may have been, it seems clear that some versions of the teachings of the Buddha and elements of Buddhist culture had made their way into both northern and southern China as early as the first century CE. One rather obvious question is, what kind of Buddhist ideas, texts, and cultural artifacts made it into China?

Before answering this question we should first pause to recall that in addition to the complex network of Buddhist ideas, concepts, teachings, texts, and monastic practices, one of the other important cultural exports of Indian Buddhism was its artistic productions and religious rituals. It is easy to overlook the fact, especially in the rarefied air of the academic, intellectual, and philosophical study of Buddhism, that before everything else, Buddhism is a way of life practiced by particular followers (both lay and ordained), at a particular time, in a particular location, and for particular reasons. In other words, it is a particular response to the peculiar circumstances of one's life and a chosen means for dealing with the day-to-day issues, questions, problems, and situations that one faces in everyday life. I do not think this point can be stressed enough. In fact, I want to insist that in addition to the logical coherence and consistency of the ideas and beliefs of a way of life, the other most persuasive reason for someone to consider adopting a new and different way of life (assuming freedom of choice and no coercion) is the quality of life manifested in the particular practices of those who are already committed to following that way of living.

The historical evidence for this is, of course, the missionary efforts of all of the world's great religious and philosophical traditions, where in addition to the persuasiveness of their teachings, many have been convinced to adopt a new way of life based on the persuasive power of the lives of their practitioners. This is especially true among the masses and those who tend to be less well-educated than the social and political elite, who possess the power, if not always the intelligence or will, to effect broad social changes within their own communities. The practical consequences of this distinction are that new ways of thinking and acting are able to make inroads into a society in one of two different ways.

First, there is the top-down method of appealing to and persuading the leaders and rulers of a community who, in turn, influence and direct their followers and subjects. Second, there is the bottom-up method of appealing to the masses of a community who, in turn, influence and urge their leaders to adopt their way of doing things. Of course, nothing prevents anyone from pursuing both methods at the same time, and it is often the case that both are employed in order to persuade the entire community of the effectiveness of one's new way of life. Nevertheless, the actual, real world situation of a community, for example, the China into which Buddhism spread at the beginning of the Common Era, often involves a "negotiated" compromise or "middle way" between these two methods, where the "final" but ongoing result is a dependently arisen event in which the people and their leaders, and the community as a whole continuously forge their communal identity in their daily and ongoing interactions as a group.

I am so convinced of the pedagogical advantages of this model for understanding social change, as well as by its fittingness when applied to the history, spread, and development of Buddhism, that I want to use it to help explain the Chinese assimilation of the teachings of the Buddha.

One of the easiest ways to conceptualize the history and development of Buddhism in China is to think of it as a series of negotiated compromises, or as a series of attempts to find a "middle way" between two extreme or opposed positions. For example, I think it is possible to distinguish "high" and "low" forms of Buddhism (as we did above), "city" and "country" forms of Buddhism, and "strict" and "relaxed" ways of following the teachings of the Buddha. The first pair of opposites refers to the differences between the educated, scholarly elite and the ordained monastic followers of the Buddha and the masses of common, ordinary lay-practitioners. The second pair of extremes refers to the differences between the kinds of Buddhism found in major cities, especially, important centers of political power, and the outlying, rural versions of Buddhism. The third pair of contending positions refers (at least in theory, if not always in practice) to the differences between those who rigidly follow the precepts and disciplinary rules prescribed by the Buddha and his early followers (i.e., ordained monks and nuns) and those who take a more pragmatic approach to the rules for Buddhist practice (i.e., ordinary lay followers). The resultant form of Buddhism in any community possessing these distinct ways of following the *Dharma* will be a dynamic compromise or "middle way" between these competing extremes of theory and practice.

While obviously an oversimplification, this way of thinking about both Buddhism in China and Chinese Buddhism has the advantage of applying the Buddha's own method of finding a "middle way" between extreme positions, as well as clarifying a remarkably complex phenomenon. It also helps distinguish the various forms of Buddhism that were present in China. For my purposes I want to suggest the following additional "extremes" or contending positions that were reconciled in the Chinese assimilation of Buddhism: the *Arhat* model of enlightenment and the *Bodhisattva* model of enlightenment; the meditation model of practice and the action model of practice; the easy road to enlightenment and the difficult road to enlightenment; the sudden form of enlightenment and the gradual form of enlightenment; the textual study model of learning and insight and the direct experience model of learning and insight; the Buddha as present after his *Parinirvana* view and the Buddha as absent after his *Parinirvana* view; and finally, the single path to the goal of Buddhist practice and the multiple paths to the goal of Buddhist practice.

Before considering the Chinese Buddhist path between these extremes, I want to return for a moment to my previous comments with respect to the top-down and bottom-up models for how new ways of thinking and acting are able to make inroads into a society, and the related idea that the technical teachings behind Buddhist practices had already made significant advances in China by way of other cultural expressions of its beliefs and ideas, especially the art, religious rituals, and the extraordinary powers of its followers.

As previously noted, many scholars believe there were probably two separate lines of transmission of Buddhism from India into China. Although almost nothing is known with certainty about these first encounters, there can be little doubt that many Chinese people, both political leaders as well as common folks, were intrigued by Buddhism and the practices of its followers.

Despite its advanced system of social organization, its own rather accomplished history of philosophical and religious thinking, and perhaps because of its natural and cultivated tendency to focus on its own ethnocentric concerns, the Chinese were fascinated by something that was by their own cultural standards new and interesting. As William LaFleur[1] and others have pointed out, Buddhist art and other Indian cultural artifacts were unlike anything the Chinese had ever seen or made themselves. Although the Chinese had their own religious arts and rituals, they were fascinated by the religious practices of the Buddhists, the extraordinary powers and prowess of its followers, and the new and intriguing ideas it espoused with respect to the meaning and purpose of life, the fundamental

---

[1] LaFleur (1988), pp. 21–22.

nature of reality, morality, and what happens after death. In particular, the Chinese appear to have been attracted to the Buddhist ideas about *kamma*, *samsara*, rebirth, interdependent arising, and perhaps, most significantly, to the Buddha's idea that one could through one's own efforts cultivate both one's mind and one's character in order to become a sage (a traditional Chinese goal of life) and realize *Nibbana* (the Buddhist goal of life).

As far as the top-down and bottom-up models for how these new ways of thinking and acting were able to make inroads into Chinese society, it is not difficult to see how the different levels of China's hierarchically arranged society might respond in different ways to these new and exotic ideas and teachings. In fact, there are conflicting "official" stories about how the teachings of the Buddha were first brought to China.

Richard Robinson, Willard Johnson, and Thanissaro Bhikkhu[2] claim that Chinese Buddhists preserved a story that their beliefs and practices were brought to China at the instigation of Emperor Ming Ti (ruled from 58–75 CE) of the Later Han dynasty, whose curiosity about Buddhism had been piqued by a dream. They quickly add, however, that other historical records indicate that the teachings and ideas of the Buddha were more likely brought into Han China by Central Asian merchants, traders, and monks, who established monasteries within their own immigrant settlements in the major Chinese cities along the Silk Road.

Regardless of the actual methods of transmission, it should not be difficult to imagine that while these high level interactions were taking place at court and in the major cities of China, other more common and everyday interactions were happening throughout the cities and in the countryside between ordinary Chinese citizens and Buddhist merchants, traders, and monks. As a result, it is easy to see how the beliefs and practices of Buddhism could make inroads in China from the top down and from the bottom up.

In short, Buddhism appeared to offer the people of China something new and useful. Its ideas and practices offered the Chinese help and solutions to some of their most basic questions and problems in life, and it did so in ways which were simultaneously different from their traditional beliefs and practices and also in some important respects consistent with and complementary to their own religious and philosophical sensibilities. It is to the

---

[2] Robinson et al. (2005), p. 176.

particular workings out of these relationships between indigenous Confucian and Daoist ideas and the teachings of the Buddha that we now turn our attention.

Confucianism and Daoism

From the outset it is important to keep in mind that the assimilation of Buddhism in China did not happen overnight. Most scholars suggest a time frame of at least half a century or longer as the Chinese negotiated their understandings, interpretations, and ultimate acceptance of this "foreign" way of thinking and living. In fact, almost all scholars would agree that the golden age of Buddhism in China occurred during the Tang Dynasty (618–907), when despite a few severe setbacks, it enjoyed lavish royal patronage and its monasteries acquired significant political influence as well as large pieces of property and enormous wealth. Nevertheless, it is also important to keep in mind that Buddhism's acceptance and success in China was anything but guaranteed.

Among the numerous obstacles that it had to overcome were language problems, textual difficulties, ideological differences with indigenous Chinese philosophical and religious traditions, imposing geographical factors, and the social, economic, and political upheavals brought about by the gradual decline and subsequent collapse of the Han dynasty (206 BCE–220 CE). It is clearly well beyond the scope of this text to consider all of these elements in any detail, so we shall limit our attention on the linguistic, textual, and ideological obstacles.

The common thread that connects the linguistic, textual, and ideological obstacles to the reception of Buddhism in China is the simple fact that aside from little direct contact and limited direct experiences between Buddhists and non-Buddhists, there were major language barriers in both directions. In general, the Chinese knew little Sanskrit and the merchants, traders, and monks knew little Chinese. In this context, as is eminently clear to anyone who has ever traveled abroad and tried to get around with only limited knowledge of the local languages and customs, it is not difficult to imagine that there were serious misunderstandings and only limited comprehension. Moreover, given the technical nature of most religious and philosophical discourse as well as the numerous and often conflicting texts that purported to contain the authentic teachings of the Buddha, it is easy to imagine that the level of mutual understanding was rather low indeed. And all of this is further complicated by both the geographical size and regionalization of China in not only physical terms but also social and cultural terms as well, and the subsequent effects of all of this on the various and widely differing locations into which Buddhism first made its appearance there. In particular, the major differences between the northern and southern regional circumstances are not to be underestimated – especially given their subsequent historical differences in understanding and interpreting the texts and ideas of Buddhism.

Peter Harvey[3] and other scholars have claimed that one of the key events and causes (if not conditions) of the successful adoption, adaptation, and eventual assimilation and ascension of Buddhism to its place as the major religion of all classes in China, was the decline and fall of the Han dynasty. Harvey claims that the collapse of the Han dynasty led to "a crisis of values due to the apparent failure of Confucianism,"[4] and he suggests that the uncertainty caused by the political, social, economic, and cultural instability of this event provided a perfect opportunity for Buddhism to fill the vacuum created by this situation. He also notes that in some ways the circumstances of the decline and fall of the Han dynasty mirror or parallel the circumstances of the origins of Buddhism in India.

Recall that in **Chapter 1** we noted that Siddhattha Gotama, the man who would become the historical Buddha, was born into a society in the midst of great social and political changes. His was a time when the certainties of traditional ways of thinking and living were being challenged by the new and unsettling problems arising out of the breakdown of tribal federations and the development of powerful monarchies and vibrant urban centers. Siddhattha also lived in the midst of a transition from an agrarian, village-based economy to a city-based form of life with all of its attendant problems and possibilities.

The situation in China at the time of the collapse of the Han dynasty was remarkably similar. It was a time of great political, social, and economic change. It was also a time of great anxiety and uncertainty as the tried and trusted traditional ways of thinking and living were no longer functioning. The average Chinese citizen as well as their more sophisticated and educated leaders must have wondered how things could have gone so wrong.

---

[3] Harvey (1990), p. 149.   [4] Ibid.

They must have wondered how and why things that had lasted over four hundred years could no longer be counted on, and they also must have worried about how things would go in the future. Amidst all of these questions and uncertainties, they turned to the ideas and teachings of Buddhism as a new source of answers and values that could help them make sense of things and deal with the circumstances in which they found themselves. The collapse of the Han dynasty and the appearance of teachings about a "new" and fundamentally different way of life forced them to rethink their traditional values and their own obviously unsuccessful way of living. In short, the fresh ideas, teachings, and practices of Buddhism provided a perfect opportunity to re-examine and re-evaluate the practical value and now uncertain truth of the established beliefs and traditional practices of Daoism and Confucianism.

If we begin with the ideas of Confucius, it is not an exaggeration to suggest that in general the Han dynasty survived and flourished for as long as it did, at least in part, as a result of its anointing and championing of Confucius and his moral principles and values as state orthodoxy. In fact, the Confucians of the Han dynasty seem to have worshiped him as an "uncrowned king," and they engaged in ritual sacrifices to him because they believed that he was in an important moral sense the founder of a new dynasty.

Xinzhong Yao[5] reports that during the Han dynasty the scale and importance of the sacrifice grew from bestowing hereditary fiefs to his descendants, to state-sponsored repair of Confucius' home town temple, to his designation as a "Duke" and the issuing of a decree that sacrifice to him was to be linked with sacrifices to the Duke of Zhou, one of the greatest political figures of ancient China. Emperor Ming issued an order in 59 CE that sacrifices to Confucius were to be made at all educational institutions. In 492 Confucius was given the title "the Venerable Ni, the Accomplished Sage," in 630 the founder of the Tang dynasty decreed that all districts and counties must establish temples in honor of Confucius, and in 657 Confucius was given the title "the Perfect Sage, the Ancient Teacher."[6]

All of these facts confirm the social, political, educational, and cultural importance of Confucius, but they do not reveal anything about his philosophical significance. When we turn to his teachings, we discover that he

---

[5] Yao (2000), p. 204.   [6] Ibid.

stressed a number of profound and interrelated ideas including: the cultivation of filial piety and respect for one's parents, ancestors, and family; self-cultivation and the pursuit of social harmony; giving one's best effort in all situations and circumstances, especially in educational and political matters; learning to play one's role in society and being a reliable citizen or a respected community leader; and finally, cultivating moral excellence by respecting social and religious rituals and making one's way by being a student of the *Dao*. For those in power, especially, the teachings of the Buddha must have appeared to undermine these traditional Confucian and Chinese values.

First of all, the life of a celibate, mendicant monk is clearly opposed to the Chinese cultural ideal of getting married, starting a family, and producing male offspring. Such a life also does not appear to offer any tangible benefit to the community in terms of productive labor, and actually imposes a burden on those who do work in order to support those who do not. Moreover, it includes additional economic and military costs to the community, because monks were typically excused from military service and many people supported monasteries with gifts of land and other goods that would have normally been given to the state or at least been taxed by the state. Politically, monks and their monastic communities raised concerns about their loyalty and obedience to the rulers and the community as a whole because they were initially and usually viewed as autonomous groups who were not bound by any civil or lay authority.

In addition to these social, political, and economic concerns, there were serious ideological differences between Confucianism and some fundamental principles of Buddhism. First of all, Buddhist ideas about *kamma*, *samsara*, and rebirth were not only inconsistent with, and perhaps contrary to the teachings of Confucius, they also lacked sufficient evidence to be accepted. Confucians and Daoists alike were committed to the idea that one's fate in life was controlled at least to some extent by one's own choices and actions, but more importantly by *Tian* or the *Dao* or "the will of Heaven," and not by *karma*. Confucians also were critical of the Indian and Buddhist idea of rebirth, because it appeared to undermine their own practices of ancestor veneration. The same Confucians would have been suspicious and highly critical of worshiping or venerating the Buddha, who was clearly not an authentic Chinese ancestor.

Nevertheless, it would obviously be incorrect to maintain that everything in the ideas, teachings, and practices of Buddhism was completely incompatible with either Confucianism, or Daoism, or Chinese cultural sensibilities in general. The average Chinese person living during the first and second centuries of the Common Era needed to look no farther than the immanent decline and impending collapse of the Han dynasty to realize that something was gravely wrong with current events. Whatever the ultimate causes of that devastating situation may have been, the subsequent assimilation and ascension of Buddhism to its heights in the golden age of the Tang dynasty is more than sufficient historical evidence to show that clearly some things in Buddhism were minimally acceptable to both the Chinese elite and the masses of common folks.

According to the bottom-up model of assimilation, it seems quite clear that among the reasons why Buddhism was able to make itself acceptable to the masses of common folks, especially those who lived in rural areas, was that they were very impressed by the supposed magical powers of the Buddhist practitioners. This is not surprising, given their longstanding folk religious beliefs and practices. In addition to the special powers that the Buddhists displayed, Peter Harvey[7] claims that their teachings were also seen as being more popularly orientated, and hence more egalitarian than those of Confucianism. There also can be little doubt that one of the most persuasive reasons to common folks for adopting Buddhism is that it offered a message of hope and the possibility of release from circumstances and conditions that were fraught with pain, suffering, anxiety, and unhappiness – in a word – *dukkha*. It offered a series of rituals and practices that were relatively easy to perform, similar to their own ordinary folk religion and Daoist practices, and economically affordable, especially for those of limited means. Finally, it seemed to offer or at least promise powerful supernatural assistance with respect to the ultimate end of the lives of its followers in the form of *Bodhisattvas* who had not only vowed to help all beings but who could also transfer merit to help their devotees. For the average Chinese person living through the ravages of the collapse of the Han, these very practical things had to seem quite persuasive, especially given their current circumstances.

According to the top-down model of assimilation, on the other hand, one of the reasons why Buddhism was able to make itself acceptable to the educated elite and the political leaders of China was that once the linguistic

---

[7] Harvey (1990), p. 149.

problems were overcome, the collapse of the Han, the division of China into separate kingdoms, and the different transmission routes as well as different forms of Buddhism being transmitted along those routes, all provided an opportunity for Buddhists to adapt their teachings to the local Chinese cultures and conditions.

In order for the educated elite to understand the teachings of the Buddha it was not enough to hear them, they wanted texts to study, meditate upon and interpret. Among the first translations, which were begun around the middle of the second century of the Common Era in the capital of Loyang, were short practical texts and handbooks on meditation, mindfulness, and breathing techniques. Other early texts included the *Small Perfection of Wisdom Sutra* and a *Land of Bliss Sutra*. These texts were not technical philosophical treatises but how-to manuals meant to guide one into Buddhist meditative practices.

Donald Mitchell[8] points out that these texts were particularly popular because like Confucianism, and especially the Daoism of that time, they stressed inner cultivation and refining of one's spirit. In fact, despite Daoist disappointment with the Buddhist's inability to provide the elixirs and practices that would lead to the kind of immortality and union with the *Dao* that many Daoists sought, the first wave of textual translations used Daoist terms, concepts, and ideas in order to convey Buddhist ideas. While initially useful, it is easy to see how this practice would and did lead to much confusion about exactly what the Buddha taught and what were actually Daoist ideas and interpretations. And the problem was only magnified later when both Indian and Chinese monks brought more and different texts into China. In fact, the split into the northern and southern kingdoms after the collapse of the Han dynasty as well as the different transmission routes also played a major role in the development of the kinds of Buddhism in China.

In the north, where the social and political disruption caused by the collapse of the Han dynasty was worse than in areas south of the Yangzi river, the Chinese eventually lost all political control for almost three years to foreign rulers who decided to use Buddhism as a state religion. In these circumstances, Buddhist monks played the role of religious leaders and they often became political and military advisers as well. As a result, the primary

---

[8] Mitchell (2002), p. 180.

focus of Buddhism in the north tended to be on ritual and individual practice at the service of the state.

In the south, on the other hand, where many of the political and educated elite fled after the loss of the northern kingdoms, their focus tended to be on the textual and literary study of Buddhism. In these circumstances, Confucian and Daoist scholars worked to translate and understand the written teachings of the Buddha. In fact, during this time, Chinese scholars such as Tao-an (312–385) and others collected, catalogued, and produced critical editions of Buddhist texts. They also began to realize that there were many gaps and translation difficulties with the texts they had. Eventually, Chinese monks went to India to bring back more reliable texts, and others worked as translation teams to improve their understanding of the texts and their teachings.

In general, Buddhism appealed to the Confucian elite because it offered practical political advice, and some of its most basic ideas – mental cultivation, interdependent arising, social harmony, and sagehood – were not only consistent with Confucian teachings but also extensions of them.

In a certain sense, the same could be said about the Daoist response to Buddhism. First- and second-century Buddhism appealed to the Daoist elite because it offered ideas that were consistent with its own ideas about harmonizing oneself with the *Dao*, acting naturally and spontaneously, and pursuing longevity or immortality through alchemy, dietary practices, and meditative union with the *Dao*. In fact, many of the key terms and concepts of Daoism and Neo-Daoism that were popular at this time were used to translate many important Buddhist ideas. We have already noted the kinds of problems and difficulties this caused for the Chinese in their efforts to understand the teachings of the Buddha. However, it is important to keep in mind that these very same problems and difficulties also allowed the Chinese to creatively adopt and adapt Indian versions of Buddhism to their own peculiar situations and circumstances. It is to one of the most important and influential adoptions and adaptations that we now turn our attention.

Bodhidharma

The rather extended discursion on the historical background of Buddhism in China in the previous section has been necessary to set the stage for the appearance of Bodhidharma and his teachings on Buddhism as well as to help frame and explain the position and contributions of Huineng. The former is a perfect example of a typical Indian Buddhist monk and missionary who came to China to spread the teachings of the Buddha, while the latter is one of the more important and influential indigenous Chinese Buddhists. Although they represent just a single tradition within the spectrum of Buddhist teachings, as a pair they provide a perfect illustration of two essential features of the historical unfolding and development of Buddhism outside of India. On the one hand, they represent the historical origins of the *Dhamma* in India. On the other hand, they represent the ongoing process of adoption, adaptation, and assimilation of Buddhism as it was transmitted to places and communities beyond India. It is for these reasons, as well as their specific interpretations of the Buddha's teachings, that I selected Bodhidharma and Huineng as exemplars of one Chinese form of Buddhism.

According to traditional accounts, Bodhidharma was probably born some time around the middle of the fifth century of the Common Era, the third son of a South Indian king of the warrior caste. After becoming a Buddhist, he was instructed by Prajnatara, the supposed twenty-seventh patriarch of the Chan tradition, who sent him to China to teach and spread the *Dharma*.

Bodhidharma arrived via the sea in southern China some time around the end of the fifth or beginning of the sixth century. After getting situated in the port city of Nanhai (now Canton) and having presumably studied the Chinese language, eventually he was invited to meet with Emperor Wu of the Liang dynasty – one of the most generous and lavish political patrons of Buddhism in Chinese history. It is unclear exactly how many times Bodhidharma met with the emperor, but the tradition reports two significant interactions.

First, as is easy to imagine given the emperor's charitable and philanthropic activities on behalf of the Buddhist faith (i.e., building temples, translating texts, and supporting monks, nuns, and other lay followers), he asked Bodhidharma about the supposed merit of his religious works. Unexpectedly, Bodhidharma responded by denying that there was any merit in these actions. Somewhat surprised, the emperor then asked a second question about the truth and purpose of Buddhism. At this point, Bodhidharma replied with an even more puzzling and baffling response about the Buddhist teaching on emptiness. Since all things including merit and even the teachings themselves lack any fixed nature or essence, they can be spoken of conventionally, but ultimately they are beyond the categories of truth and falsity, and meaning and purpose.

According to Bodhidharma, Buddhism is not about anything the emperor thinks it is about. It is about a way of thinking and acting in the world that is beyond the ordinary, unenlightened ways the emperor and all other ignorant beings think and act. Realizing that the emperor was either unable or unwilling to understand him, and not wanting to jeopardize his mission and his life, Bodhidharma left the imperial court, headed north, crossed the Yangzi river and took up residence near the Shaolin temple on Mount Song.

At this point, the tradition reports that Bodhidharma proceeded to spend the next nine years engaged in a kind of meditative practice referred to as "wall-gazing." The most common understanding of this practice is that he simply sat facing the wall of a cave in order to quiet and focus his mind, minimize distractions, and overcome the mind's habitual defilements and obstructions to awareness, clarity, and enlightenment. Yet there is more to this practice than simply sitting and purifying one's mind, as we shall shortly see.

Obviously many Buddhist monks both from India and in China taught and practiced yogic meditation, but one of the more interesting historical and philosophical questions is why Bodhidharma rather than any other monk became so famous for his version of the *Dharma* – especially since the tradition that traces its lineage back to him did not begin to flourish until roughly two hundred years after his death.

One can imagine lots of possible answers to this question, ranging from truths about Bodhidharma himself and his personality, to features and qualities of his teaching and practices, and perhaps other external factors such as social, political, and even religious and philosophical circumstances that could have limited the extent of his influence. For example, although the tradition indicates that Bodhidharma had only a small number of students, it also reports that it was some time during his "wall-gazing" practices that Bodhidharma found his successor and *Dharma*-heir, Huike, who was so determined to study under him that after being ignored and rejected a number of times, cut off his arm and offered it to Bodhidharma in exchange for his teaching and as a way to demonstrate his total, unrelenting commitment to the *Dharma* and its practice. Even if this story is only partly true, it gives some rather clear indications about the kind of man Bodhidharma was and the kind of student he was looking for.

This same tradition not only records other obviously apocryphal stories about Bodhidharma (i.e., that out of frustration over his drowsiness and in order to avoid falling asleep while meditating, he pulled off his eye lids, and when he disposed of them tea plants grew on the spot; that his wall gazing and yoga practice was so intense and prolonged that eventually his legs withered away from excessive sitting – this is the origin of the Japanese Daruma doll; that on finding the monks of Shaolin temple unable to defend themselves against local thieves, he taught them physical exercises and the martial arts techniques of self-defense known as *kung fu*; and that he did not die until he was 150 years old) but it also attributes numerous texts to him. Most contemporary scholars,[9] however, are of the opinion that aside from a brief biography, two short letters, and a few recorded dialogues, only the *Two Entrances and Four Practices* (or the *Outline of Practice* as it is also known) contains Bodhidharma's authentic teaching. We shall try to answer our previous question about why Bodhidharma became so famous by examining this text.

The basic teaching of the *Two Entrances and Four Practices*[10] is that there are two entrances to the Buddhist path: principle/reason and practice; and there are four practices: patiently enduring suffering, recognizing and following causes and conditions, seeking nothing, and living in accord with or practicing the *Dharma*.

The former – entering by principle/reason – means seeing things as they really are and fully realizing that all beings share the same nature. The problem, according to Bodhidharma, is that we fail to do this precisely because the "adventitious dust" of false sensations and concepts either misleads us or we allow ourselves to be misled by it. In other words, cognitive delusions or defilements interfere with our ability to see things as they really are. Yet, Bodhidharma claims that we can correct this misapprehension by firmly abiding in unwavering wall-gazing, grasping the basic identity of all things, and not being concerned with or distracted by written texts.

The first part of Bodhidharma's solution to our ignorance of the true nature of things is to engage in the kinds of disciplined, meditative practice

---

[9] Broughton (1999) and Hershock (2005).   [10] Broughton (1999), pp. 9–12.

he was said to have done himself during his nine years of wall gazing. In this respect, one ought to be reminded immediately of the historical Buddha and the kind of practice he did in order to achieve enlightenment. The second part of his solution to our ignorance is presumably a reference to the fruit of such practice.

Peter Hershock helpfully suggests that, "the 'principle' of Bodhidharma's teaching consists of opening oneself to the patterns of relationship or interdependence obtaining among all things and seeing in these patterns their one true nature."[11] He also insists that this activity is not "seeking identities" or "common natures" or "essences" or even thinking distinctions among various "things," but instead it is "recognizing that they participate in a shared meaning, each uniquely contributing to a profoundly common movement."[12] In short, for Hershock, entering Bodhidharma's Buddhist path by way of "principle" is actively realizing partnership with all things, or as the historical Buddha taught following the night of his enlightenment, realizing interdependent arising and seeing things as they really are. The third part of Bodhidharma's solution to our delusion is related to a traditional verse attributed to him about what Chan Buddhism is:

> A special transmission outside the scriptures;
> Without depending on words or letters;
> Pointing directly to the human mind;
> Seeing into one's own true nature, and the attainment of Buddhahood.

This verse is traditionally understood to express the idea that in Chan practice, textual study is of limited and secondary importance. What is important in the Chan tradition is that insight and enlightenment – overcoming ignorance and seeing things as they really are here and now – arise by direct mind-to-mind transmission from teacher to student or master to pupil. In fact, the entire tradition traces its roots all the way back to Mahakasyapa, an immediate follower of the historical Buddha who, as the tradition records, became instantly enlightened as a consequence of grasping the Buddha's meaning when Sakyamuni held up a flower as part of one of his teachings.

The second entrance to the Buddhist path, entering by practice, is meant to give specific, practical advice about how one can live the Buddha's

---

[11] Hershock (2005), p. 85.   [12] Ibid.

teaching. According to Bodhidharma, the four practices (i.e., patiently enduring suffering, recognizing and following causes and conditions, seeking nothing, and living in accord with or practicing the *Dharma*) actually include all other practices. In fact, only the slightest reflection on them is necessary to confirm that they appear to be just a variation on the Buddha's Four Noble Truths.

Patiently enduring suffering or suffering injustice means realizing that things and circumstances are the results of *karma*. In other words, encountering adversity provides an opportunity to enter the Buddhist path by allowing one to see and understand why things are the way they are and how one has already contributed to the way things are and how they are going to be.

Adapting to the causes and conditions of circumstances extends our understanding of our selves as *anatta* – lacking a self – and our understanding of circumstances as being interdependently arisen from karmic causes and conditions. In short, the way things really are ultimately depends on the complex network of causes and conditions that "I" and my circumstances interdependently bring into existence.

All "things," as we saw in **Part II**, are the results of their causes and conditions, and when "things" change, as they always do, the processes and events continue. To see "things" as they really are, i.e., as ongoing processes, events, or happenings, and not reified, unchanging objects is to transcend the limitations of habitual ignorance, and to be unmoved by the joys and sorrows of attachment to impermanent "things." It is, as Bodhidharma says, to be "mysteriously in accordance with the path."[13]

"Seeking nothing" is what those who, like the Buddha himself, are fully awake do. Those who are fully awake realize that all "things" are empty of "selves," and hence not worthy of pursuit or desire or sufficient to satisfy craving for them. But those who are deluded and ignorant do not and cannot see this truth. Habitual ignorance and false dualistic thinking lead them to believe that there is a fundamental metaphysical difference, distinction, or gap between themselves and the "things" around them which they lack and from which they are separated. As a result, they are always looking for something, desiring something, and seeking something. In other words, not seeing things as they really are – interdependently arising and mutually

---

[13] Broughton (1999), p. 10.

and dynamically contributing to one another – they fail to comprehend the full extent of the problem caused by the process of wanting or craving.

To want or crave for some "thing" is to believe that both "you" and that "thing" have an essence or nature that can be possessed and enjoyed. But the truth, at least for the Buddha and Bodhidharma is that you can never be satisfied by what you lack and desire, because there really is no "thing" to be sought and no "you," in the sense of a fixed self or soul, to be satisfied. To realize this truth is, for Bodhidharma, to stop seeking, and to understand that "seeking nothing is joy."[14] It is to realize fully that seeking nothing truly is the practice of the path.

The fourth practice is the practice of according with and actually living the *Dharma*. It is, so to speak, the place where the tire of Buddhism meets the road of everyday life. It is the day-to-day making, living, and walking of the Buddhist path. To engage in this final practice is not only to see and understand but also to put into action and live the truths of emptiness, unattached interdependent arising, and *anatta*. In fact, Bodhidharma insists that the truly enlightened person who fully understands the Buddha's teaching on no-enduring-self will live the *Dharma* in the exact opposite way of habitually ignorant and deluded seekers and desirers – with a spirit of generosity and giving – asking nothing and attached to nothing. Moreover, such a person of insight benefits both themselves and others and lives the life of a *Bodhisattva* – an enlightenment being or Buddha-to-be – who cultivates the six *paramitas* or "moral virtues and perfections" (i.e., generosity, morality, patience, effort or zealous striving, meditation or focused mind, and wisdom or insight) that help all beings overcome the *dukkha* of *samsara* and realize the liberation of *Nirvana*.

Not surprisingly, at the very end of his account of the *Two Entrances and Four Practices* Bodhidharma offers both practical advice about how to eliminate false, ignorant, and deluded thoughts, and a profound and powerful insight into just what Buddhist practice really is. With respect to the former, he maintains that mindfully practicing the six perfections eliminates false, ignorant, and deluded thoughts. In other words, in sentiments reminiscent of the traditional Buddhist conception of the relationships among the various elements of the Eightfold Path as well as the Buddha's teaching on interdependent arising, correct practice leads to correct thoughts, and

---

[14] Ibid., p. 11.

correct thoughts lead to correct practice. However, he also immediately adds in a way that is perfectly consistent with the Confucian and Daoist notions of *wu-wei*, and in what was to become typical Chan and Zen *koan* practice, that this kind of practice is really practicing nothing at all.

For Bodhidharma and his Chan followers, Buddhist practice is not a matter of doing anything at all. It is not about rewards, benefits, goals, outcomes, and merit – as Emperor Wu mistakenly thought. On the contrary, it is about doing nothing, seeking nothing, craving nothing, and thinking nothing – *now*. In short, in profound simplicity, it is about realizing here and now, in this very moment, wherever you happen to be, that that is the place of awakening and enlightenment. The locus of enlightenment is within us in the one true nature that all beings mutually contribute to as we realize it in enlightened thoughts, words, and deeds. It was precisely this vision of the *Dharma* as well as his robe, his bowl, and a copy of the *Lankavatara Sutra* that Bodhidharma bequeathed to his *Dharma*-heir Huike and his subsequent followers in the Chan and Zen tradition.

Huineng

According to the traditional lineage of its patriarchs, Huineng (638–713) was the sixth patriarch of the Chan version of Chinese Buddhism, and its first native-born *Dharma*-heir. As we have just seen, the Chan Chinese lineage is said to have begun with the Indian monk Bodhidharma, who was the teacher of Huike (487–593), who was the teacher of Sengcan, who was the teacher of Daoxin (580–651), who was the teacher of Hongren (601–674), who chose Huineng as his successor and *Dharma*-heir. Bodhidharma himself is also claimed as the twenty-eighth patriarch of the Indian line of Chan patriarchs, which traces its roots all the way back to the Buddha's disciple, Mahakasyapa.

Although little is known with certainty about Huineng, and even more controversy surrounds the origins, content, and historical accuracy of the supposed record of his teachings, i.e., *The Platform Sutra of Huineng*, there is relatively little disagreement within the Chan tradition itself about his importance as the Chinese transmitter of the teaching and practice of "sudden enlightenment." In fact, I do not think it is incorrect to suggest that, assuming for the sake of argument there is just one authentic Chan teaching and lineage, Huineng and "his" teachings play a pivotal role in preserving and transmitting the one, true Chan interpretation and practice of Buddhism. In other words, he stands at the critical juncture when the Chan tradition was, at least from its own point of view, in danger of departing from its original and correct understanding of the Buddha's *Dharma*.

The basic facts of the traditional account of Huineng's reception of Bodhidharma's robe and bowl from the fifth patriarch Hongren are easy enough to relate. According to the tradition, in order to select his successor Hongren decided to test his pupils' understandings of his teaching by proposing a poetry contest in which each would write a verse displaying their level of insight and grasp of his teaching. The community of monks, who presumably knew something about each other's abilities decided as a group to let the chief monk and brightest student, Shenxiu (600–706) write the verse without any competition. After reportedly overcoming serious self-doubts about his ability as well as distressing concerns about possibly failing to display a profound enough grasp of his master's teaching, Shenxiu eventually wrote the following verse on the monastery wall:

> The body is the Bodhi tree;
> The mind is like a bright and clear mirror and stand.
> At all times we must diligently wipe and polish it,
> And must not let any dust collect.

After reading the verse Hongren publicly praised it and instructed the other monks to recite it. However, having determined who its author was, Hongren privately told Shenxiu that his verse unfortunately expressed less than perfect understanding of his teaching.

At around the same time, Huineng, a poor, uneducated, and illiterate southern woodcutter who had himself attained sudden enlightenment while overhearing some verses of the *Diamond Sutra*, and who had earlier arrived at the East Mountain monastery to study with Hongren, overhears the monks reciting Shenxiu's verse and immediately realizes that it does not express the deepest insight into the master's teachings or the Buddha's *Dharma*.

It is also important to note that Huineng's arrival and reception at the East Mountain monastery had been less than hospitable. The tradition reports that even though Hongren initially cast aspersions on his southern roots and lack of education, he was sufficiently impressed by Huineng's retort "although there are northern and southern men, north and south make no difference to their Buddha-nature or in enlightenment,"[15] that he decided to put him to work in the kitchen without ordaining him.

Having been informed about the poetry contest and realizing the limited understanding of the only entry submitted, Huineng decided to ask a fellow monk to write the following verse on the competition wall:

> Bodhi originally has no tree;
> The bright mirror also has no stand.
> Buddha-nature is forever clear and pure;
> Where is there any room for dust?

After reading the new verse Hongren publicly criticized it, but he also decided to dismiss the painter who had been preparing the competition wall to paint scenes from the *Lankavatara Sutra*. In short, he decided to keep the verse instead of the scenes from the *sutra* and inquired about its author. Eventually Hongren discovered that Huineng was the author of the verse and called him to his room, where because of the politics of the monastery and the real possibility of Shenxiu's jealousy, he privately bestowed upon Huineng the robe and bowl that originally belonged to Bodhidharma, thereby making him his *Dharma*-heir, and immediately sent him into hiding back in southern China.

The subsequent history following this rather messy affair is that Shenxiu eventually proclaimed himself the sixth patriarch and he became the leader of what came to be known as the "Northern School" or gradual enlightenment school of Chan Buddhism. At the same time, Huineng was also thought to be the sixth patriarch of what came to be called the "Southern School" or sudden enlightenment school of Chan Buddhism. Ultimately, the dispute between the competing schools was settled at a council in 796 when the emperor chose in favor of the Southern School and as a result Huineng was finally recognized as the "true" sixth patriarch of the Chan tradition.

As for Huineng himself, he was eventually ordained and attracted many students who also became important figures in the Chinese lineage of the Chan tradition. In fact, his importance and contribution to establishing the authentic and enduring line of the Buddha's *Dhamma* in China is confirmed not only by the reputations of his former students but also by the traditional story that when he died, Bodhidharma's robe and bowl were sealed into his tomb. The latter account is traditionally interpreted as confirming the

---

[15] *The Sutra of Huineng*, p. 68.

ultimate authority and continuing validity of the Chinese lineage. With respect to the former, we need look no farther than Shenhui (670–762), one of the most influential followers of Huineng, who in addition to being a former student of Shenxiu, was not only credited with starting the Northern–Southern Schools controversy, but also was responsible for helping persuade the emperor to decide the matter in Huineng's favor.

What is particularly fascinating and, more importantly, relevant about these events is that they give some clear indications about the kinds of issues involved in the Chinese adoption and adaptation of Buddhism. The story of Huineng, the content of his teachings, and the ultimate victory of the Southern School of Chan Buddhism provide a window on the social, political, and philosophical terms of the debate as Buddhism was being assimilated into China. They also provide a perfect illustration of the background and context against and in which Chinese versions of Buddhism were worked out. In fact, I want to suggest a Buddhist-inspired way of reading this moment from the history of Chan Buddhism that will allow us both to see it on its own terms and also help us to appreciate the broader issues involved in the transmission, evolution, and general development of Buddhism in China.

Chinese Buddhism

I think it is relatively easy to see that from the point of view of philosophical matters, some of the central issues involved in this snapshot from the Chan story of Chinese Buddhism include: the nature and origin of enlightenment, the nature and qualities of the mind, the nature and significance of meditation, the relationships among emptiness, mind, consciousness, and Buddha-nature, the role of Buddhist practice and its connection to the goal of Buddhism, the nature of the *Dharma* and its authentic transmission, the student–teacher relationship, the nature and role of authority, and of course, the idea of *upaya* or skillful means.

Two features of this list of phenomena should stand out. First, there is little or no mention of many of the ethical and moral matters outlined in the Four Noble Truths or the Eightfold Path. Second, the identified phenomena are in fact principally and primarily concerned with metaphysical and epistemological matters. These features confirm two truths about the Chinese assimilation of Buddhism. First, they highlight the reality that at least one form of Chinese Buddhism was clearly inclined to interpret the Buddha's teachings as being primarily concerned with metaphysical and epistemic matters. Second, these same facts reinforce and help support the central thesis of this book that the single most important or most basic insight of the historical Buddha was the claim, so plainly affirmed by the Chinese Chan tradition, that who we are and what we think exists is a function of our mind and its cognitive powers and activities. Peter Hershock confirms this when he asserts with respect to the *Diamond Sutra* and its role in Huineng's enlightenment that, "what we take things or people to be tells us more about the quality and horizons of our own awareness than about anything else."[16] In short, the Buddha and the Chan tradition both think it is our mind and our uses of it that determine how we see and understand our self, the world, and other things.

In addition to these basic elements of the snapshot, I also want to suggest that when these metaphysical and epistemological matters are joined to a consideration of the social and political circumstances, as well as a consideration of the various authoritative texts that have been cited in passing, we get a broader and more richly detailed picture of the Chinese assimilation of Buddhism.

As for the social circumstances involved in the Chinese Chan reception and interpretation of Buddhism, it should be clear from our earlier discussions of the top-down and bottom-up models that there were at least two fundamentally distinct lines of social adaptation: the former, top-down model, involved the ruling class and the educated elite strata of society, and the latter, bottom-up model, involved ordinary, common folks. The Chan stories of Bodhidharma and Huineng clearly involve features and characteristics from both levels.

From the point of view of politics and institutions, it should be clear, especially from the ultimate success of Huineng and the initial failure of Bodhidharma, that the fate of philosophical views sometimes depends on and is often determined by forces and factors well beyond the mere clarity, coherence, and plausibility of the teachings themselves. This should not, however, be surprising given the Buddha's general teaching on interdependent arising, and the specific interpretations of it by both Bodhidharma and Huineng. According to the latter, as we have seen,

---

[16] Hershock (2005), p. 96.

literally every "thing" is the result of interdependent arising and the complementary causal participation of all "things" to the production of ongoing events and processes.

Finally, as far as the texts themselves are concerned, the *Lankavatara Sutra*, the *Diamond Sutra*, the *Two Entrances and Four Practices*, and *The Platform Sutra of Huineng* all helped fix the central concerns and focus of the Chinese Chan tradition. Each in its own way addresses the issues raised at the beginning of this section.

For example, the *Lankavatara Sutra* which has traditionally been associated with Bodhidharma, a supposed master of the text, and was mentioned in the story of Huineng's verse, was an influential work within the Yogacara tradition in India. Aside from these facts, the text itself is important for a number of reasons. First, the text, like many Chinese translations of Indian texts, appears to have changed over time because there are various versions of it. Second, its unsystematic treatment of different topics also raises questions about the ultimate meaning and interpretation of Buddhist texts. Its central teachings involve issues about how the Buddha is present in and available to all beings, emptiness and the way to realize it, consciousness and its role in and relationship to experience, *karma*, rebirth, interdependent arising, and awakening or enlightenment. In fact, part of its solution to questions about how the various *Sutras* are to be read and understood is to emphasize the idea of *upaya* or skillful means. This idea was used to explain the apparent inconsistencies in the Buddha's teachings and the Buddhist *Sutras* by drawing an analogy with a doctor and various sick patients. According to the analogy, the Buddha, as a doctor trying to bring the mind from ignorance to enlightenment, had to offer different forms of medicine for the different medical conditions of his patients. In other words, because different people are in different stages of ignorance and suffering from *dukkha*, the Buddha offered different kinds of help for their various conditions. His teachings and the *Sutras* are just so many different forms of mental medication.

Another way to think about the idea of *upaya*, especially in the context of the Chinese Chan appropriation of Buddhism, is to realize that because the Buddha's *Dharma* can really only be experienced, it is possible to talk or write about it as an experience in many different ways. Understood in this way, the various *Sutras* are simply useful guides to the many different avenues for arriving at the same destination.

The *Diamond Sutra*, like the *Heart Sutra*, is one of the *Perfection of Wisdom* texts in Mahayana Buddhism. In addition to being known as the text that initiated Huineng's enlightenment or awakening, this *sutra* is concerned with the Buddhist notion of emptiness and the relation of all beings to mind. Like the *Lankavatara Sutra*, the *Diamond Sutra* is also a difficult and puzzling text to understand. In fact, some scholars have suggested that it is not meant to be read and studied like other texts, but that it was actually designed for meditation purposes – both to guide one on the path to enlightenment and to reveal the truth of the way things really are (i.e., their emptiness and dependence on mind).

We have already considered the *Two Entrances* and some important elements of *The Platform Sutra*. What is particularly fascinating and puzzling about the latter is that it is considered a *sutra*, but it does not contain any direct teaching or sermon of the historical Buddha. In addition to the same questions and problems caused by the various versions of it, the text also begins with an anomalous autobiography of Huineng. Among its various teachings are its concerns with the relationship between Buddhist practice and enlightenment, the relationship between the mind, ignorance, and seeing things the way they really are, and the question of gradual versus sudden enlightenment. Some scholars have suggested that its lack of a direct sermon by the historical Buddha is an indication and final confirmation of the authenticity of Chinese Buddhism.

The *Lotus Sutra*

At this point, it should not be surprising that the same kinds of issues, ideas, topics, concerns, and their various relationships can be seen in the Chinese appropriation of many other Buddhist texts, including the highly influential *Lotus Sutra*. As a result, I want to conclude this chapter by briefly sketching the transition from Indian forms of Buddhism in China to the development of other indigenous Chinese forms of Buddhism and I want to use the *Lotus Sutra* and its reception as a final example of the sinicizing of Buddhism.

It is customary[17] in presenting the history and development of Buddhism in China to begin by noting that at its outset, it is possible to identify at least

---

[17] See for example, Mitchell (2002), pp. 185–190.

half a dozen Indian schools of Buddhism in China. The common feature among these various schools is that they were simply Indian forms of Buddhism geographically and ideologically transplanted into China. Among these schools were: the Sarvastivada-inspired Kosa school, the Sautrantika-inspired Satyasiddhi school, the Lu Vinaya school, the Tantric Zhenyen school, the Madhyamaka Sanlun school, and the Yogacara Fazang school. The indigenous or homegrown forms of Chinese Buddhism, on the other hand, are indicative of a uniquely Chinese experience of Buddhism. Its most famous schools were: the T'ient'ai school, whose central text was the *Lotus Sutra*, the Huayen school, whose central text was the *Avatamsaka Sutra*, the Chan school that we have been considering throughout this chapter, and the Jingtu or Pure Land school.

If, for the sake of space constraints, but also because of its influence, we concentrate on the *Lotus Sutra* and its reception in China alone we discover another text that is concerned with the various issues raised above. The *Lotus Sutra*, which is among the earliest Mahayana scriptures, is arguably the most important and influential Buddhist text throughout Asia. However, despite its range of influence, its teachings are anything but obvious. The text itself cautions us that the wisdom of the Buddha is profound and difficult to understand. In fact the teachings are so difficult and obscure that George Tanabe[18] has described the *Lotus Sutra* as a text "about a discourse that is never delivered" and a "preface without a book." According to Burton Watson, the reason for this is that "Mahayana Buddhism" – recall Bodhidharma's verse on Chan Buddhism – "has always insisted that its highest truth can never in the end be expressed in words, since words immediately create the kind of distinctions that violate the unity of Emptiness."[19]

Nevertheless, even if the ultimate and complete truth is beyond expression, the central teachings of the *Lotus Sutra* are concerned with questions about the various paths and goals of Buddhist teachings and practices, the ontological status and accessibility of the Buddha, skillful means, the character development of *bodhisattvas*, and the importance and value of religious devotion and religious ritual practices. According to the T'ien-t'ai school of Buddhism (and later the Tendai school in Japan), the *Lotus Sutra* represents

---

[18] Tanabe (1989), p. 2.   [19] Watson (1993), p. xx.

the final and highest teaching of the historical Buddha precisely because it recognizes that the teaching itself is inexpressible.

Given this background, it should not be surprising that the *Lotus Sutra* teaches that although the Buddha initially taught three paths to liberation (i.e., the *Arhat* path, the *Pratyekabuddha* path, and the *Bodhisattva* path), there is actually only one path and one vehicle to the single goal of Buddhahood. The *Lotus Sutra* also teaches that the other paths were merely instances of *upaya*, and that the Buddha is really present and available to help all followers of the one true vehicle or *Ekayana*. According to this teaching, the ultimate goal of Buddhism is not what the Buddha's earliest followers understood it to be, namely, *Nibbana*, but instead, it is the realization of one's Buddha-nature or Buddhahood, which is beyond words and concepts and can only be directly experienced in acts of devotion.

The *Lotus Sutra* also rather provocatively predicts an age of decline and end to the *Dharma* in history. This prediction and the subsequent development of new and different forms and teachings of Buddhism is meant to explain and confirm the Buddha's own recognition of the limitations of the various vehicles and hence his use of skillful means to teach the *Dharma*. In short, it helps one make sense of the various competing and sometimes inconsistent teachings, practices, and Buddhist schools in the world. In this regard, at least, the history and development of Buddhism in China is a microcosm of its subsequent spread to and assimilation in other parts of Asia and the rest of the world.

At this point, I do not think it is incorrect to suggest that the complicated dynamics of philosophical issues, social, political, and institutional forces and factors, in conjunction with hermeneutical questions and interpretations related to authoritative texts and their teachers, all mutually contributed to the complex phenomenon called "Chinese Buddhism." In short, all of these factors causally affected and influenced the various forms that Buddhism was to take as it was incorporated and assimilated into the Chinese philosophical and religious worldview. The story of the Chinese Chan tradition from Bodhidharma to Huineng that we have outlined in this chapter is just one case in point. The same kinds of issues were also involved in the Japanese reception and assimilation of Buddhism as it made its way from China to Korea and finally into Japan. It is to a consideration of these matters, with special emphasis on the development of Pure Land Buddhism, that we turn our attention in the next chapter.

Things to think about

1. How did Buddhist ideas conflict with and complement traditional Chinese ideas?
2. What effect did the kinds of texts first introduced into China have on the development of Chinese Buddhism?
3. According to Bodhidharma, what must one do to be a Buddhist? Do you accept his account? Why or why not?
4. What is at stake in the "sudden" vs. "gradual" enlightenment dispute? Which position seems correct to you and why?
5. What are the similarities and differences between Bodhidharma's and Huineng's versions of Buddhism?

10 Pure Land Buddhism

"Local" Buddhism

One especially fruitful way of considering the history and development of Buddhism in general and Pure Land Buddhism in particular is to think of both as a series of ongoing and interrelated attempts to respond to the specific concerns and particular problems of the people and cultures they came in contact with. Since people and their concerns and problems as well as their cultures vary from place to place and across time, it should not be surprising that local forms of Buddhism would be different from one another. At the same time, however, it should be clear that regardless of time or location, all humans are faced with the same kinds of universal circumstances and situations. All of us are born, live, and eventually we die. All of us, to greater or lesser degrees, have concerns, fears, and worries about practical needs involving food, clothing, and shelter. All of us engage in thoughts, words, and deeds whose consequences affect not only ourselves but also those around us. And sooner or later all of us wonder what is going to happen when we die. This commonality of experiences across time and locations helps explain, in part, why the various forms of Buddhism noted above also have common features or elements despite their particular differences.

The reality of this situation is confirmed by the study of Buddhism as it made its way from India into China, and from China into the rest of Asia and the world beyond. In fact, at this point, we have had the opportunity to consider the continuity and changes in Buddhism from its origins in the teachings of the historical Buddha, through the development of its traditions and canon, to its assimilation in a foreign culture in China. One of the purposes of this chapter, therefore, is to continue to trace the development and growth of Buddhism as it was transmitted from China into Japan. Given the considerations already raised above, we should expect to encounter at least two things. First, we should expect to find new forms of Buddhism in response to new local situations and circumstances. I plan to show how this is true of the different forms of Pure Land Buddhism in both China and Japan. Second, we also should expect to see some of the same enduring features of Buddhism as well. I think this will become more obvious when we consider particular Chinese and Japanese responses to questions about the Buddha's method of teaching, the nature of enlightenment and *Nirvana*, the importance and role of meditation, and the Buddha's compassion and causal powers.

Two approaches to the development of the *Dharma*

Although the actual spread and development of Buddhism in China was far more complex and complicated than the simplified account presented in the previous chapter would indicate, one advantage of concentrating on the early evolution of the Chan lineage and the teachings of just two of its most important and influential patriarchs or *Dharma*-heirs, Bodhidharma and Huineng, is that it allowed us to consider some of the historical, social, and cultural circumstances surrounding the ongoing development of the *Dharma* as it made its way eastward from India into China. A second advantage of this approach is that it allowed us to consider both the underlying continuity in the teachings as well as the doctrinal development initiated by teachers who could trace their authority and *Dharma*-ancestry all the way back to the historical Buddha. In this sense, I want to suggest that **Chapter 9** was an account of the development of the *Dharma* from the point of view of its teachers and heirs. Precisely because Bodhidharma and Huineng were identified as *Dharma*-heirs of the historical Buddha, they were recognized as legitimate teachers and interpreters of Sakyamuni's thoughts and ideas. As a result, the authority of their pedagogical pedigree validated the content of their teachings.

A second, alternative approach to the development of the Buddha's *Dharma* is to consider the logical development of the teachings themselves, independent of the authority of their teachers. According to this approach, one can consider either the internal consistency of the teachings in whole or in part, or the external extension of the teachings to new and different situations and circumstances not previously covered by the particular teachings in question.

For example, I think it should be sufficiently clear from our discussion of the Chinese Chan tradition that despite its teachings' decidedly intellectual and metaphysical leanings, it clearly advocated a pragmatic and practical approach to questions about the method and means to enlightenment, especially in the monastic setting. Understood in this way, at least, it is not difficult to see the teachings of either Bodhidharma or Huineng as reaffirming the historical Buddha's insistence on the importance of putting his teachings into practice in daily life rather than being concerned with abstruse metaphysical questions and problems.

At the same time, however, it should be evident from our consideration of the top-down and bottom-up models of assimilation discussed in **Chapter 9** that the monastic roots of the Chan tradition are more clearly part of the former model than the latter. In fact, as far as its teachings are concerned, its major shortcoming is that it does not provide a method of practice that is readily available to ordinary lay followers of the Buddha. Its emphasis on the master–student relationship as the ideal method for conveying the *Dharma* and enlightenment is effectively beyond the reach of most lay practitioners. As a consequence of this limitation some Buddhists began to consider other methods of conveying the Buddha's teachings to those who were outside the ordained monastic community. What they were seeking was a method of practice that was at once simple, practical, manageable, and also authentically Buddhist. In short, the practice they were seeking had to be consistent with the basic teachings of the Buddha and also adapted to the circumstances of his followers who were neither monks nor nuns.

One of the easiest ways to achieve this end was to study the *Suttas*, reflect on the basic ideas of the Buddha's teachings, consider their history and development, and apply them to contemporary questions and problems by logically extending them to new situations and circumstances.

As in previous chapters, I want to recommend thinking about the history of this process as a series of transitions involving the study of various *Sutras*, the pursuit of numerous methods of maintaining and cultivating contact with and awareness of the Buddha, and the ongoing search for a simple, single method of practice that would grant all beings access to the Buddha's wisdom, compassion, and power.

In the particular cases of the monks and lay followers of the Buddha in China and Japan, I think it is clear that this is precisely the method employed by those who were responsible for developing Pure Land Buddhism. By studying various Mahayana *Sutras* (i.e., especially the *Lotus Sutra*, as well as the *Prajnaparamita Sutras*, the *Longer* and *Shorter Sukhavati-vyuha Sutras*, and the *Amitayurdhyana Sutra* or *Meditation Sutra*), by reflecting on their teachings and extending their ideas through their own writings, commentaries, and practices, Pure Land masters in China and Japan were able to make important and enduring contributions to the Buddhist tradition.

Given this account of the origin of Pure Land Buddhism, the purpose of this chapter is to trace the ongoing development of the Buddha's *Dharma* as it moved from China into Japan in its Pure Land forms. We shall accomplish this task by applying the logical assessment approach discussed above to its teachings. First, we will begin by focusing on the historical and philosophical roots of the Indian sources of Pure Land ideas. Second, we shall continue our consideration of the complex issue of the relationship between texts and doctrines and discipline and practice by considering the influence of the *Lotus Sutra* and the *Longer* and *Shorter Sukhavati-vyuha Sutras*. Finally, we will make the subject matter of the second task more concrete by giving special attention to the logic of some of the key ideas and teachings of Pure Land Buddhism in both China and Japan.

The origins of Pure Land Buddhism

Although the exact origins of Pure Land Buddhism are somewhat unclear, there is little doubt that its roots are intertwined with the beginnings of the Mahayana tradition in India. According to most contemporary scholars, what was to become Pure Land Buddhism in China, Korea, and Japan actually began as a form of Indian devotional practice centered on particular *Sutras* in response to practical problems and philosophical questions caused by ongoing reflection on the Buddha's teachings and his *Parinirvana*.

In order to get some sense of the kinds of issues and questions involved in the development of Mahayana Buddhism, imagine for a moment that you have had the opportunity to listen to the teachings of the historical Buddha, Sakyamuni. In fact, imagine that you were young enough to have had the opportunity to listen to him speak on a number of different occasions, over the course of many years, and that you have come to believe that what he teaches is true. At some point, however, you begin to realize as the Buddha continues to age that he is getting closer to death. As far as human experience is concerned, you know it is absolutely certain or at least that there is good inductive evidence for the belief that all human beings and all living things die. So you conclude that the Buddha will die, and eventually he does. At this point you are faced with at least two problems or questions: first, what happens to people, including the Buddha, after they die; and second, following the Buddha's death and *Parinirvana*, where can you go for help when you have questions about his teachings?

The answer to the first question, as we have seen, depends on whether the people in question are enlightened or not, whether they have achieved or realized *Nirvana*, and just what *Nirvana* is. There appear to be a number of possible answers to the second question. In fact, the problems and challenges surrounding both questions are exacerbated by the fact that you seem to recall that the Buddha taught different things on different occasions to different audiences. In other words, his teachings were not always logically consistent and even his closest followers offered different and conflicting accounts of them. Moreover, even if you could make logical sense of his teachings, and simultaneously harmonize his followers' explanations, you also realize that given the current state of affairs in the world (i.e., a world characterized by impermanence, *dukkha*, and no-enduring-self) as well as your own intellectual and moral limitations and shortcomings (i.e., defilements – greed, hatred, and delusion), it is simply impossible or at least highly unlikely that you shall ever be able to achieve the goal that the Buddha described and presumably has realized. Desperate and exasperated you ask yourself what a devoted follower is supposed to do.

This thought experiment is not difficult to imagine. In fact, I want to suggest that it pretty accurately captures what many of the Buddha's followers must have experienced after his death and presumed *Parinirvana*.

Parinirvana – questions and problems

The Pali canon reports in various texts that the Buddha told his followers that he had given them all that was necessary to achieve the same end that he was about to realize, and that all they needed to do was to follow the *Dhamma* and work diligently for their liberation from *samsara*. That advice, however, presupposes at least two important conditions: first, that the *Dhamma* itself was not inconsistent (i.e., that it makes logical sense and was able to be practiced); and second, that one has the ability, opportunity, motivation, and perseverance to pursue its goal, especially when circumstances and/or character traits make it difficult or almost impossible to do so. Let's take a look at each of these conditions more closely.

As we have seen, one traditional Buddhist response to the charge that the *Dharma* is not consistent is the Buddha's teaching on *upaya* or skillful means. According to this teaching, any time there is an apparent discrepancy between any two teachings of the Buddha, the solution to the problem is to recall that the Buddha suited his message to his audience and therefore he often gave different answers to different listeners. A second, more sophisticated response to this situation goes farther and distinguishes conventional truths from ultimate truths while also recognizing and emphasizing the significance of ignorance and its effects on the cognitive powers of the individual. Any pair of apparently inconsistent teachings must first be checked as possible instances of *upaya*, and then their truth-values can be evaluated against the conventional-ultimate truth standards of the *Dharma*. Assuming that these are satisfactory responses to cases where the *Dharma* appears to be logically inconsistent, we are still left with the problem of difficulties that arise from either poor environmental conditions or character flaws or both.

I want to suggest that one of the more important sources of Pure Land Buddhism can be traced to solutions to this second set of conditions for following the Buddha's advice. I also want to maintain that the issues involved in the development of Pure Land Buddhism are directly related to the kinds of questions, doubts, and worries that all of us have when we lose someone we love and admire. In this respect, they are related to the beliefs we have about what happens after death and the kinds of existence that are possible or likely in that state. Finally, I want to propose that they closely correspond to the experiences students typically have when their teachers are suddenly unavailable.

As I suggested earlier, it is not difficult to imagine that one of the more pressing and ongoing issues that the followers of the Buddha had to deal with after his death was their personal loss and profound questions about his existence. They had to deal with the fact that their teacher and guide was no longer readily available and therefore they needed to explain the senses or ways in which one could say that the Buddha was available to aid and instruct them. And both of these concerns were further complicated by a history of speculation and theories about what is or may be the case not only in this world but also in other worlds, if they exist. These are obviously difficult and problematic situations, involving profound questions, but eventually we all must come to terms with them, just as the followers of the Buddha did.

Some preliminary responses

As far as we know, the earliest Indian and Buddhist responses to questions about the circumstances and conditions in which one seeks liberation from *samsara* were directly related to broader views about the metaphysical and cosmological structure of reality. Without going into the details of these theories, it is important to realize that Buddhism inherited much of its own cosmology from prevailing Indian accounts of the nature, origin, and structure of the universe. According to these speculative accounts, which are remarkably similar to some Western cosmological theories about the universe, the cosmos is infinite in both space and time, and as a whole it undergoes recurring cycles and patterns of evolutionary progress and gradual decline. Traditional Buddhist cosmology contends that space is full of an infinity of universes or "world systems." In fact, Paul Williams[1] points out that within this network of "worlds" an individual world known as a *Buddhaksetra* – "Buddha Land" or "Buddha Field" – is a place where a Buddha exerts his causal powers in ways that are analogous to how a king exercises political control throughout his kingdom. The basic line of reasoning used to support these claims seems to have originated, at least in part, with speculative questions about what happened to the Buddha after his death and his *Parinirvana*.

As we saw in **Chapter 8**, some of his early Mainstream followers insisted that as a result of his *Parinirvana* the historical Buddha was, like a flame that is blown out, completely extinguished upon his death. They also maintained that questions about where he is or where he went after his death are simply misguided and ignorant. Others, however, who eventually became known as Mahayana Buddhists not only rejected this account of the Buddha's realization of *Nirvana* and extinction as inconsistent with his teachings on compassion, but they also claimed that *Bodhisattvas* and Buddhas do not go out of existence or become extinguished when they realize *Nirvana* or achieve Buddhahood.

Those who accepted this account of the historical Buddha's *Parinirvana* appear to have been influenced by the *Jataka Tales* of his previous lives and to have engaged in devotional practices centered on the ritual worship of his bodily relics, as well as pilgrimages to the various sacred sites associated with his teaching activities. They also seem to have practiced meditating on the various qualities of the Buddha in order to visualize his presence, and part of this activity included chanting or reciting his name either silently or aloud. Finally, they came to believe that the Buddha himself had the spiritual power to save them by guiding them to his "Pure Land." In other words, by emphasizing the Buddha's compassion and the efficacy of his teachings, they asserted that he and other Buddhas and *Bodhisattvas* remain in existence – in this world or some other *Buddhaksetra* – to help all beings achieve

---

[1] Williams and Tribe (2000), pp. 181–184 and especially footnote 23, pp. 268–269.

liberation from *samsara*. The reason why they are needed, of course, is the declining moral state of the world as well as ubiquitous human weakness.

The logic of this argument appears to be that since Buddhas and *Bodhisattvas* continue to exist and exercise causal powers (which must be true because the *Sutras*, i.e., especially *The Lotus Sutra*, say so and the logic of devotional practices requires it), they must exist somewhere, and that "some-where" is a *Buddhaksetra* or Pure Land. Assuming for the sake of argument that this line of reasoning is coherent and persuasive, it still does not tell us anything about the particular features of the *Buddhaksetra*, and it also does not tell us anything about the activities of the Buddhas and *Bodhisattvas* who occupy them. It is to these particulars that we now turn our attention.

Buddhas and *Buddhaksetras*

Not surprisingly, Mahayana Buddhists appear to disagree about the parti-cular features of Buddha Lands. In order to help clarify these disagreements we can distinguish those that relate to the Lands themselves, and those that are concerned with the means and methods for gaining access to them. With respect to the former, one line of thought asserts that since a Buddha is purified of all attachments and defilements, the place where he exists must also be pure. This idea appears to be the source of the Chinese term "*Jingtu*" – "Pure Land" – which was used to translate the idea of *Buddhaksetra*.

One problem with this rendering of "*Buddhaksetra*," however, is that little reflection is required for one to realize the rather obvious truth that our world is anything but pure. In fact, what is clear and evident to our senses seems to entail by the "logic of Pure Lands" that neither Buddhas nor *Bodhisattvas* exist here or at least that the historical Buddha lacked the power to purify it. Some Buddhists claimed that the second alternative seemed clearly false or at least highly doubtful, and so it must be the case that Buddhas and *Bodhisattvas* exist somewhere else from where they offer help to beings in our world. Moreover, the Buddhists who affirmed the first disjunct also maintained that its truth confirmed the need for an explana-tion of how those beings living in such a world could realize liberation through the help of "absent" Buddhas and *Bodhisattvas*. This is precisely what they believed was contained in the *Longer* and *Shorter Sukhavati-vyuha Sutras*, the *Amitayurdhyana* or *Meditation Sutra*, and their accounts of Pure Land Buddhism that we shall be examining shortly.

At the same time, other Buddhists, who accepted the idea of Buddha Lands, rejected the idea that such places must necessarily be pure. In other words, as they saw things, not all *Buddhaksetras* are Pure Lands. In fact, they distinguished three types of *Buddhaksetras*: pure, impure, and mixed. They also appear to have offered alternative explanations for the relative purity or impurity of these Lands. On the one hand, they seem to have recognized that lack of purity, whether complete or mixed, is not inconsistent with the ongoing efforts of *Bodhisattvas* who are continually working through compassionate actions to purify their Lands in preparation for becoming Buddhas. On the other hand, some texts, such as the *Vimalakirti Sutra*, insist that the purity and impurity of the Buddha Lands is actually a feature of the minds of those who inhabit them and not the Lands themselves. In other words, all *Buddhaksetras* (whether there is only one or many) are Pure Lands, and their seeming impurity is actually a function of the impurity of the minds of those who occupy or meditate on them and not a feature of the Lands themselves.

While this latter explanation is certainly plausible and also consistent with the central thesis of this book about the importance of the mind in shaping and knowing reality, its explanation of the purity and impurity of a *Buddhaksetra* seems clearly contrary to ordinary sense experience (assuming, of course, that there are good reasons for thinking our senses are reliable), especially in the case of our world. In fact, it seems to present us with two fundamentally different and radically incompatible conceptions of the nature of our world.

According to the first conception, the nature of things in the world is a function of the beings of those things that compose it, and it is completely independent of the mind's idea of it. According to the second conception, on the other hand, the nature and features of the things in the world is completely determined by the mind's way of seeing them. The differences between these two conceptions could not be starker and the philosophical consequences of affirming one rather than the other more momentous.

Buddhists who subscribe to the second conception of the world want to affirm the all-important role of the mind in the Buddha's teachings. They eventually became known as Yogacara Buddhists, and they had a direct influence on the development of certain Pure Land ideas, as we shall see shortly.

Those who subscribe to the first conception, however, want to affirm the Buddha's realism and empiricism. They insist that the Four Noble Truths and Eightfold Path are teachings about the way things are in the world and not claims about the mind or its functioning. They also insist that the Buddha's unrelenting realism entails dealing with things as they are. For these Buddhists, the Buddha's First Noble Truth is that everything is *dukkha*, and the sad truth is that he has died and is no longer in the world. The point of his teachings is to help us realize these facts and learn to deal with them. No other teachings are necessary or required – just as the Buddha said.

Interestingly enough, however, this same line of reasoning also helps support the "new" idea, originally conceived in China and more fully developed in Japan (though ascribed retroactively to the Buddha's foresight), that since the Buddha has "left" this world, that fact helps explain why his teachings and influence are degenerating and waning over the course of time.

As previously noted, this notion of "the end of the *Dharma*," *mofa* in Chinese, or "the last days of the *Dharma*," *mappo* in Japanese, played an important role in the development and justification of Pure Land Buddhism. Those who accepted this line of thinking eventually worked out various accounts of the locations of the Pure Lands and the Buddhas who occupy them and the means and methods for gaining access to them. The most famous of these is the Pure Land of Amitabha Buddha, which is located in the west and known as Sukhavati. We shall consider this Buddha and his Pure Land shortly.

At the same time, other Buddhists disagreed with this account of our world and its apparent lack of a Buddha. According to these Buddhists, who were influenced by the Yogacara ideas discussed above, the historical Buddha, Sakyamuni, can be said to have purified our world through his teachings and compassionate actions. What they mean by this assertion is that what Siddhattha realized on the night of his enlightenment was that this world is already pure. The reason that it "appears" to be impure is that it is not seen by an enlightened mind. Those who fail to realize that this world is already pure are simply misled by their own habitual ignorance and false thinking. This state of ignorance is exactly what the Buddha's enlightenment removed and his teachings were meant to address.

In other words, it is not, strictly speaking, the world that is the problem, it is how we view it – with a mind clouded by ignorance, defilements, and habituated patterns of false and erroneous thinking – that causes us to see it and things incorrectly. In this respect, one should be immediately reminded of Peter Hershock's claim in the previous chapter apropos Huineng's enlightenment that "what we take things or people to be tells us more about the quality and horizons of our own awareness than about anything else."[2] This way of understanding the world and the mind's relationship to it also highlights one of the fundamental differences among Buddhists with respect to the features of the Buddha Lands.

With respect to the disagreements among Buddhists about the means and methods for gaining access to a *Buddhaksetra*, it should not be surprising that there are different and competing accounts of how one gains access to a Buddha Land.

According to various Mahayana *Sutras*, there appear to be at least half a dozen different ways to gain access to a Pure Land: meditative practices, visualization techniques, chanting or reciting the name of the Buddha who exercises power over the Land, sincere acts of faith in the power and compassion of the Buddha whose Land it is, purification of one's mind in order to realize that one is already in a Pure Land, and various combinations of these methods in conjunction with strict moral practices.

Paul Williams[3] suggests not only that one way to visit a Buddha Land is by meditation, but also that the very idea of a Pure Land had some connection with the experiences of visions seen in meditation. According to his account, *buddhanusmrti*, or "recollection of the Buddha,"[4] is a meditative technique whose roots can be traced all the way back to one of the oldest Buddhist texts of the Pali canon, the *Sutta Nipata*. In that text, one of the Buddha's followers reports that even though he cannot follow the Buddha physically because of his age and bodily troubles, there is no time when he is not in the Buddha's presence because he is always with him in his mind's awareness. In other words, meditating on the Buddha and his qualities has the power of making him visible and present to the mind in the same way that he was visible and present to the eyes and body. In fact, Williams claims that one of the reasons motivating the development of the practice of Buddha-recollection was regret at living in an age after the life of the Buddha had passed.[5] It also appears likely that this same meditative approach to the Buddha's presence helped inspire the visualization practices of other Mahayana *Sutras*.

---

[2] Hershock (2005), p. 96.   [3] Williams and Tribe (2000), p. 183.
[4] Williams (1989), pp. 217–220.   [5] Williams and Tribe (2000), p. 183.

A second means of access to a Buddha in a Pure Land is by certain visualization techniques. This method of access is explained in the *Pratyutpanna Sutra*, where as a result of extended reflection and deep meditation on Amitabha (Buddha of Infinite Light) or Amitayus (an alternative name for Amitabha meaning "Infinite Life") Buddha and his Pure Land, Sukhavati, the meditator is literally able to see the Buddha and receive his teaching.

The third method of access to a Buddha in a *Buddhaksetra* is by chanting or reciting aloud the name of the Buddha who exercises power over the Land where one is seeking to be reborn. For example, in order to be reborn in Sukhavati, one must recite or chant Amitabha's name – "*Namo Omito-Fo*" in Chinese or "*Namu Amida Butsu*" in Japanese ("Praise to Amitabha Buddha"). However, there are two important differences between the Chinese and Japanese understandings of the *Nien-fo* and *Nembutsu* (Buddha-recitation) practices. The former, at least initially, appears to have been part of a broader conception of practice that emphasized the personal powers of the practitioner. According to this conception, one recites the name of the Buddha in order to calm, purify, and concentrate the mind as well as to create karmic connections to the Buddha and his Pure Land. The specific goal of the practice then is to guarantee through one's own efforts that one will be reborn in that Buddha's Pure Land and subsequently achieve *Nirvana* from there. This form of practice also seems to have involved visualization of an image of the Buddha, and meditation on the Buddha's name and virtuous qualities.

The latter, Japanese approach, on the other hand, completely depends on the compassion and assistance of Amitabha/Amida Buddha and does not recognize any causal power or karmic contribution on the part of the practitioner. According to this conception, the practice of reciting the Buddha's name is directly related to a set of vows pledged by the Buddha Amitabha while he was still a *Bodhisattva*. *The Longer Sukhavati-vyuha Sutra* reports that the *Bodhisattva* Dharmakara promised (as one of almost fifty vows) that if after becoming a Buddha any sentient being who desired to be born in his *Buddhaksetra* and called his name even ten times, and was not reborn there, then he would not achieve enlightenment and become a Buddha. The fact that he ultimately became Amitabha Buddha entails, however, that his promise must have been kept, and therefore those who desire to be reborn in Sukhavati and who call upon Amitabha Buddha will in fact be reborn there.

Without at the moment going into any more of the specific differences among the various forms of Chinese and Japanese Pure Land Buddhism, it should be obvious that there are many intriguing questions and important philosophical issues involved in the details of these practices for gaining access to Pure Lands. Among other things, these questions and issues involve matters ranging over such topics as exactly how many times the name must be invoked (answers range from a single time to constantly), the kinds of dispositions, intentions, and attitudes required for proper recitation of the Buddha's name (i.e., sincerity, profound faith, and a fervent desire to be reborn in his Pure Land according to *The Longer Sukhavati-vyuha Sutra*), the relation of *Nien-fo* and *Nembutsu* practices to other kinds of moral and immoral actions (i.e., following the Eightfold Path or engaging in inappropriate actions), and the specifications of *karma* (i.e., the *Bodhisattva*'s, the Buddha's, and the individual practitioner's), self-power and other-power, and the logic and possibility of merit transfer, to name just a few. However, despite these important issues, what is particularly interesting about the development of the Pure Land Buddhist traditions in China and Japan is their ongoing commitment to respond creatively to metaphysical and epistemological topics and difficulties.

Given the Buddha's teaching on interdependent arising as well as the history of the development of Buddhism that we have been considering throughout the last two chapters, it should not be surprising that questions about *Buddhaksetra* were not considered in isolation from other issues. In fact, the various accounts of the particular features of Buddha Lands that we have been outlining were worked out in conjunction with other issues related to them. One of the more pressing metaphysical and epistemological issues was the question of the Buddha's ongoing existence and efficacy.

Trikaya – the Buddha's three bodies

At roughly the same time that the various accounts of the Buddha Lands were being worked out, other questions about the ontology of the historical Buddha were also being addressed. As we have seen, according to the earliest Mainstream followers of the Buddha, Siddhattha Gotama was born and lived as a human being, with a human body, and having achieved *Parinirvana*, he escaped *samsara* and was extinguished. However, subsequent Mahayana followers of the Buddha insisted that his enlightenment and realization of *Nirvana* allowed him to transcend the conventional categories of *samsara* and *Nirvana*, and that as a result he realized a higher state or condition than is shared by all Buddhas.

According to Mahayana Buddhists, the Buddha's great powers of concentration and meditation allowed him to realize various "spiritual" powers, including the power to generate subtle bodies through which he could communicate the *Dharma* to beings on other planes of existence and in other parts of the universe. As a result of these ideas, some Mahayana Buddhists developed the idea that the Buddha has the power to present himself in three distinct bodily forms or modes of being: first, there is his Truth or *Dharma* Body or *Dharmakaya*, in virtue of which the Buddha is both the whole of his perfected qualities, as well as equal to the unchanging truth or "suchness" of all things (i.e., the Buddha as synonymous with ultimate reality and Buddha-nature or Buddhahood); second, there is his Enjoyment Body or *Sambhogakaya*, which refers to his cosmic or celestial form by which he is "present" in his Buddha Land; and third, there is his Emanation Body or *Nirmanakaya*, by which he appears on earth as an instance of *upaya* in order to instruct ignorant human beings in the *Dharma*.

The purpose of these distinctions appears to be twofold: first, they help explain, clarify, and extend the notion of skillful means by presenting the various ways in which the Buddha can be experienced by those who are puruing his way of life; and second, they provide the metaphysical explanations for the various ways in which the Buddha can be said to exist and act, especially in the context of his Buddha Land. In fact, when the idea of the Buddha's "three bodies" is considered within and against the context of the history of Pure Land Buddhism, I think it helps clarify the conceptual developments of Buddhism. In order to make these developments more obvious we shall briefly consider the particular ideas and teachings of some forms of Pure Land Buddhism in China and Japan.

Chinese Pure Land Buddhism

Before considering the basic ideas of Chinese Pure Land Buddhism it may be helpful to review briefly the situations and circumstances, and questions and problems that gave rise to Pure Land thinking. As we have seen, the most troubling and problematic situation facing the early followers of the Buddha was his death and *Parinirvana*. In addition to practical questions about what to do in response to this fact, how to organize themselves, and the kinds of lives they should live, they were also faced with more profound philosophical questions about the meaning of his teachings and the relationships among the various ideas used to convey his *Dharma*.

One can imagine that the Buddha's death produced a spectrum of responses in his closest followers. Those who completely accepted his authority and teachings presumably took him at his word and thought that he had achieved *Nirvana* and that they would too if they just followed his path. On the other extreme, those who doubted, questioned, or rejected his authority and teachings were probably still in doubt about his final status. Those between these extremes likely had a mixed reaction, accepting what seemed true and wondering about what seemed doubtful.

As far as we know, it appears that initially his followers were able to organize themselves into monastic communities without too much trouble. However, problems soon began to arise with respect to differing interpretations of his teachings. One particularly important question involved the status and practices of lay followers.

On the one hand, there was little disagreement about the basic elements of monastic practices. As we have seen, Buddhist monks following the example of the historical Buddha engaged in ascetic practices, meditation and visualization techniques, begging for alms, and teaching. In order to train themselves for these practices they also engaged in textual studies of his teachings and devotional activities. Those who were able to engage in these practices presumably looked forward either to a better rebirth or the realization of *Nirvana*. On the other hand, the early monastic followers of the Buddha, at least initially, only offered his lay followers the promise of merit and a better rebirth if they helped support the more difficult life of the monks. However, some began to question the appropriateness of this "second class" teaching, especially within the context of discussions about the power and compassion of the Buddha.

According to this line of thinking, simultaneous reflection on the overwhelming power of the Buddha, the difficulty of the monastic path, and the pervasiveness of human weakness and ignorance leads one to realize that the possibility of achieving the goal of Buddhist practice is quite literally beyond the grasp of most human beings. Those who were particularly moved by considering the Buddha's compassion could not reconcile this fact with their belief that he intended to teach and help all beings realize *Nirvana*. In order to overcome this shortcoming in the Mainstream interpretation of his teachings, Mahayana Buddhists developed their own broader conception of practices that were easier to engage in and more readily available to lay followers. These practices included devotional activities such as prayers and invocations as well as pilgrimages to sacred sites that were designed to help those not inclined to monastic practices to overcome both the external obstacles and internal impediments to the ultimate realization of their goal. Pure Land Buddhism is the direct result of this line of thinking.

When we turn to the Chinese context into which the early Pure Land ideas were introduced, two features in particular are important for understanding their reception and assimilation: first, the politically unstable environment in the post-Han era created such deplorable conditions that most people were looking for any kind of hope in the future; and second, Pure Land teachings about a better situation after this life were remarkably consistent with the neo-Daoist pursuit of life after death. Other Pure Land teachings about the value of meditation, and the promise of improving one's mind and life also resonated with Chinese sensibilities. In short, the logic of Pure Land teachings conformed to their experiences.

One way of making sense of the Chinese appropriation of Pure Land ideas is to begin with a question about the role of faith or belief in accepting the Buddha's teachings. There appear to be four moments or steps in this process. First, one must be exposed to or hear the teaching. Second, one must understand the ideas being conveyed by thinking about and reflecting on them. Third, one must decide to put the ideas into practice. Fourth, one learns the truth about the ideas by experiencing the results of their practice.

Initially, the Chinese were told that Pure Land Buddhism provided a method for purifying the mind that would not only improve the quality of their minds, but also would allow them to receive help from the Buddha. As a result, the first version of Pure Land practice in China was a support group for those who wanted to test the devotional promises and meditative benefits of its teachings. After some success with its practices, its initial Chinese followers began to propagate its teachings by emphasizing the easiness of its practice in comparison with the difficulty associated with the traditional path. As they saw things, meditation and visualization techniques in conjunction with devotional invocations of the Buddha provided an easy path to help those who were seeking rebirth during a time of moral decay. Although there were disagreements among themselves with respect to specific practices, in general, Chinese Pure Land Buddhists maintained that simply by calling on the Buddha, they could avail themselves of his power and thereby be born into a Pure Land from which they could subsequently work out their final realization of *Nirvana*.

In other words, assuming for the sake of argument that Buddhists are correct about rebirth, and that an infinity of past lives entails the real possibility of an unlimited amount of evil committed by an unenlightened being, and further that the current state of affairs in the world is not exactly conducive for engaging in practices that even in the best of circumstances are quite difficult, if not practically impossible for even the most dedicated and committed of it followers, they reasoned that in order for there to be any real possibility for the masses of unenlightened beings to be liberated from *samsara*, some kind of external help was absolutely necessary to save them from unending death and rebirth. As a result, they maintained that Pure Land practices involving meditation, visualization, devotional practices, and faith in the Buddha and his teachings, in conjunction with the vows of Amitabha Buddha guaranteed that even those who were ignorant and defiled could escape *samsara* and be reborn in a Pure Land.

Understood in this way, the logic of the Chinese Pure Land conception of the goal of Buddhism is that since even a good rebirth in heaven in this world system is rebirth in *samsara*, and since enlightenment in an age of the decline of the *Dharma* is highly unlikely, it is not possible to achieve *Nirvana* directly from this world. But if the Buddha is to be trusted and his teachings are to be believed, one can overcome these obstacles by having a sincere faith in his power and by firmly resolving to be reborn in his Pure Land so that one can receive his help and eventually be liberated from *samsara*. Unlike some medieval Western philosophers and theologians such as Augustine and Anselm who thought that faith leads to understanding, Chinese Pure Land Buddhists thought that faith leads to liberation in a Pure Land. Japanese Pure Land Buddhists, however, rejected even the slightest suggestion that the individual had any "self-power" in these matters, and they insisted that the logic of Pure Land thinking entailed that everything was dependent on the "other-power" of the Buddha. It is to this conception of Pure Land thinking that we now turn our attention.

Japanese Pure Land Buddhism

In order to help clarify the Japanese response to the teachings of the Buddha it is important to keep in mind that like China it received his teachings in two ways – at the level of common folks and at the level of scholars and government officials. It is also necessary to understand that by the time the Buddha's *Dharma* made its first appearance in Japan in the sixth century of the Common Era it had been significantly altered as it made its way through China and Korea. Without going into the details of this transformation, let it suffice to say that by the time it made its first official appearance in Japan, it was promoted as a source of worldly benefits, including material goods, bodily health, political power, and military success.

Like their Chinese predecessors, the Japanese were initially overwhelmed by the sheer volume and variety of texts and teachings attributed to the Buddha. As one can imagine, eventually each of the various Indian and Chinese schools of Buddhism made its way into Japan. One of the central concerns for the Japanese was to make sense of these different, competing, and sometimes clearly inconsistent interpretations of the Buddha's ideas. Given this context and background, therefore, I think it is useful to think of the Japanese development of Pure Land Buddhism (and Zen and Nichiren as well) as a search for a single form of practice available to all practitioners who happen to find themselves living through *mappo* – the degenerate age of the *Dharma*.

As indicated above, the most basic difference between Chinese and Japanese forms of Pure Land Buddhism is their disagreement over the question of "self-power" and "other-power." While Chinese Pure Land Buddhists generally recognized some role for "self-power" in choosing to believe or have faith in the Buddha and his teachings, Japanese Pure Land Buddhists disagreed and emphasized both the "other-power" of the Buddha and the complete and total unworthiness and powerlessness of the individual. In other words, by taking the teaching on *mappo* seriously and joining it with a realistic assessment of human ignorance and frailty, Pure Land Buddhists in Japan came to the conclusion that the only way to be liberated from *samsara* is through the saving "other-power" of the Buddha. They also argued that their interpretation of Pure Land ideas was more consistent with the original teachings of the Buddha, especially his teaching on *anatta*, because as they understood the idea of no-enduring-self, it was not only contrary to the Buddha's teaching but also logically incoherent to hold that a follower of the Buddha had any "self-power" whereby they alone could choose to have faith in the Buddha.

When we turn to the specific ideas of Japanese Pure Land Buddhism, it should come as no surprise that it shares many of its ideas with its Chinese predecessors. For example, many of its earliest practitioners were attracted to Pure Land ideas promoting the intellectual and spiritual benefits of its meditative practices. They also were attracted to its promises with respect to rebirth. At the same time, however, they were unclear about the relationships among the various forms of practice accompanying the oral invocation of the Buddha's name. On the one hand, Pure Land Buddhism as they initially understood it seemed to require nothing more than the oral recitation of the Buddha's name in order to convey its meditative benefits as well as to guarantee rebirth in a Pure Land. On the other hand, some forms of Pure Land Buddhism seemed to require extensive meditation, complex visualization techniques, ascetic practices, a disciplined moral life, and other devotional activities. Eventually the Japanese developed two distinct but related forms of Pure Land Buddhism.

The first form, *Jodu Shu* (i.e., Japanese for "Pure Land"), was founded by the Tendai monk Honen (1133–1212). According to his version of Pure Land Buddhism, the oral invocation of the Buddha's name is sufficient to convey meditative benefits in this life and rebirth in a Pure Land in the next life. Given the current state of affairs in the world (i.e., *mappo*), Honen claimed that the only effective practice that could guarantee one a rebirth in a Pure Land was to keep the Buddha's name fixed in the mind at all times and to recite it aloud as often as possible. In addition to the recitation, however, he also insisted that one must have a sincere, deep faith in the power of the Buddha, and a firm resolution to be reborn in a Pure Land. All other practices are simply beyond human capacity, especially when it is considered within the context of the final age of the *Dharma*.

The second form of Pure Land Buddhism, *Jodo Shinshu* (i.e., "True Pure Land"), was founded by Shinran (1173–1262), a former student of Honen. Like Martin Luther, Shinran appears to have had a profound sense of his own weaknesses and moral unworthiness. Given these beliefs, and the Buddha's teaching on *anatta*, he reasoned that it was not only impossible to do any action whose merit could entail access to a Pure Land, but also that everything was ultimately a function of the Buddha's power and grace. He seems to have believed quite frankly that an honest and realistic assessment of one's own weaknesses, limitations, and defilements will necessarily lead one to the conclusion that there is only one being, the Buddha, who can help one achieve liberation from *samsara* by granting access to his Pure Land. In fact, he claimed that the desire to recite the *Nembutsu* even once was itself a gift from the Buddha. As a result, Shinran claimed that he (and not Honen) had discovered the one practice – accepting the Buddha's help in sincere and humble faith and with joyful thanksgiving – that was required for access to the Pure Land.

It should not take much reflection for the reader to realize the serious implications of this view. While one of its virtues is its apparent simplicity and ease of practice, nevertheless, among its more glaring weaknesses is the fact that it offers no justification or rationale for behaving morally. In fact, if Shinran is correct moral actions such as following the Eightfold Path are completely superfluous to realizing enlightenment or gaining access to a Pure Land. Such a consequence is not only inconsistent with common-sense conceptions of morality, but also clearly contrary to the explicit teachings of the historical Buddha.

Yet, in Shinran's defense, one could argue that the original teachings of the Buddha were delivered under far different circumstances and conditions, and that different times and situations, especially those obtaining in *mappo*, call for new and expedient teachings. In that sense, at least, one could legitimately claim that True Pure Land Buddhism, like the Buddha's own teachings, was merely a raft to the distant shore of enlightenment, or *Nirvana*, or in particularly bad times, the next best thing – a Pure Land.

Despite this obvious shortcoming, Pure Land Buddhism and True Pure Land Buddhism did not lack for followers. In fact, their common focus on and development of meditation and visualization techniques in conjunction with their pursuit of a single form of practice to gain access to a Pure Land, realize enlightenment, and ultimately achieve Buddhahood had a lasting effect on the subsequent history of Buddhism. This is especially true as Buddhism finally made its way into Tibet in the seventh century CE, and as Pure Land Buddhism continued to develop and establish itself as one of the most popular and influential forms of Buddhism in the world. Nevertheless, its apparent shortcomings should inspire the reader to consider carefully the important connections between the metaphysical and epistemological teachings of Buddhism and their ethical implications and consequences. We shall have the opportunity to do this in a preliminary way when we consider the development of Buddhism in Tibet in **Chapter 11**, and then more consciously when we conclude the book by focusing on two of its more important and recognized contemporary teachers, the Dalai Lama and Thich Nhat Hanh.

Things to think about

1. What specific issues related to the Buddha's *Parinirvana* motivated Pure Land thinking?

2. What are the basic differences between Chinese and Japanese Buddha-recitation practices and beliefs?

3. What kinds of particular, practical questions arise from the "logic of Pure Lands?"

4. In what way(s) is Pure Land Buddhism an attempt to make Buddhist practices less burdensome? In what sense is Pure Land Buddhism "easy"? How is this situation related to the ongoing development of other philosophies and religions?

5. What are the similarities and differences between *Jodu Shu* and *Jodo Shinshu* Buddhism? Which account seems better to you and why?

11   Tibetan Buddhism

Key terms and teachings

Bodhicitta: Sanskrit term for "thought of enlightenment/awakening."
In Mahayana Buddhism it refers to the enlightened mind of a *bodhisattva*.
Dharani: Sanskrit term for an extended *mantra* used to focus the mind
and help it retain teachings.
Guru: Sanskrit term for "teacher," commonly found in the Vajrayana
tradition.
Dalai Lama: Literally "Great Ocean" (*dalai*) "Teacher" (*lama*), the title
designates the temporal and spiritual leader of Tibet. The Mongol ruler,
Altan Khan, originally bestowed the title upon the "third" Dalai Lama.
Mahamudra: Sanskrit term for "Great Seal," in Vajrayana Buddhism it
refers to the meditative practices that lead to enlightenment, and insight
into the unity of wisdom and compassion and *samsara* and emptiness.
Mandala: Sanskrit term for a sacred circle that symbolically represents
the world and what exists. In Tantric Buddhism it is thought to represent
the mind, body, and speech of a Buddha and is used in meditation
practices.
Mantra: Sanskrit term for sacred sounds that are thought to possess
supernatural/spiritual powers.
Mudra: Sanskrit term meaning "seal" or "sign," it refers to a symbolic
gesture using the hands or body to represent an aspect of the Buddha's
teaching.

Why study Tibetan Buddhism?

The purpose of the final two chapters of **Part III** is to complete our account
of the "Development of the *Dhamma/Dharma*" by considering the features of
Tibetan Buddhism and the particular ideas and teachings of two influential

229

and popular teachers of contemporary Buddhism – the Dalai Lama and Thich Nhat Hanh.

Aside from the historical and chronological order of its development, there are at least two additional reasons for considering Tibetan Buddhism. First, its focus on the teacher–student or master–disciple relationship helps highlight this important teaching in Buddhism. In this respect, the history and ideas of Tibetan Buddhism help link **Chapters 9** and **10**, which focused on the development of the Chinese and Japanese traditions, with **Chapter 12**, which is specifically concerned with the particular teachings of the Dalai Lama and Thich Nhat Hanh. In other words, the Tibetan focus on the importance of the teacher–student relationship allows us to return to a consideration of the specific teachings of particular teachers who not only see themselves but also who are seen by their followers as authentic transmitters of the Buddha's *Dharma*.

Second, the Tibetan Buddhist focus on meditation, mental cultivation, and visualization techniques in realizing enlightenment or awakening or one's Buddha-nature is another important piece of evidence in support of the claim that the Buddha's single most important teaching is concerned with reorienting one's mind and one's thinking in order to see "things" as they really are.

Nevertheless, it is important to keep in mind that there also are good reasons for being cautious about one's claims about Tibetan Buddhism because of limited reliable texts as well as ongoing scholarly debates and disagreements about both its development and its relationship to Indian Buddhism, Tantric ideas, and Chinese forms of Buddhism. As a result, this chapter has three specific purposes: first, to consider the Indian and Tantric sources of Tibetan Buddhism; second, to examine some of the basic ideas of Tibetan Buddhism; and third, to provide the historical and intellectual context for the ideas and teachings of the Dalai Lama.

Sources of Tibetan Buddhism

It is customary to distinguish two historically distinct transmissions or disseminations of Buddhism into Tibet. The "first transmission" occurred roughly between the seventh and ninth centuries of the Common Era and is associated with King Songtsen Gampo (d. 650) whose Chinese and Nepalese wives were Buddhists. This first wave of Tibetan Buddhism was, according to Peter Harvey,[1] a combination of monastically based Mahayana Buddhism, initiated by the Indian monk and scholar Santaraksita (705–788) of the Buddhist monastic university in Nalanda, India, and the Tantric mysticism and rituals taught by the Indian yogin Padmasambhava (fl. eighth century), who is generally recognized as the founder of the Nyingma School of Tibetan Buddhism. As a result, it is not inaccurate to suggest that the subsequent history and development of Tibetan Buddhism is the working out of the, sometimes contentious, relationship between monastic and Tantric forms of Buddhism.

The "second transmission" of Buddhism occurred during the tenth and eleventh centuries, and is typically dated from the second major influx of Indian monks and scholars, including Atisa (982–1054), and the subsequent development of the Kadam, Kagyu, and Sakya Schools of Tibetan Buddhism. The last major school of Tibetan Buddhism, the Geluk-pa or "Virtue"-School, which eventually replaced both the Kadam and "New Kadam" Schools, traced its intellectual roots to the works of the Indian scholars Asanga (fl. fourth century, founder of the Yogacara school of Indian Buddhism), Vasubandhu (younger brother of Asanga and Yogacara philosopher), Candrakirti (fl. seventh century, Madhyamaka philosopher and logician), and Dharmakirti (fl. seventh century, Indian Buddhist logician and epistemologist). As a result of its political connections with the Mongolian court in the sixteenth century its leading teachers or *gurus* (who were believed to be both the reincarnations of their predecessors and the emanations of Avalokitesvara) were given the title "Dalai Lama" – "teacher (lama) whose wisdom is as deep as the ocean (dalai)" or "wisdom as deep as an ocean teacher."

Before considering some of the basic ideas involved in the assimilation and development of the Tibetan form of Buddhism, it may be helpful to consider its Indian Tantric roots as well as its relationship to its own indigenous pre-Buddhist thought and religion.

Pre-Buddhist Tibetan beliefs

Although shrouded in mystery and a subject of considerable uncertainty because of a lack of early textual sources and serious scholarly disagreements

---

[1] Harvey (1990), p. 145.

about its subsequent relationship to Buddhism – against which it was defined, distinguished, and in some sense constructed – the (perhaps?) indigenous intellectual and religious ideas of Tibet prior to the advent of Buddhism are conventionally referred to as "Bon." Whatever its particular beliefs and practices may have included (i.e., royal funeral ceremonies and a cult of dead kings, magical practices for controlling supernatural forces and powers, and some belief in rebirth), it seems safe to say that it was against and in contention with these ideas and practices that Buddhism made its initial headway into Tibet. In fact, what is particularly interesting about the spread of Buddhism into Tibet is its striking similarity to the earlier spread of Buddhism into places such as China and Japan.

As we have seen, even though we distinguished "high" and "low" forms of Buddhism as it made its way into both China and Japan, it was not until the political leaders of these countries embraced and supported it that its assimilation was assured. In other words, it seems to be an empirical fact of history that political support for a religion or philosophy is a *sine qua non* for its enduring success, if not its initial acceptance. In the case of Buddhism, this was true not only in China and Japan but in Tibet as well. However, it is also true that broad popular support can and does have a significant effect on the viability of a religion or philosophy. We have already seen how this occurred in China and Japan in their different forms of Buddhist ideas and practices, and the same thing appears to have happened in Tibet. In the latter case, traditional accounts report that it was a series of Tibetan "*Dharma*" Kings who were responsible for the initial transmission and propagation of Buddhism. At the same time that Tibetan kings were embracing Buddhist ideas and practices, ordinary "Bon" believers were being introduced to Buddhist ideas that were, at least in part, somewhat similar to their own beliefs and practices. It is to a consideration of each of these circumstances that we now turn our attention.

Bon beliefs and practices

As far as we know, Bon practitioners appear to have participated in rituals related to royal funeral ceremonies, and these services seem, at least in theory, to have been motivated by beliefs about rebirth. They also appear to have engaged in magical, ritual practices for controlling supernatural forces and powers. In fact, some scholars have suggested that these activities seem to have been supported by animistic and/or shamanistic beliefs and practices. In other words, Bon practitioners appear to have been committed to the belief that certain rituals and practices could pacify spirits, control the weather, heal various kinds of sickness, and even guarantee various kinds of material success.

Although little is known about specific Bon rituals, it is not difficult to imagine that they would have included various kinds of ritual instruments, physical actions, and appropriate words as well as the assistance and direction of recognized experts or adepts, who could properly conduct the ritual and "guarantee" its benefits. Whatever the exact nature of the practices may have been, what is important for understanding the assimilation and development of Buddhism in Tibet, especially with regard to its Tantric elements, is the fact that ordinary Tibetans were apparently already predisposed by their "own" beliefs and practices to understand and accept those forms of Buddhism that included ritual and magical practices. This is exactly the kind of Indian Tantric Buddhism that made its way into Tibet during both of its transmissions.

The "official" Buddhism of the "*Dharma*" kings

At roughly the same time that this "low" or "popular" form of Indian Tantric Buddhism was being spread throughout Tibet, a second, "high" or "elite" form of monastic Buddhism was also being disseminated at the official governmental level. As previously noted, this form of Buddhism is traditionally associated with the activities of the Tibetan "*Dharma*" kings, especially, Songtsen Gampo, who in deference to his wives first "opened" Tibet to Buddhism, and later King Trisong Detsen (fl. late eighth century), who was a devout Buddhist himself, and who sought to spread the *Dharma* throughout Tibet, and finally, King Relpa Chen (fl. early ninth century), whose royal patronage in building numerous monasteries and temples not only contributed to the growing political power of the Buddhist *Samgha*, but also eventually led to a confrontation with the Tibetan aristocracy in which the king was assassinated by his political rivals and his successor King Lang Dharma (d. 842) was himself subsequently assassinated by, surprisinglyly enough, a Buddhist monk.

The political chaos caused by these assassinations traditionally marks the end of the "first transmission" of Buddhism to Tibet. During the next century and a half, while the "official," government-supported form of Buddhism was being suppressed, Buddhist beliefs and practices continued to be maintained and transmitted by lay practitioners and their teachers. In fact, this "low" form of Buddhism appears to have been an important link between the first transmission of Buddhism in Tibet and its second transmission at the end of the tenth and beginning of the eleventh centuries. We shall return to this point in a moment.

Eventually, after some form of political stability was finally restored in the mid-to-late tenth century, Tibetan rulers again became interested in learning more about Buddhist beliefs and practices. What is traditionally referred to as the "second transmission" of Buddhism is typically associated with a new influx of Indian monks and scholars, one of the most famous of whom was Atisa, who arrived from the monastic university at Nalanda and whose mission was to renew and re-energize the teachings and practices of the *Dharma* in Tibetan monasteries.

Atisa is especially renowned for his broad understanding of Indian Buddhism, his insistence on traditional monastic training, his emphasis on personal *Dharma* transmission between a teacher and student, and for his synthesis and integration of *Abhidharma*, Mahayana, and Tantric forms of Buddhism. Each of these distinct forms of Buddhist teachings and practices was to have a profound effect on the emergence of Tibetan Buddhism, as we shall see. In fact, the end of the "second transmission" is usually associated with the formation of the four major "Schools" of Buddhism in Tibet, which happen to share many ideas and practices that can be traced back to *Abhidharma*, Mahayana, and Tantric forms of Buddhism. Among these three forms of Buddhism, however, arguably the most important for the development of Tibetan Buddhism was Indian Tantric Buddhism because of the role it played in linking the two transmissions.

At this point in our study of the history and development of Buddhism, however, it should be clear that there are important and fundamental differences between what we have for the sake of convenience designated as "high" and "low" forms of Buddhism. The former, as we have seen, is associated with monks, monasteries, organized meditation practices, and the translation and study of texts and commentaries. The latter, on the other hand, is especially associated with rites and rituals, material support of monks and their monastic communities, and some forms of individual prayer and ritual and meditation practices. Nevertheless, despite these differences, there are also commonalities between these distinct forms of Buddhist practice.

In the case of Tibet, I want to suggest that one of the most important common features of "high" and "low" Buddhism was their interest in Tantra. It is to an examination of the basic ideas and features of this form of Indian Buddhism that we now turn our attention.

Indian Tantric Buddhism

It is not possible in the remaining pages of this chapter to give anything more than a general account of Tantric Buddhism[2] because of space constraints, limited availability of textual sources, the complexity of the subject matter itself, and finally, changing scholarly attitudes and views of the topic. What we do know with some degree of certainty may be summarized as follows.

The roots of Indian Tantra appear to be anchored in ancient devotional traditions and practices that can be traced through esoteric ritual and meditation texts that purport to aid their practitioners in identifying with a deity or "being united" – either literally or imaginatively – with such a being. The term "*tantra*," which is related to the words for "thread" and "weave," refers to both texts that contain ritual instructions and the practices themselves. One particularly clear and helpful way of thinking about Tantric texts and practices[3] is to see them as various ways and means of "weaving" a new vision, a new experience, or a new understanding of reality.

The basic idea is that these texts and rituals provide their practitioners with the shortest and most effective path to experiencing and realizing the truth about the fundamental nature of reality, however that "reality" is ultimately conceived. In its peculiarly Buddhist form, "*tantra*" refers to the texts and ritual practices that claim to provide the most direct method for achieving enlightenment, or realizing one's Buddha-nature.

Perhaps the easiest way to understand Tantric Buddhism is to think of it as a set of ritual practices involving the mind, the body, and one's actions that are intended to help one understand and experience the unity and

---

[2] For a particularly clear account to which I am indebted see Williams and Tribe (2000), pp. 192–244 and their suggestions for other sources in footnote 2, p. 271.

[3] Mitchell (2002), p. 160 and Robinson et al. (2005), p. 130.

connection between one's consciousness or mind and one's Buddha-nature. In other words, through the exercise of certain esoteric practices involving ritual actions and visualization techniques, one is enabled to experience, understand, and subsequently live the compassionate life of an enlightened being. What this means in most basic terms is that Tantric Buddhist practices provide a unique method and strategy for transforming one's consciousness, which in turn transforms one view of reality and the way things are, and which ultimately helps one realize in the quickest and most effective means possible that one is, in virtue of one's Buddha-nature, already enlightened or awakened. Ignorance, of course, is the cause of our failing to realize this. As a result, Tantric Buddhism provides the requisite meditative techniques by which one can overcome one's habitual ignorance and become what one already is – an enlightened being – a Buddha.

Inspired by Donald Mitchell's[4] account, the basic ideas behind the specific practices associated with the various forms of Tantric Buddhism are rather easy to enumerate if not to exercise. Their features include the following intellectual and moral commitments: first, a willingness to turn away from attachment by recognizing and accepting the Buddha's teachings on *dukkha*, impermanence, *anatta*, and *karma*; second, a resolve to work with a teacher or *guru* who has the skill and knowledge (based on his own practice, experience, and realization) required to help one realize liberation and enlightenment; third, a firm pledge to arouse *bodhicitta*, i.e., the enlightened mind of a *bodhisattva*, and thereby vow to realize one's Buddha-nature or achieve Buddhahood for the welfare of all beings; fourth, the unrelenting intention to purify one's mind as well as one's thoughts (through meditation on and visualization of mental and material *mandalas*), words (through the recitation of various *mantras* and ritual *dharanis*), and deeds (through *mudras* and other ritual bodily movements); fifth, an attitude of prayerful supplication for the assistance of other enlightened beings (i.e., celestial Buddhas and *Bodhisattvas*); and sixth, a fastidious performance of the prescribed rituals in order to guarantee their efficacy.

Only a moment's reflection on these features of Tantric Buddhism should be necessary to indicate what was to become one of the most basic issues in Tibetan Buddhism: the relationship between meditation and moral actions in achieving enlightenment. On the one hand, it appears that one could

---

[4] Mitchell (2002), pp. 162–164

reasonably interpret these features of Tantric Buddhism as simply so many intellectual, cognitive, or mental activities. They do not seem to require any specific kinds of behavior or action beyond the rituals themselves, and the fact that they are part of one's practice where one is committed to working with a *guru* and a specific *Tantra*, seems to imply that it is the meditative work and visualization techniques that are the most important elements of the practice. On the other hand, despite the lack of moral specificity, it is clear that there is a rather undeniable "practical" element in the list of commitments. Although the Four Noble Truths and Eightfold Path are not explicitly mentioned, it would not be too difficult to show how they are implicitly present and entailed by some of the ideas enumerated above.

A second, related issue in Tantric Buddhism involves the question of whether the Tantric practices outlined above produce their effects suddenly, instantaneously, and immediately, or whether their success requires an extended period of continuing and ongoing practice and meditation such that one would describe their benefits as being gradually realized over time. In fact, this question provides a perfect opportunity to consider in more detail some of the features of the various forms of Indian *Tantra*, and then to show how these features were interpreted and understood in Tibet.

Tantras and their benefits

One of the best ways to understand Tibetan Buddhism is to think of it as the project and process of coming to grips with a wide variety of Buddhist texts, commentaries, and traditional practices from both India and China simultaneously. In this respect, "high" Tibetan Buddhism in particular can be seen as an attempt to make sense of a jumble of competing and often incompatible texts, claims, authorities, and sets of traditional ritual practices. The Tibetan canon, which we shall consider shortly, is the eventual result of these efforts. At this point, however, I want to complete our consideration of the Tantric background to the Tibetan assimilation and adaptation of its various kinds of beliefs and ritual practices.

It is customary to distinguish at least four (and sometimes five) distinct kinds of *Tantra* collections. According to Robinson, Johnson, and Thanissaro,[5] an eighth-century Buddhist commentary initially distinguished three classes

---

[5] Robinson et al. (2005), p. 130.

of Tantras: *Kriya* (Action) *Tantras*, *Carya* (Performance) *Tantras*, and *Yoga* (Union) *Tantras*. A subsequent text divided the *Union Tantras* into *Yoga Tantras*, *Higher Union Yoga Tantras*, and *Unexcelled Union Yoga Tantras*. Finally, Tibetan Buddhists combined the *Higher Union* and *Unexcelled Union Tantras* into what they called the *Anuttara Yoga* (Unsurpassed Union) *Tantra*, which is now considered the fourth kind of *Tantra* in addition to the original three classes distinguished above.

Action Tantras, which ultimately came to be viewed as preparatory texts, contain *mantras* that are specifically concerned with material success and worldly benefits. According to Tantric beliefs, the words of the *Action Tantras* themselves and other ritual words called *mantras* and *dharanis* possess a "spiritual power" which can be accessed by the recitation of them in order to bring about various kinds of material benefits, such as bodily health, good crops, good weather, protection from one's enemies, and ultimately even enlightenment itself. In a very basic sense, the *Action Tantras* may be thought of as a collection of ritual chants that have the power to bring about effects either in the world (as magic spells and special incantations are thought to do), or in oneself as a result of meditative transformation.

Performance Tantras, or *Practice Tantras* as they are sometimes called, are the second class of *Tantras* concerned with material success and worldly benefits, but they also include important initiation rites and specific instructions from a *guru* who is not only a master of a particular *Tantra*, but also an adept who has the power to transmit his mystical knowledge to his student. Unlike *Action Tantras*, this group of *Tantras* contains initiation rituals in which the practitioners seek to identify themselves with the Cosmic Buddha, Vairocana, who is thought to be the source of existence of all things. By ritually uniting with the cause of all being, practitioners visualize themselves as enlightened beings, who through their identification with Vairocana are able to affect and control things in the material world. In simple terms, these *Performance Tantras* help their practitioners transform themselves through visualization techniques so that they can act in the world with the power of an enlightened being.

Yoga Tantras go beyond *Carya Tantras* and offer their practitioners the opportunity to fully realize Buddhahood. The initiation rituals of these *Tantras* include visualization techniques and the use of a *mandala* or sacred diagram to help their initiates to become quite literally one with the body, mind, and speech powers of a Buddha. *Yoga Tantras* purport to help their practitioners achieve worldly, material success, spiritual awakening, and full realization of Buddhahood.

The fourth class of *Tantras*, the *Anuttara Tantras*, or "Highest" and "Supreme" form of *Tantras* include initiation rituals and other practices that involve sexual yoga and various kinds of unconventional practices and behaviors that are intended to help their practitioners overcome dualistic ways of thinking and behaving as well as to participate in the "power" of "forbidden" things. There are two distinct lines of interpretation of these *Tantras*.

One line of interpretation is more "theoretical" or "abstract" and focuses on the symbolism of the practices and the mere visualization of the unconventional behaviors. A second line of interpretation, on the other hand, insists on the actual performance of the unconventional behaviors, and maintained a secret, oral tradition that was concealed from the uninitiated. This last class of *Tantras* also stresses the importance of women and the role of females in helping practitioners transcend dualistic thinking and conceptualizations. In fact, many of these *Tantras* equate the pleasure and bliss of ritual sexual union and orgasm with the mental and psychological states experienced in enlightened or awakened thinking.

Conceived of as a whole, one might usefully think of the four classes of *Tantras* as sets of teachings, rituals, meditative practices, visualization techniques, and behaviors intended to help their practitioners quickly and effectively realize the goal of enlightenment, awakening, or Buddhahood. In general, they begin with *mantras* and *mudras* that purport to have the power to bring about material success in ways that are remarkably similar to the practices of contemporary athletes who employ the power of positive thinking, meditation, and concentration, and various kinds of pre-game rituals to ensure their own success. They also employ rituals and visualization techniques that allow their users to imaginatively "practice" and virtually "experience" what it is like to be an enlightened being. Finally, some *Tantras* appeal to both male and female principles, either in theory only, or in actual ritual sexual practices, to represent and realize the unity of skillful means or moral actions (i.e., the male or masculine) and wisdom (i.e., the female or feminine).

With respect to the last point, in particular, it should not be surprising to learn that many scholars hold the view that Tantric Buddhist teachings and practices probably originated outside of traditional or "orthodox" monastic centers as a form of practice engaged in and taught by "unorthodox" yogins. As with other forms of Buddhism, it also should not be difficult to imagine that there were numerous texts and commentaries that accompanied the various kinds of *Tantras*. As I previously indicated, translating, interpreting, reconciling, and assimilating all of these texts were some of the most basic activities of Tibetan Buddhists. In fact, the Tibetan canon eventually came to include two sets of scriptures: the *Kanjur* or "translated words and teachings of the Buddha," and the *Tenjur* or "translated commentaries and treatises on the Buddha's teachings." The former contains Buddhist *Vinaya*, various Mahayana *sutras*, and numerous *Tantras*, which were traditionally said to have contained the secret teachings of the Buddha. The latter includes *Abhidharma* texts, numerous commentaries on the teachings of the Buddha, and treatises on various topics, including, astrology, grammar, medicine, and other crafts.

In addition to these textual matters, Tibetan Buddhism was also concerned with serious philosophical questions and issues related to the meaning and interpretation of the texts and their ideas, and practical questions about how one was to put the Buddha's teachings into practice. The former involved profound questions about how to understand emptiness, Buddha-nature, awakening, and enlightenment, and in particular, important questions about the relationship between conceptual thinking and enlightenment, and the value and role of moral practices and compassion for achieving enlightenment. The latter, on the other hand, was typically answered in one of two ways: either by traditional monastic communities and practices or by specific teacher–student or master–disciple relationships. It is to a consideration of each of these elements of Tibetan Buddhism that we now turn our attention.

Tibetan philosophy and practices

As in China and Japan before it, Buddhism in Tibet may be characterized as an attempt to come to terms with a vast array of teachings, ideas, texts, authorities, and practices all of which claim to be authentic representations of the Buddha's *Dhamma*. In order to help make sense of this complex phenomenon, I previously suggested making a distinction between "high" and "low" forms of Buddhism. If we return to this earlier distinction between the different forms of Buddhism in Tibet, I now want to suggest that the "high" form of Tibetan Buddhism is more precisely Tibetan philosophy, which can best be thought of as an exercise in textual exegesis. This form of Tibetan Buddhism is concerned with analyzing texts, ideas, and arguments, and harmonizing the various sources of the Buddha's teachings.

Given the large number of Mahayana *sutras* that eventually made their way into Tibet, it should not be surprising that much of Tibetan philosophy is concerned with particular questions about such Mahayana themes as the nature of emptiness, the teaching on "Two Truths," Buddha-nature, and the ways and means to achieve enlightenment. We shall be examining the different Tibetan answers to the last issue shortly.

At the same time that these technical philosophical issues were being clarified and addressed by the "high" form of Tibetan Buddhism that is typically associated with monastic communities and universities, a "low" form of Tibetan Buddhism was coming to grips with specific issues related to ordinary Buddhist practices. As previously indicated, this form of Tibetan Buddhism was worked out in the day-to-day relationships between teachers and students and masters and disciples. In a very real sense then, Tibetan Buddhism is best thought of as the union of these two forms of "high" and "low" Buddhism. In short, it is simultaneously both the pursuit of wisdom through textual study and the daily practice of Tantric meditation and compassionate action under the guidance of one's teacher. We shall provide particular examples of the all-important teacher–student relationship when we consider the schools of Tibetan Buddhism, especially the Geluk-pa School and its leader, the Dalai Lama.

The question of enlightenment

One of the most important issues in Tibetan philosophy is the question of the relationships between meditation and enlightenment or practice and awakening. In simple terms, the issue is whether various kinds of meditative practices engaged in over the course of many years in conjunction with textual study and moral practices are absolutely necessary for enlightenment, or whether enlightenment or awakening is the immediate and instantaneous result of a momentary, direct insight into the nature of the mind itself without any kind of intervening mental conceptualization or practice.

The historical roots of the issue can be traced back to a rather famous eighth-century "debate" between the Indian Buddhist monk, Kamalasila, a student of the renowned scholar Santaraksita who had been invited by King Trisong Detsen to help establish the first Buddhist monastery in Tibet, and a Chinese monk, who seems to have practiced and taught a form of Chan Buddhism. In fact, the reference to the Chan tradition is also important because it should bring to mind our previous discussion in **Chapter 9** of the Chinese Chan tradition, its own related debates, and the story of its roots which it claims can be traced all the way back to the historical Buddha's disciple Mahakasyapa who was immediately enlightened when the Buddha showed him a flower. So in an important way, the historical roots of the Tibetan debate actually go all the way back to the earliest teachings of the Buddha himself.

Aside from questions about the exact nature of the Tibetan "debate" and even who "won," the basic dispute appears to have been a fundamental disagreement between a Chinese or Chan (and perhaps, ultimately Indian?) interpretation of enlightenment as the result of a "sudden" awakening or direct insight into one's Buddha-nature or Buddha-mind brought about through meditative practice and expressed in enlightened living, and an (other?) Indian interpretation of enlightenment as the "gradual" and ongoing process of incremental growth in wisdom and compassion that takes years and usually many lifetimes to complete and perfect.

According to the traditional Tibetan account,[6] the Chinese/Chan position was that enlightenment literally has nothing to do with morality, and in fact, its realization is directly impeded by concerns about good and bad actions, and thoughts and worries about following rules and precepts. True awakening, it is said, can only be realized with the elimination of all conceptual thinking, and all discursive reasoning. By its very nature, enlightenment is a momentary, instantaneous, and immediate insight or awareness. In fact, it is not a "thought" at all – it is an experience, a happening, an event – and, as a result, there is certainly nothing "gradual" or incremental about it.

The Indian response, of course, is that if the Chan interpretation of enlightenment is correct, then it can happen in the absence of thinking (on the assumption that not having thoughts entails that one cannot be thinking), and more importantly, it undermines all the teachings and practices that have been handed down by the Buddhist tradition. But, as

---

[6] See Williams (1989), pp. 193–197 for a clear summary of the "debates."

Kamalasila claimed, since both conjuncts of the consequent are obviously false, the antecedent must also be false as well.

There are obviously other claims that could be made in support of each position, and in fact, there appear to be strong and plausible cases for each side of the debate. However, the king was ultimately persuaded by Kamalasila's position, and subsequently declared that everyone should follow the Indian interpretation of enlightenment and moral practice.

In light of the king's decision, I want to maintain that it is possible and indeed helpful to think of the subsequent history of Tibetan Buddhism as the unfolding of the basic tension expressed in this debate. On the one hand, there appear to be good philosophical and historical reasons for thinking that the Chinese/Chan interpretation is not completely wrong-headed. At the same time, however, there appear to be equally good reasons for accepting the Indian "gradualist" view of enlightenment as well. In fact, I want to suggest that the different schools of Tibetan Buddhism that developed as a result of the "second transmission" are really just subtly different takes on the great eighth-century debate.

For example, the Nyingma School, which interestingly enough, came to be associated with Kamalasila and his teacher Santaraksita, espoused an approach to enlightenment, *dzogchen*, which in many respects was quite like the Chan interpretation of enlightenment. *Dzogchen* meditation practice, which is unique to the Nyingma School, is anchored in the belief that the essence of mind or consciousness is originally and innately pure, free from defilements, and non-dual. In other words, it distinguishes the source of our ordinary mental activities, which include making distinctions, forming mental habits, and generating various kinds of thoughts and actions, from the ultimate source of mind or consciousness, which is in itself empty of all natures and features. This "essence of awareness," so to speak, is always already awake or enlightened, and waiting to be realized for what it already is. In order to experience this source of awareness directly and immediately all that is required is the stilling of the ordinary, ignorant mind and its usual, habitual, and unenlightened mental activity. A *guru* who has already achieved this insight and awakening is also necessary to guide one in the specific techniques required for calming one's "everyday" mind and helping one experience the pure awareness of mind itself or one's Buddha-nature.

Given this characterization of *dzogchen* I think it should be clear that it includes features from both sides of the "Great Debate." On the one hand, the fact that the practice includes a teacher who helps one with the specific techniques for calming the mind clearly indicates that there is a "gradualist" element to the practice. On the other hand, the fact that the essence of mind is already awake or enlightened is consistent with the teachings of the "sudden" interpretation of enlightenment. A similar kind of "borrowing from both sides" can be seen in the other schools of Tibetan Buddhism as well.

One of the Kagyu School's most important teaching and practices centered on the *mahamudra* meditation technique aimed at helping one realize both the emptiness of all phenomena and the intrinsic luminosity of all things. As in *dzogchen* meditation, one must work with a *guru* to calm one's ordinary mind and thereby eliminate the defilements that cause inappropriate thoughts, words, and deeds. According to this school's practice, the ultimate insight into the emptiness of all things helps one realize the undefiled state of the mind itself, which is beyond, above, or outside of *samsara* and the emptiness of phenomena.

The Sakya School teaches that *samsara* and *Nirvana* are actually identical and falsely distinguished by unenlightened thinking. On this interpretation, the enlightened mind realizes that the defilements of *samsara* are simply so many obstacles to a mind that is originally free of defilement and impediments to awakening. With the help of an awakened teacher one is able to embark on the meditative and Tantric path that will end in the realization that one has, so to speak, become what one already was all along – awake or enlightened.

Finally, the Geluk School, to which the Dalai Lama belongs and whose roots can be traced back to the Kadam School, emphasizes the study of texts and *sutras* as well as obeying the *Vinaya*. According to the teachings of this school, one must gradually enter the path that will ultimately lead to enlightenment. In a certain sense, it advocates a literal step-by-step process of engagement with Buddhist ideas that moves methodically from the Four Noble Truths, through the Eightfold Path, to the Mahayana ideal of the *bodhisattva*, and finally to the Vajrayana realization of Buddhahood or Buddha-nature. In the final analysis, according to this approach, to see with an undefiled mind that all things are ultimately empty is to realize the wisdom of the Buddha and therefore to act with the Buddha's compassion.

To help make things a little more concrete, the current Dalai Lama summarizes our cognitive situation in this way: first, we need to realize that we naturally, spontaneously, and ignorantly form concepts that we uncritically think entail that the "things" we are thinking about have essences or natures or selves; second, this wrong or ignorant view leads to the development of unwholesome emotions and desires that are directed to these seemingly enduring "things;" third, these afflicted emotions, desires, and cravings lead to inappropriate thoughts, words, and deeds, that produce negative karmic consequences; and fourth, liberation and enlightenment from this state is possible only by following the path described above, by meditating on emptiness, and acting with compassion. Not surprisingly, he also advocates visualization techniques and meditation on the processes of death and rebirth in order to focus the mind on the truths about emptiness and interdependent arising. The ultimate purpose of his teaching is to help others to realize the value and importance of compassion and its intimate connection to wisdom.

It seems clear from this account of the Dalai Lama's teachings that he would say that he is simply following the traditional Tibetan interpretation of the "gradual" path to enlightenment. In fact, there can be little doubt that he advocates a form of practice that is specifically concerned with reorienting one's thinking about the world and the way "things" really are. I hope to make this point more clear when we consider his teachings in more detail in the next chapter.

Nevertheless, I also think it should be quite clear from the accounts of the other schools' approaches to practice and enlightenment that there are clearly "sudden"-interpretation elements in their teachings. What all of this seems to indicate is that the truth about Tibetan Buddhism, like its Chinese and Japanese predecessors, appears to be that it is simultaneously the product and process of trying to come to grips with a seemingly overwhelming and clearly incommensurable collection of texts, teachings, ideas, and practices.

At the same time, its most important insight and enduring message is its continuing insistence that *both* wisdom and compassion, *both* meditation and moral practice are necessary for enlightenment and authentic Buddhist practice. Philosophy, or "the love of wisdom," and the purely intellectual study of texts and ideas alone are not enough for a faithful Tibetan Buddhist, one must also engage in the appropriate kinds of practices or moral actions as well – just as the historical Buddha himself did. That, I want to suggest, is precisely the message of two of the Buddha's more popular contemporary disciples – the Dalai Lama and Thich Nhat Hanh, whose ideas we shall be examining in the next chapter.

Things to think about

1. How were pre-Buddhist Tibetan beliefs and practices helpful in the assimilation of Buddhism?
2. What is the role of a *guru* in helping a student achieve enlightenment and engage in Tantric practices?
3. Why do some *tantras* use sexual yoga and other unconventional moral practices?
4. How is the Tibetan eighth-century debate related to the "sudden" vs. "gradual" debate in China?
5. How are the various Tibetan Schools just different takes on the eighth-century debate?

12 Two forms of contemporary Buddhism

Key terms and teachings

Engaged Buddhism: A form of Buddhism developed by Thich Nhat Hanh and others that combines the meditative practices of the monastic life with the practical demands of compassionate action in the world. Its point and purpose is for its practitioners to realize that wisdom and knowledge must eventually lead to enlightened action and service.

Mindfulness: The art of living mindfully is the practice of living in the present moment. It is the meditative technique of keeping one's consciousness alive to the present reality in the present moment. In short, it is the process and activity of cultivating awareness and restoring the mind to its original undistracted state.

Echoing the Buddha

The primary purpose of this chapter is to complete our account of the "Development of the *Dhamma/Dharma*" by considering some of the ideas and teachings of two of the most popular (at least in the West) contemporary teachers of Buddhism – the Dalai Lama and Thich Nhat Hanh. In this chapter I want to show how their teachings and interpretations of Buddhist ideas echo the historical Buddha's teaching that it is our mind and our uses of it that determine how we see and understand our self, the world, and other things. The secondary purpose of this chapter is to complete my case for the claim that the Buddha's most basic teaching is concerned with our minds and our uses of it. In fact, I plan to show that both purposes are interrelated, because as I read them, the Dalai Lama and Thich Nhat Hanh are perfect examples of contemporary Buddhists who reaffirm the historical Buddha's most basic and important teaching. Finally, I want to show

how each in his own way is inspired by the Buddha's life and teaching by insisting that knowledge and wisdom (i.e., "seeing things as they really are") must be perfected in enlightened compassionate practice. In other words, I take it that both the Dalai Lama and Thich Nhat Hanh think that you really only enter the path of transforming your mind and your life when you actually put into practice the things you believe and understand. In short, I want to suggest that the Buddha, the Dalai Lama, and Thich Nhat Hanh are all committed to the same view that practice makes perfect, and that questions and concerns about metaphysics and epistemology must ultimately give way to ethics and enlightened living of the *Dharma*.

The Dalai Lama

There are many ways to approach the ideas and teachings of the Dalai Lama. One of the easiest ways is to consider them within the context of his life. First of all, he is the temporal leader of the Tibetan government-in-exile. In this respect, we could consider his social and political activities as the leader of a country that is currently occupied by Chinese military forces. Second, according to traditional Tibetan beliefs and practices, he is also recognized as the spiritual leader of the people of Tibet and as such he is thought to be both the reincarnation of his predecessor, the thirteenth Dalai Lama, and an incarnation of Avalokitesvara, the Buddha/*Bodhisattva* of Compassion. In this capacity, he is considered the highest *lama* or teacher of the Tibetan cultural tradition. He is, as a result, the *de facto* spokesman for Tibetan Buddhism and so we could consider his religious and philosophical teachings in themselves, independent of their relationship to the facts and context of his life. A third possibility is to consider how his religious and philosophical ideas inform his social and political activities. This third approach has the advantage of uniting his beliefs and practices and also provides us with an opportunity to see how the Dalai Lama himself lives a life of wisdom and compassion.

His life

Lhama Dhondrub was born (July 6, 1935) to a farming family in a small village in northeastern Tibet. Following traditional Tibetan beliefs and cultural practices, it was determined that he was the reincarnation of the thirteenth Dalai Lama and he was renamed Jetsun Jamphel Ngawang Lobsang Yeshe Tenzin Gyatso. Tenzin Gyatso began his monastic education at the age of six, assumed political control of Tibet at the age of fifteen as Chinese forces were advancing into Tibetan territory, completed what is roughly equivalent to a doctorate in Buddhist philosophy when he was twenty-five years old, and eventually fled to India where he was given political asylum.

His social and political activities since 1960 have been concerned with working with the United Nations and other countries to persuade the Chinese government to respect the human rights, autonomy, and cultural traditions of the Tibetan people. He has worked tirelessly to protect the lives of his people, to preserve Tibetan culture, and to promote peace and happiness throughout the world. In 1989 he was awarded the Nobel Peace Prize for his ongoing efforts to promote a non-violent resolution to the political situation in Tibet, and he continues to travel, speak, and write about human rights, inter-religious understanding, and world peace.

His teachings

In addition to these social and political activities, the Dalai Lama has continued to study and teach Tibetan Buddhism. He has written numerous books on philosophical and ethical issues and topics, including, love, compassion, relationships, forgiveness, the meaning of life, the art of happiness, and most recently the convergence of science and spirituality. He also has a deep and abiding interest in the study of science, and is especially interested in the relationship between Buddhist thought and practice and the methods and procedures of contemporary science. In fact, one of his most recent books, *The Universe in a Single Atom*, and his continuing support of and participation in the Mind & Life Institute and Mind & Life conferences highlight his view that science and spirituality have not only an opportunity but also a moral obligation to work collaboratively to help improve the human condition.

According to the Dalai Lama,

> I say this because I believe strongly that there is an intimate connection between one's conceptual understanding of the world, one's vision of human existence and its potential, and the ethical values that guide one's behavior. How we view ourselves and the world around us cannot help but affect our

attitudes and our relations with our fellow human beings and the world we live in. This is in essence a question of ethics.

Scientists have a special responsibility, a moral responsibility, in ensuring that science serves the interests of humanity in the best possible way.[1]

There can be little doubt from this quotation that the Dalai Lama accepts the Buddha's teaching that who we are and what we think exists is a function of our mind and its cognitive powers. At the same time, the quotation also supports the notion that the Buddha went further than a merely metaphysical or epistemological claim and insisted that one's understanding of the self, the world, and others, when fully perfected, leads to actions whose moral qualities are commensurate with the level and depth of insight of one's mind. That is, the greater one's intellectual penetration into the way things really are, the greater one's obligation to engage in morally appropriate kinds of actions. In short, the Dalai Lama, following the Buddha, seems to think that moral action is the fruit of intellectual insight, and that this is especially true in the case of scientists. What exactly is his evidence for these claims?

In *The Universe in a Single Atom* and other writings the Dalai Lama reports that science has always fascinated him and that his interest in science began with technology and how things – toys, watches, a movie projector, and the automobile – work. At the same time that he was tinkering with mechanical objects he also was spending considerable amounts of time studying and memorizing Buddhist philosophy, scriptures, and rituals, as well as meditating for roughly eight hours every day. Eventually, after conversations with numerous professional scientists, he says he noticed similarities in the spirit of inquiry between science and Buddhist thought, and that he was particularly fascinated by the parallels between the scientific form of empirical investigation and those forms of study he learned in his Buddhist philosophical training and his own contemplative meditative practice.

As the Dalai Lama sees it, "science moves from empirical experience via a conceptual thought process that includes the application of reason and culminates in further empirical experience to verify the understanding offered by reason."[2] In this respect, at least, he was struck by how similar the methodology of science is to the advice the Buddha offered his followers

---

[1] Gyatso (2005b), p. 207.   [2] Ibid., p. 23.

when he insisted that they should test the truth of what he said through reasoned examination and personal experiment. In fact, he is so convinced of the truth and reliability of this empirical methodology that he has claimed that,

> If science proves some belief of Buddhism wrong, then Buddhism will have to change. In my view, science and Buddhism share a search for the truth and for understanding reality. By learning from science about aspects of reality where its understanding may be more advanced, I believe that Buddhism enriches its own worldview.[3]

There can be little doubt from these claims that the Dalai Lama is firmly convinced that Buddhism and science share a basic methodology that helps its practitioners arrive at the truth and "see things as they really are." The basic difference between them, however, is, as the Dalai Lama has noted, that scientific investigation proceeds by experiment, using instruments that analyze external phenomena, while Buddhist contemplative investigation proceeds by the development of refined attention, which is then used in the introspective examination of inner experiences.[4] Nevertheless, it is clear that both approaches share an empirical method that the Dalai Lama is convinced can be used to "see things as they really are." In fact, his commitment to this empirical or scientific method is also seen in his interest and participation in the Mind & Life Institute and its conferences.

According to its mission statement, "The Mind and Life Institute is dedicated to fostering dialogue and research at the highest possible level between modern science and the great living contemplative traditions, especially Buddhism. It builds on a deep commitment to the power and value of both of these ways of advancing knowledge and their potential to alleviate suffering." Its vision is to "establish a powerful working collaboration and research partnership between modern science and Buddhism – the world's two most powerful traditions for understanding the nature of reality and investigating the mind." And its purpose is to "promote the creation of a contemplative, compassionate, and rigorous experimental and experiential science of the mind which could guide and inform medicine, neuroscience, psychology, education and human development."[5]

---

[3] Gyatso (2005a).   [4] Gyatso (2005b), p. 24.
[5] Mind & Life website at www.mindandlife.org.

In essence, the Mind & Life Institute and its various programs are an organized and ongoing discussion forum between the Dalai Lama and Western scientists who are interested in the convergence and collaborative opportunities that exist between Buddhism and contemporary science. Although its past conferences have studied a broad spectrum of scientific issues and topics, including, the cognitive sciences, the neurosciences, emotions and health, sleeping, dreaming, and dying, physics and cosmology, quantum physics, the nature of matter and the nature of life, its central and enduring topic has been the mind and the brain and their relationship. In fact, its most recent conference, in the fall of 2005, "Investigating the Mind: The Science and Clinical Applications of Meditation," was concerned with how medicine and science can benefit from a collaborative bi-directional dialogue with Buddhism and other contemplative traditions about attention and awareness, meditation, mindfulness, mind/body interactions, the nature of pain and suffering, the cultivation of compassion and self-compassion, and the potential for the training of human faculties for learning, growing, healing, and emotion regulation across one's lifespan.

According to the Conference Program, recent clinical trials and research studies showing that meditation can result in stable brain patterns and changes over both short- and long-term intervals suggest the potential for systematic driving of positive neuroplastic changes via intentional practices cultivated over time. In other words, meditative practices, which are commonly used in the clinical treatment of stress, pain, and an entire range of chronic diseases in both medicine and psychiatry, are now being studied as techniques that might potentially promote greater overall mental and physical health and wellbeing.

Although the scientific study of meditation is relatively new, there is a growing body of empirical data that suggests at least a correlation (if not a causal link) between meditative practices, and in particular, mindfulness exercises, and one's ability to deal with stressful, painful, and unhealthy conditions and circumstances. In fact, experimental investigations being conducted by neuroscientists, psychologists, and practicing contemplatives are beginning to reveal the brain's extraordinary capacity for plasticity (i.e., its ability to change its structure or be reoriented) and its ability to promote both physical and mental healing and other important human qualities such as compassion.

The Buddhist contribution to all of this, of course, is its twenty-five centuries of contemplative practices in which the mind is used to understand the nature of reality and to "see things as they really are." At the same time, it has had an ongoing compassionate commitment to help humans deal practically and concretely with the negative aspects of the human condition and thereby improve our lives. The particular Tibetan Buddhist contribution to this discussion, as we saw in the last chapter, and as evidenced by the continuing efforts and activities of the Dalai Lama, is its insistence on the unity of theory and practice, the unity of wisdom and compassion, and the unity of contemplation and action.

The Dalai Lama, like the historical Buddha before him, claims based on his own experience that there is an important and necessary connection between meditative practices and compassionate action. As I suggested in **Chapter 2**, the Buddha and the Dalai Lama are committed to the view that meditation, like weight training for the body, has the power to improve and strengthen the mind and its faculties. In fact, an enlightened mind, following the Buddhist idea of interdependent arising, has the power not only to see things as they really are but also to direct our thoughts, words, and deeds with compassion and loving-kindness. The Dalai Lama says he knows this from personal experience because he spends at least six and sometimes eight hours of every day in prayer and meditation. The proof of his claims is, so to speak, in his thoughts, words, and actions. He continues to practice and teach what he calls his simple religion and philosophy – kindness, and he continues to insist that if you want to be happy then you must practice compassion. In a very real sense, then, the source of his actions is his spiritual practice, and the source of his spiritual practice is his compassionate actions. In short, the Dalai Lama is committed to the view that our thoughts and actions are intimately connected and interdependently related, in the same way that spirituality or spiritual practice and science or scientific investigation are related. At the end of *The Universe in a Single Atom*, he asserts that,

> At its best, science is motivated by a quest for understanding to help lead us to greater flourishing and happiness. In Buddhist language, this kind of science can be described as wisdom grounded in and tempered by compassion. Similarly, spirituality is a human journey into our internal resources, with the aim of understanding who we are in the deepest sense and of discovering

how to live according to the highest possible idea. This too is the union of wisdom and compassion.[6]

Given these remarks, it should be clear that the ultimate justification for the Dalai Lama's claims about the "moral responsibility" of scientists is the Buddha's teaching about interdependent arising, and the connection between wisdom and compassion. The former, as we have seen, encourages us to look beyond the "thing itself" to its field of relationships as the enlightened way of seeing "things" as they really are. The latter, of course, is seen and confirmed in the daily lives of the Buddha's followers.

In the particular case of the Dalai Lama, from his earliest monastic training, through his ongoing efforts to help the people of Tibet, and his continuing efforts to understand and promote the convergence of science and spirituality, he has endeavored to put his understanding of Buddhist wisdom into compassionate practice. He has, like the historical Buddha before him, tried through his thoughts, words, and deeds to give others a vision of the world in which our various, partial, incomplete, and ignorant ways of understanding ourselves, one another, and our universe can be brought together in an enlightened and compassionate service of humanity. The same kind of vision, motivation, and enlightened practice can be found in the life of the Vietnamese Buddhist monk, Thich Nhat Hanh. It is to a consideration of his ideas and practice that we now turn our attention.

Thich Nhat Hanh

Like the Dalai Lama, there are many ways to approach the ideas and teachings of Thich Nhat Hanh. One could, of course, consider them within the context of his life and see how they developed in response to the situations and circumstances in which he lived. One could also consider them directly in his written works without reference to the particular circumstances in which they arose. A third possibility is to consider how his religious and philosophical ideas inform his social and political activities. This third approach, like our approach to the ideas and teachings of the Dalai Lama, has the advantage of uniting his beliefs and practices and also provides us with an opportunity to see how Thich Nhat Hanh tries to live a life that combines contemplative wisdom and compassionate action.

---

[6] Gyatso (2005b), p. 208.

His life

Thich Nhat Hanh was born Nguyen Xuan Bao in central Vietnam in 1926 and entered a Buddhist monastery at the age of sixteen. His principal form of monastic training was in Zen Buddhism and he was ordained as a monk in the Vietnamese meditation school in 1949. "Thich" is the name and title given to all monks in the Vietnamese Buddhist tradition, and is a transliteration of the Sakya clan name. As a result, the name and title implies that he is a member of the family of the historical Buddha. His ordination or *Dharma*-name, "Nhat Hanh," means roughly "one/best action" or "highest conduct." His students and friends refer to him as "Thay," which is Vietnamese for "Master" or "Teacher."

Nhat Hanh's reputation in the West is based, in part, on his "one action" of helping to found and develop the "engaged Buddhism" movement. He is also recognized for his influence on the development of Western Buddhism, especially its meditative elements, and for his unique approach to modern Zen practice where he combines traditional Zen teaching methods with ideas from contemporary science and psychology. His life and work in the "engaged Buddhism" movement have been an ongoing attempt to combine the meditative practices of the monastic contemplative life with the practical demands of compassionate action in the world. One could, I think, best characterize his life as the "one action" of promoting peace and human rights through the union of meditative practices aimed at inner transformation and social action for the benefit of society. In fact, it is not an exaggeration to suggest that his life and teachings are in a fundamental way an enlightened and compassionate response to the social, political, and military circumstances of Vietnam during the last half of the twentieth century.

Following his ordination, Nhat Hanh worked in two arenas: first, he was actively involved in the revival and reform of Buddhism in response to French colonial rule and the growing perception among some Buddhists that monks and nuns were too far removed from the social realities of Vietnam; and second, he helped those suffering from the consequences of the ongoing political and military struggles in Vietnam. In the first arena he was named Editor-in-Chief of *Vietnamese Buddhism*, the journal of the Unified Buddhist Association, and he worked to encourage the unification of the various schools of Vietnamese Buddhism. Although suffering various setbacks, his efforts in this arena were eventually realized with the founding of the United Buddhist Church of Vietnam in 1964.

Perhaps his most significant activity in the second arena was the founding of the School of Youth for Social Services (SYSS), a student group of peace workers who were sent into villages to help those suffering from the ravages of war. The students in the school were trained to help the villagers with their educational, health, and economic needs, and practiced what Nhat Hanh called "engaged Buddhism." The point and purpose of "engaged Buddhism" was for its practitioners to realize that wisdom and knowledge must eventually lead to enlightened action and service. In order to demonstrate the importance and necessary connection between wisdom and action Nhat Hanh himself taught at the Institute of Higher Buddhist Studies in Saigon during the week and worked in its surrounding villages on the weekend. Eventually he formed a religious order for his fellow social workers, "The Order of Inter-being," and authored a series of Fourteen Mindfulness Trainings to help them put into practice what they studied at school.

In 1966 Thich Nhat Hanh received *Dharma* transmission from his teacher and he was authorized to teach as a Zen master. He subsequently traveled to the United States where he had once studied comparative religion, and taught Vietnamese Buddhism and continued his work as a peace activist. After a series of conversations with civil rights activist Martin Luther King, Jr., whom he personally persuaded to publicly oppose US involvement in Vietnam, King decided to nominate him for the Nobel Peace Prize in 1967 for his ongoing pacifist activities against the Vietnam War.

Since 1982 when he founded the Plum Village Buddhist Center in France, Nhat Hanh has continued to work with the Order of Inter-being and teach his mindfulness trainings and "engaged Buddhism." Despite his age, he works tirelessly to promote peace and to end the social, political, and economic conditions that contribute to world violence. He continues to travel, teach, and give retreats throughout the West (and even recently was granted permission to return to his own country from which he had been exiled because of his anti-war activism) and has established monasteries and *Dharma* Centers in the United States (in California, Vermont, and Mississippi) and Europe. He also is a prolific author and poet and continues to publish his ideas and teachings in both English and Vietnamese.

His teachings

Thich Nhat Hanh has authored more than eighty-five books of prose and poetry on various topics, including, anger, Jesus and the Buddha, inter-being, monastic training, happiness, love, community, prayer, commen-taries on various Buddhist *Sutras*, and consciousness and the mind, but he is perhaps best known for his writings on meditation practices, mindfulness training, and, of course, the practical application of these activities for reducing and eliminating human pain and suffering.

Given the context of his life and work, it should not be difficult to imagine that his most important ideas and teachings are concerned with working for and establishing peace. In fact, it is quite clear that his most basic teaching is that mindfulness is the key to developing peace both in oneself and in the world.

According to Nhat Hanh, compassionate action is and must be anchored in a meditative insight into the interrelatedness or interconnectedness of all things. Inspired by the Buddha's own meditative practices, his teaching on interdependent arising, and his actions after his enlightenment, Nhat Hanh insists that compassionate action is the fruit of meditative practices and mindfulness of the interrelatedness of all beings. In other words, it is the basic insight into what he calls the "inter-being" of things that allows one to see and understand that suffering anywhere is suffering everywhere, and that what I ignorantly and mistakenly take to be "my" suffering is actually symptomatic of the broader suffering of all beings. As a result, Nhat Hanh teaches that to realize the truth that all things arise interdependently is to see that the only appropriate response to suffering is empathy and compassionate action. It is precisely this union of insight and action, or wisdom and compassion, that Thich Nhat Hanh practices and teaches to the members of the Order of Inter-being and anyone else who is willing to work for social change by engaging in personal transformation. His first and most basic lesson is teaching "the art of mindful living."

According to Thich Nhat Hanh, mindfulness or the art of living mindfully is the practice of living in the present moment. He writes,

In Buddhism, our effort is to practice mindfulness in each moment – to know what is going on within and all around us. When the Buddha was asked, "Sir, what do your monks practice?" he replied, "We sit, we walk, we eat." The questioner continued, "But sir, everyone sits and walks, and eats." And the Buddha told him, "When we sit, we know we are sitting. When we walk, we know we are walking. When we eat, we know we are eating."[7]

Given this initial characterization of mindfulness, one cannot help but be immediately reminded of what Maurice Walsh and other scholars claim "is generally regarded as the most important *Sutta* in the entire Pali Canon,"[8] the *Satipatthana Sutta* or the *Discourse on the Foundations of Mindfulness*. In that text, the Buddha declares,

> There is, monks, this one way or direct path to the purification of beings, for the overcoming of sorrow and distress, for the disappearance of pain and sadness, for the gaining of the right path or true way, for the realization of *Nibbana* – namely, the four foundations of mindfulness.
>
> What are the four? Here monks, a monk abides contemplating the body as a body, ardent, fully aware, and mindful, having put aside covetousness and grief for the world. He abides contemplating feelings as feelings . . . He abides contemplating mind as mind . . . He abides contemplating mind-objects as mind-objects, ardent, fully aware, and mindful, having put aside covetousness and grief for the world.

In the course of further explaining the contemplation of the body and its postures, the Buddha adds,

> Again, a monk, when walking, knows that he is walking, when standing, knows that he is standing, when sitting, knows that he is sitting, when lying down, knows that he is lying down. In whatever way his body is disposed, he knows that that is how it is.

In fact, in his descriptions of the remaining foundations of mindfulness, the Buddha insists that the mindful monk knows and is fully aware of his feelings, his mind, and its mind-objects, and also abides detached and not grasping at or clinging to anything in the world. He concludes the *Sutta* by promising that anyone who develops the four foundations of mindfulness even for as little as seven days will realize either Arahantship in this life, or the state of a non-returner, i.e., someone who is reborn in a higher world from which he subsequently attains *Nibbana* without ever returning to the human world.

[7] Nhat Hanh (1995), p. 14.   [8] Walshe (1995), p. 588.

The problem, however, as Thich Nhat Hanh and anyone who has ever tried to practice the Buddha's teaching and the art of mindfulness realizes is that, "Most of the time, we are lost in the past or carried away by future projects and concerns."[9] In other words, most of the time we are simply so preoccupied with worries and concerns about what has happened in the past and what might have been and what is going to be taking place in the future and what might be, that we are completely and totally unaware of what is happening *here* and *now* in the present moment.

For example, how many times have you taken your car somewhere and arrived, and suddenly realized that you cannot recall how you got there? How many times have you been having a conversation with someone when suddenly you realize that you have not heard a single word they have said? Or, how many times have you absentmindedly done any activity (like driving your car while talking on the cell phone) and suddenly realized that you simply were not paying attention to what you were doing? All of these examples are the exact opposite of what the Buddha and Thich Nhat Hanh mean by the foundations of mindfulness and the art of living mindfully.

Sister Annabel Laity[10] has pointed out that Thich Nhat Hanh has often taught that our mind is like a television set with many different channels, and that in the present moment we can choose the channel that we want to watch. She also notes that the Buddha taught that there are fifty-one different kinds of mental formations (including love, joy, hate, jealousy, feelings, and perceptions), and that it is up to us to choose which formation or program we want to watch. The problem, however, she notes, is that most of the time we do not consciously choose which program we are watching because we allow our minds to channel surf, or we watch the same old program out of habit. In fact, the Buddha compares the mind in this state to a "monkey":

> Just as a monkey roaming through a forest grabs hold of one branch, lets that go and grabs another, then lets that go and grabs still another, so too that which is called "mind" and "mentality" and "consciousness" arises as one thing and ceases as another by day and by night.[11]

And Thich Nhat Hanh employs the same analogy and claims that, "The mind is like a monkey swinging from branch to branch through a forest,

---

[9] Nhat Hanh (1995), p. 14.   [10] Nhat Hanh (2005), p. 18.   [11] *Samyutta Nikaya*, p. 507.

says the Sutra."[12] The reason this happens, of course, is because we simply are not mindful and have not practiced the art of mindfulness. That is precisely what Thich Nhat Hanh encourages us to do – even for just a few minutes each day – and he offers a number of different exercises or ways to do this in his book, *The Miracle of Mindfulness: A Manual on Meditation.*

If we take him seriously and try to practice being mindful by focusing on our breathing, or paying attention to what we are doing while making tea or washing the dishes or even cleaning our room, then just as we can improve our strength by spending time working out in the weight room, we can train our minds to be more mindful. In fact, Thich Nhat Hanh claims that by mindfully meditating on subjects like interdependence, compassion, the self, emptiness, and non-attachment, or walking mindfully, or mindfully visiting a cemetery, or even generating compassion and loving-kindness for the person we hate or despise the most, we will realize that "Those who are without compassion cannot see what is seen with the eyes of compassion."[13] He also insists that those who mindfully cultivate compassion and loving-kindness eventually begin to develop a level of wisdom or a state of mind called "non-discrimination mind" in which there is no longer any distinction made between subject and object.[14] Such a person sees things in a deeper and more profound way, and, quite literally, sees what those whose minds are clouded by false and ignorant views cannot see.

---

[12] Nhat Hanh (1975), p. 41. It should be noted that Thich Nhat Hanh appears to be referring to the *Sutra of Mindfulness* as the source of the monkey analogy, but it does not occur in that text. The actual reference is the *Nidanasamyutta* or the *Connected Discourse on Causation* or the later Mahayana Sutra, *The Bequeathed Teachings of the Buddha*, which says, "The mind is the lord of the five senses and for this reason you should well control the mind. Indeed, you ought to fear indulgence of the mind's (desires) more than poisonous snakes, savage beasts, dangerous robbers or fierce conflagrations. No simile is strong enough to illustrate (this danger). But think of a man carrying a jar of honey, who, as he goes heeds only the honey and is unaware of a deep pit (in his path)! Or think of a mad elephant unrestrained by shackles! Again, consider a monkey, who after climbing into a tree cannot, except with difficulty, be controlled! Such as these would be difficult to check; therefore hasten to control your desires and do not let them go unrestrained! Indulge the mind (with its desires) and you lose the benefit of being born a man; check it completely and there is nothing you will be unable to accomplish. That is the reason, O bhikkhus, why you should strive hard to subdue your minds" (translation by The Buddhist Association of the United States).

[13] Nhat Hanh (1975), p. 108.   [14] Ibid., p. 57.

If we return for a moment to the analogy with the weight room, in the same way that someone who diligently works out eventually develops the strength to lift what the ordinary person cannot lift, the person who persistently practices the art of mindfulness inevitably develops the ability and power to see and understand what the ignorant and unenlightened person simply cannot see or know.

According to Thich Nhat Hanh, mindfulness is keeping one's consciousness alive to the present reality in the present moment. It is the art of keeping your attention focused on whatever it is that you are doing, being alert and ready to handle ably and intelligently any situation that may arise.[15] In short, it is the life of awareness, and the point of one's meditative practice is to extend mindfulness from one's meditative sessions to one's daily life.

As Nhat Hanh sees it, mindfulness frees us from distractions, forgetfulness, and dispersion of the mind and makes it possible to live fully each minute of life.[16] Understood in this way, meditation both reveals and heals. On the one hand it gives us the power "to see things as they really are." On the other hand, it restores the mind to its true self or Buddha-nature and helps one find joy and peace in this very moment.[17] That, in essence, is what Nhat Hahn thinks mindfulness is for and also what enlightenment is all about.

Mindfulness is the process and activity of restoring the mind to its original undispersed state. In this state of awareness the false views of the separateness and distinctness of the self and all "things" is overcome and one realizes what Peter Hershock[18] aptly calls "liberating intimacy" – a state beyond the false and conventional subject-object distinction in which we experience a "serene encounter with reality"[19] and are no longer pushed or pulled by anything. This is what Thich Nhat Hanh claims is our "true mind" – our true self – the Buddha – "the pure one-ness which cannot be cut up by illusory divisions of separate selves, created by concepts and language."[20] This is also, he insists, the gate to compassionate action, because "when your mind is liberated your heart floods with compassion."[21] Those who see with the eyes of compassion finally and fully realize that "the life of each one of us is

---

[15] Ibid., p. 14.   [16] Ibid., p. 15.   [17] Ibid., p. 36.   [18] Hershock (1995).
[19] Nhat Hanh (1975), p. 60.   [20] Ibid., p. 42.   [21] Ibid., p. 58.

connected with the life of those around us,"[22] and so they live and act accordingly.

In the last chapter[23] of *The Miracle of Mindfulness* Thich Nhat Hanh retells a short story from Tolstoy that he believes captures the experience of those who practice mindfulness in every moment. Without going into the details of the story, its point is that those who have fully achieved an ongoing state of mindfulness are able to answer the following three all-important questions: first, What is the best time to do each thing?; second, Who are the most important people to work with?; and third, What is the most important thing to do at all times? The answers, as the story and Nhat Hanh indicate, are: now, the person you are with, and making them happy – for that alone is the pursuit of life, and that alone will bring peace. Given these answers, it should not be difficult to see why he thinks "engaged Buddhism" is what the historical Buddha taught and lived.

Conclusion

As we come to the end of our account of the "Development of the *Dhamma/Dharma*" I think it should be sufficiently clear that Thich Nhat Hanh and the Dalai Lama both insist that whatever else one might say about the Buddha and his teachings, authentic Buddhism is ultimately about how one lives one's life. This is not to deny that both think that the mind and how we use it plays an important and foundational role in how we see and understand our self, the world, and other things. This should be obvious from their teachings on the importance and value of meditation as well as their interest in the study of the mind and consciousness and the art of living mindfully.

Nevertheless, it is also important to keep in mind that both are firmly committed to the view that beyond the realm of philosophical speculation and scientific study, beyond metaphysics and epistemology, Buddhism is about meditating *and* acting, knowing *and* doing, thinking *and* living. Despite the Dalai Lama's interest in the scientific study of the mind and his ongoing work with the Mind & Life Institute, the primary focus of his teaching has been and continues to be concerned with how to put the *Dharma* into practice for the welfare of all beings. The same is also true for Thich Nhat Hanh, and that, perhaps, is as it should be.

---

[22] Ibid., p. 60.   [23] Ibid., pp. 69–75.

As I noted in the **Preface**, and several times throughout the book, the Buddhist tradition reports that the historical Buddha urged his followers not to believe something because of who said it or where they heard it or where they read it, but because it accorded with their own experiences – with the way things go in life. The Dalai Lama and Thich Nhat Hahn are just two contemporary examples from a long line of followers of the Buddha who have found his ideas and teachings to be true and valuable precisely because they accord with their own experiences. I hope to have given the reader a clear enough sketch of the Buddha's life, the details of the *Dhamma/ Dharma*, and its subsequent development to inspire a similar test.

Things to think about

1. How are meditative practices, compassionate action, and happiness related according to the Dalai Lama?
2. What is the point and purpose of "engaged Buddhism?"
3. What is Thich Nhat Hanh's conception of mindfulness? What is "monkey mind" and how does mindfulness help one deal with it?
4. What is authentic Buddhism for the Dalai Lama and Thich Nhat Hanh?
5. What do you think is the Buddha's most basic and important teaching and why?

Glossary

The words compiled in this Glossary from the **Key terms and teachings** of each chapter appear in both their Pali (first) and Sanskrit or more precisely Buddhist Hybrid Sanskrit forms. Important English terms are included as well. For the sake of clarity and consistency throughout the text, I have decided to use the Pali forms when referring to the concepts and ideas of the earliest traditions of Buddhism and the Sanskrit forms for the later Mahayana developments. Since many Buddhist Hybrid Sanskrit words (i.e., *Buddha, dharma, karma, nirvana,* etc.) have already become part of the English language without their diacritical marks, I have decided not to use diacritical marks in the body of the text. They are, however, provided in this Glossary. For those looking for more details about the words and their meanings, I highly recommend Damien Keown's, *A Dictionary of Buddhism,* and Charles S. Prebish's, *The A to Z of Buddhism.*

Abhidhamma/Abhidharma: Pali and Sanskrit terms for the "higher" *dhamma/ dharma* or teachings of the Buddha. These texts are the philosophical and psychological explanations, clarifications, and commentaries on the teachings of the Buddha contained in the *suttas/sūtras.*

Anattā/Anātman: Literally "no-self," this term refers to the denial of a fixed, permanent, unchanging self or soul (*attā/ātman*). On a more general level, it refers to the Buddha's denial of any fixed or permanent substantial nature in any object or phenomenon. According to the Buddha, everything lacks inherent existence, because all things arise in dependence on impermanent causes and conditions.

Anicca/Anitya: Terms for the first of the "Three Marks" of existence according to the teachings of the historical Buddha, they mean "impermanence." Impermanence refers to the coming to be, and passing away of all conditioned phenomena, whether physical or psychological, that interdependently arises.

Arahant/Arhat: Pali and Sanskrit for "worthy one," these terms designate an enlightened individual who has overcome the cognitive and spiritual impurities that cause rebirth and has attained *Nibbāna* as the result of following the teachings of the Buddha, as opposed to having done it on their own.

Āraṇyakas: Collection of texts from the *Vedas* compiled by forest ascetics, these texts offer reflections on the meaning of ritual symbols and practices.

Āryans: Traditional name of the people who settled in northern India and whose religious beliefs and practices were recorded in the *Vedas*.

Āsavas/Āśravas: Pali and Sanskrit terms usually translated as "outflows," that refer to the defilements or impurities that cause repeated rebirths. In the Pali texts there are three or four impurities: sense desires, the desire for continuing existence, wrong views, and ignorance.

Bodhicitta: Sanskrit term for "thought of enlightenment/awakening." In Mahāyāna Buddhism it refers to the enlightened mind of a *bodhisattva*.

Bodhisatta/Bodhisattva: Literally, "enlightenment being," these terms refer to the ideal of Buddhist practice in Mahāyāna Buddhism. This ideal is derived, in part, from the *Jātaka Tales*, where the activities of the Buddha prior to his ultimate enlightenment are described. According to the Mahāyāna tradition, the *Bodhisattva* forgoes his own final enlightenment or realization of *Nibbāna* until he has helped all other beings escape *saṃsāra*. In this respect, the *Bodhisattva* is considered superior to the *Arahant* who pursues his own individual enlightenment.

Brahman: Name for ultimate reality or source of power behind all of the gods and rituals spoken of in the *Vedas*.

Brāhmaṇas: Collection of texts from the *Vedas* that explain the meaning and purpose of the Vedic rituals.

Buddha: Pali and Sanskrit title, derived from the word "*budh*," meaning to awaken, it is used for anyone who has achieved enlightenment (*bodhi*) or awakened to the truth about the way things really are. According to the Theravāda tradition, the Buddha was a human being who, as a result of sustained disciplined practice, underwent a profound religious and spiritual transformation. This conception was considerably expanded by the Mahāyāna tradition to include numerous Buddhas from other worlds. The central function of a Buddha is to teach the *Dhamma* to unenlightened beings.

Buddhakṣetra: Sanskrit term for "Buddha Land" or "Buddha Field." In Mahāyāna Buddhism it refers to a "place" where a Buddha exercises power.

Buddhānusmṛti: Sanskrit term for "recollection of the Buddha," "meditating on the Buddha," or "staying mindful of the Buddha." It is an important element of meditative practices in many forms of Mahāyāna Buddhism.

Dalai Lama: Literally "Great Ocean" (*dalai*) "Teacher" (*lama*), the title designates the temporal and spiritual leader of Tibet. The Mongol ruler, Altan Khan, originally bestowed the title upon the "third" Dalai Lama.

Dao: Chinese term for the "way"/"path" and source of all being.

Dassana/Darśana: Pali and Sanskrit words for "seeing" or "vision," they refer both to what is sought in ritual practices (i.e., seeing and being seen by the gods) and to what is sought from a teacher or spiritual guide. In a philosophical sense, these terms refer to the "system" or "view" of a given thinker and his followers.

Dasyus: Name for one of the groups or tribes of people from northern India who were assimilated by the Aryans.

Dhamma/Dharma: Perhaps the most ambiguous Pali and Sanskrit terms, they refer to the order of the universe, the nature and proper functioning of things, the basic elements of a thing, the moral law, ethical duties, and truth.

Dhammas/Dharmas: Pali and Sanskrit terms meaning "to support" or "to keep or maintain," in the *Abhidhamma* texts they refer to the individual elements or factors, both physical and psychological, that are causally responsible for the physical world and our experience of it. In a certain sense, they are the component parts from which all of reality originates.

Dhāraṇī: Sanskrit term for an extended *mantra* used to focus the mind and help it retain teachings.

Dhammakāya: Sanskrit term for the "Truth Body" of the Buddha. It is one of the three bodies of the Buddha and refers to his abiding presence in the form of his teachings and as the source of all reality.

Diamond Sutra: English name of the Mahāyāna *Vajracchedika-prajnaparamita Sūtra*. It is concerned with the perfection of wisdom and the teaching on emptiness.

Dukkha/Duḥkha: The subject of the Four Noble Truths, whose root meaning refers to an off-center wheel hub, "*dukkha*" captures the fact that life never quite lives up to our expectations, hopes, dreams, and plans. Usually translated as "suffering," it includes the broader psychological ideas of dissatisfaction, lack of contentment, discontent, pain, misery, frustration, and feeling ill at ease.

Eightfold Path: A basic summary of the Buddha's teachings in morality/*śīla* (right or appropriate speech, action, and livelihood), mental concentration or meditative cultivation/*samādhi* (right or appropriate effort, mindfulness, and concentration), and wisdom/*paññā* (right or appropriate view or understanding, and thought or intention).

Engaged Buddhism: A form of Buddhism developed by Thich Nhat Hanh and others that combines the meditative practices of the monastic life with the practical demands of compassionate action in the world. Its point and purpose is for its practitioners to realize that wisdom and knowledge must eventually lead to enlightened action and service.

Four Noble Truths: The Buddha's insight into *dukkha*; the source or arising or coming to be or cause of *dukkha* (*tanhā*); the cessation or ceasing of *dukkha* (*niroda*); and the path or way (*magga*) leading to the extinction of *dukkha*.

Four Sights: Traditional account of the cause or causes of Siddhattha's renunciation and great departure from his "princely" life to his search for enlightenment. After living a sheltered life, Siddhattha and his charioteer, Channa, leave his home and encounter an old man, a sick man, a corpse, and an ascetic wanderer. The vision of these sights led Siddhattha not only to question his original view of things but also to seek a solution to the suffering and dissatisfaction that are part of the human condition.

Gradual Enlightenment: In Chinese Buddhism this is the view of the "Northern School" that enlightenment is realized only gradually after many years of practice and meditation.

Guru: Sanskrit term for "teacher," commonly found in the Vajrayāna tradition.

Interdependent Arising: One English translation of the Pali and Sanskrit terms *Paticca-Samuppāda* and *Pratītya-Samutpāda*, these terms have been variously translated as, "dependent origination," "conditioned co-production," "co-dependent origination," "inter-dependent-origination," or "interdependent arising." Each of these is an attempt to capture the Buddha's account of causality.

Jātaka: The Pali term for "birth" and "pre-birth stories" that describe the former lives of the Buddha, Siddhattha Gotama. These tales contain more than 500 birth stories arranged in 22 books. Each claims to illustrate the qualities and actions that over the course of numerous lives prepared the way for the arrival of the historical Buddha.

Jhāna/Dhyāna: Pali and Sanskrit terms for deep meditative state or intellectual state of absorption involving direct awareness and insight into reality and experience. The Buddhist tradition identifies four to eight distinct stages or levels of meditative absorption.

Kamma/Karma: Pali and Sanskrit terms for "act," "action," or "deed," they refer to the connection between actions and their consequences that affect one's life both in this world and after death. The basic Buddhist account of action is that both appropriate and inappropriate tendencies or habits lead to actions that ultimately produce fruits or consequences.

Kōan: Zen term (from Chinese *kung-an*) literally meaning "public case." It refers to a question or puzzle that is meant to help practitioners overcome dualistic thinking and realize insight into reality.

Laṅkāvatāra Sūtra: Collection of Mahāyāna teachings, especially of Yogācāra Buddhism, focusing on the role of the mind, various forms of consciousness, emptiness, and *tathāgata-garbha* (womb of the Buddha). It was very influential in the Chan and Zen traditions.

Lotus Sūtra: English name for the *Saddhammapunarika Sūtra* which expounds the idea that there is really only one true vehicle or *Ekayāna*, and that the Buddha, out of compassion, continues to be present in the world to help those in need of his assistance.

Madhyamaka: Indian Mahāyāna Buddhist school, whose name means roughly, "middle way," traditionally thought to have been founded by Nāgārjuna. Its central metaphysical claims focused on the idea of "emptiness" or *suññatta/śūnyatā*.

Mahāmudrā: Sanskrit term for "Great Seal," in Vajrayāna Buddhism it refers to the meditative practices that lead to enlightenment, and insight into the unity of wisdom and compassion and *saṃsāra* and emptiness.

Mahāsiddha: Sanskrit term meaning "Great Master" or "Fully Perfected One," it refers to the ideal of Buddhist practice in the Vajrayāna tradition, of one who has mastered the *Tantras*.

Mahāyāna: Sanskrit word meaning "the greater way" or "greater vehicle," followers of this version of Buddhism used this term to distinguish themselves from their earlier predecessors, the Hīnayāna or "lesser way" or "lesser vehicle," most notably, the Theravāda. It is now generally thought that this form of Buddhism developed within some Buddhist communities between 100 BCE and 200 CE. Its teachings, which are located in its own *Perfection of Wisdom* (*Prajñāpāramitā*) literature, represent a major revision and reinterpretation of many fundamental ideas, concepts, and practices of "early" Buddhism. Among its most basic teachings are: emphasis on wisdom or insight (*prajñā*) and compassion (*karuṇā*), espousal of the *Bodhisattva* ideal, and development of the idea of emptiness (*śūnyatā*) as a way of expressing the truth that things do not have fixed or inherent natures or essences.

Mainstream Buddhism: Descriptive name used by Paul Williams, Paul Harrison, and others to designate non-Mahāyāna Buddhism. As Williams notes, this designation helps avoid the pejorative "Hīnayāna" and the technically incorrect and too narrow "Theravāda" to refer to the general form of Buddhism outside the Mahāyāna tradition.

Maṇḍala: Sanskrit term for a sacred circle that symbolically represents the world and what exists. In Tantric Buddhism it is thought to represent the mind, body, and speech of a Buddha and is used in meditation practices.

Mantra: Sanskrit term for sacred sounds that are thought to possess supernatural/spiritual powers.

Middle Way: Traditional English name for the enlightened path of the Buddha, *majjhima-paṭipadā* and *madhyamā-pratipad* in Pali and Sanskrit. At the most general level it is meant to capture the moral and ethical teaching of the Buddha that one's life and actions should steer a middle course between the extremes of hedonism and asceticism. In the metaphysical and epistemological realms, especially with regard to philosophical questions about human existence and human knowing, it refers to the fact that human souls are neither permanent and eternal nor annihilated, but *anattā* (i.e., lacking a fixed self) instead, and that the ultimate truth in all matters is always somewhere in the middle between extreme positions.

Mindfulness: The art of living mindfully is the practice of living in the present moment. It is the meditative technique of keeping one's consciousness alive to the present reality in the present moment. In short, it is the process and activity of cultivating awareness and restoring the mind to its original undistracted state.

Mokṣa: The ultimate goal of many forms of Indian religious and philosophical practices, this term means liberation or release from the cycle of *saṃsāra*.

Mudrā: Sanskrit term meaning "seal" or "sign," it refers to a symbolic gesture using the hands or body to represent an aspect of the Buddha's teaching.

Nibbāna/Nirvāṇa: Literally, "to extinguish" or "blow out," these Pali and Sanskrit terms refer initially to release from *saṃsāra* and the end of suffering. The Buddha reinterprets these terms to mean the extinguishing of the fires of greed, hatred, and delusion, and thus may be thought of as the goal of Buddhist practice.

Nirmāṇakāya: Sanskrit term for the "Emanation Body" or physical body of the Buddha. In Mahāyāna Buddhism it refers to the Buddha's ability to be physically present to teach the *Dhamma* to beings in *saṃsāra*.

Paccekabuddha/Pratyekabuddha: Pali and Sanskrit for a "solitary" Buddha who does not teach the *Dhamma* to other beings.

Paññā/Prajñā: In the traditional presentation of the teachings of the Eightfold Path, "wisdom" refers to the liberating knowledge of truth achieved in awakening or enlightenment. Right or appropriate view or understanding, and right or appropriate thought or intentions are the first two elements of the path to insight into the true nature of existence.

Pāramitās: Sanskrit term for "perfections" or "virtuous qualities" possessed by the Mahāyāna ideal of practice, the *bodhisattva*. These include: generosity or giving – *dāna*, morality – *śīla*, patience or forbearance – *khanti/kṣānti*, effort or zealous striving – *viriya/vīrya*, meditation or focused mind – *jhāna/dhyāna* or *samādhi*, and wisdom or insight –*prajñā*.

Paticca-samuppāda/Pratītya-samutpāda: Variously translated as, "dependent arising," "dependent origination," "conditioned co-production," "co-dependent origination," "inter-dependent-origination," or "interdependent arising" all of these refer to the Buddha's account of causality. In short, this cluster of terms refers to the law-governed dynamics of change in which the events or happenings in the world are causally conditioned by and dependent on other processes, events, or happenings.

Platform Sūtra: Chinese *sūtra* containing the biography and teachings of Huineng, the sixth patriarch of the Chan school of Buddhism.

Puggalavadins/Pudgalavādins: Pali and Sanskrit terms for "Personalists," or those who think the *puggala/pudgala:* or "person" exists as a subsistent entity.

Rebirth: Ancient Indian idea that one is reborn after death. It is usually connected to the idea of *kamma*. According to Buddhist cosmology there are six realms of rebirth: the realm of the gods or *devas*, the realm of the demi-gods, the human realm, the animal realm, the realm of the hungry ghosts, and the realm of hell. All six realms are thought to be real, but some forms of Mahāyāna Buddhism claim that they are best thought of as states of mind.

Ṛta: Indian term for the underlying structure and fundamental normative rhythm that organizes the energy and existence of all beings in the universe. It also refers to the law-like regularity and harmony of both the moral and physical spheres of the universe.

Sabhāva/Svabhāva: Pali and Sanskrit terms meaning "own-being," "self-being," substantial "self-existence," or "intrinsic nature," it is that by which phenomena or the *dhammas* are thought to exist independently of one another.

Samādhi: In the traditional presentation of the teachings of the Eightfold Path, "concentration" or "meditation" refers to the "right" or "appropriate" kinds of intellectual attitude required for sustaining one's practice of the Path. The appropriate mental states include: right or appropriate effort, mindfulness, and concentration.

Samaṇa/Śramaṇa: Pali and Sanskrit terms for anyone who leads the life of a religious mendicant or homeless wanderer. As a group, they sought religious and/or philosophical knowledge about the meaning and purpose of life and the fundamental nature of reality. They also rejected the authority and teachings of the Brahmins or the Vedic "vision." The Buddha and his followers were part of this group of religious seekers or strivers.

Saṃbhogakāya: Sanskrit term for the "Enjoyment Body" of the Buddha. It refers to the subtle body by which the Buddha is present to *Bodhisattvas* and other beings.

Saṃgha: Sanskrit word for "group," this term designates the followers of the Buddha or the Buddhist community. The Buddhist community includes ordained monks and nuns, and male and female lay followers.

Saṃyojana: Pali and Sanskrit term meaning "binding" or "fetter." The Buddhist tradition recognizes ten fetters that bind one to *saṃsāra*: belief that there is an enduring individual self, unjustified doubt with respect to the Buddha and his teachings, excessive concern with rituals and monastic and ethical rules, sensuous desire, lust or craving, hatred, ill will or aversion, craving for the Form realm, craving for the Formless realm, excessive self-love, being restless or agitated, and ignorance. The first five are known as the "lower fetters" (that bind one to the Desire Realm) and the last five are known as the "higher fetters" (that bind one to the Form and Formless Realms).

Saṃsāra: Literally "wandering on/about," this term refers to the ongoing and seemingly endless cyclical process of birth, life, death, and rebirth in ancient Indian philosophy and religion. In a more general way, it refers to the conditioned world of this life, its *kamma*, and its concomitant *dukkha*.

Sarvāstivādins: Sanskrit term for those who think that "everything exists" in the past, present, and future simultaneously.

Sautrāntikas: Sanskrit term for those who reject the authority of the *Abhidhamma Piṭaka* and instead are "followers of the *Suttas*."

Siddha: Sanskrit term for "accomplished one," this term refers to an enlightened master, teacher, or *guru* in the Tantric tradition.

Siddhattha Gotama/Siddhartha Gautama: Pali and Sanskrit name of the man known as the historical Buddha. "Siddhattha" was his personal name and "Gotama" was his family or clan name. According to the Buddhist tradition he was born into a leading political family of the Sakya clan, and was also known as "Sakyamuni" – the sage or wise man of the Sakyas.

Śīla: In the traditional presentation of the teachings of the Eightfold Path, "moral excellence" or "morality" refers to the three kinds of virtues required for the "right" practice of the path. These include: correct speech, correct action, and correct livelihood.

Sudden Enlightenment: In Chinese Buddhism this is the view of the "Southern School" that enlightenment is realized instantaneously in a single moment of insight.

Sukhāvatī: Sanskrit term for "Land of Happiness," or "Land of Bliss." It is the Pure Land of Amitabha or Amida Buddha located in the west.

Suññatta/Śūnyatā: Pali and Sanskrit terms meaning "emptiness" or "nothingness," these terms usually refer to the Mahāyāna interpretations of interdependent arising and the original state of mind, even though there is good evidence for an early Mainstream Buddhist understanding that involves the metaphysical structure of the human person. The Madhyamaka and Yogācāra schools of Mahāyāna Buddhism each offer their own, unique accounts and defenses of emptiness.

Sutta/Sūtra: Pali and Sanskrit terms meaning "thread," they refer to the sayings or discourses of the historical Buddha, though they were neither written nor compiled by Siddhattha. In the Pali canon, they are gathered into five "collections" known as *Nikāyas* (or *Āgamas* in Sanskrit), and grouped according to their lengths. The Mahāyāna canon, on the other hand, includes many more texts and compilations than the Pali *Nikāyas*.

Tanhā/Tṛṣṇā: Within the context of the Four Noble Truths, "*tanhā*" or selfish craving, grasping, wrong desire, greed, lust, and attached wanting, is the cause or root condition of *dukkha*. At its most basic level it is the drive for selfish gratification and possessiveness that fuels the fires of our suffering.

Tantras: Sanskrit term for both esoteric texts and the tradition of practices that developed around them. As a form of Mahāyāna Buddhism, these texts claimed to offer a particularly speedy means of enlightenment through a series of ritual and meditative practices guided by a *guru*.

Tathāgata-garbha: Sanskrit for "womb of the thus come one," this term refers to the Mahāyāna notion that all beings intrinsically possess the potential to become a Buddha or have a Buddha-nature.

Theravāda: Pali term, whose meaning is literally "way of the elders," this word refers to the only one of several early branches of the Buddhist monastic community to have survived to the present day. It is the dominant form of Buddhism in much of South East Asia, especially in Burma, Cambodia, Laos, Thailand, and Sri Lanka. The followers of this form of Buddhism adhere to the Pali canon, the earliest complete set of Buddhist scriptures in a single canonical language. This version of Buddhism emphasizes the monastic community or *Saṃgha*, the life of monks and nuns, and the *Arahant* as the highest ideal of Buddhist practice.

Tipiṭaka/Tripiṭaka: Pali and Sanskrit terms meaning "three baskets," which refer to the texts of the Buddhist canon. These include, the *Sutta /Sūtra Piṭaka*, or the basket of sayings or discourses of the Buddha, the *Vinaya Piṭaka*, or the basket of monastic rules and discipline, and the *Abhidhamma/Abhidhamma Piṭaka*, or the basket of higher teachings.

Trikāya: Sanskrit term for the Mahayana teaching on the "three bodies" of the Buddha.

Two Entrances and Four Practices: One of small number of works thought to contain the authentic teachings of Bodhidharma. This text is also known as the *Outline of Practice*.

Upanishad: Literally, "to sit down near," this word refers to the last part of the *Vedas*. The texts of this part of the *Vedas* consist of more purely philosophical reflections on the nature of self and the ultimate nature of reality.

Upāya: Sanskrit term for "skillful means" or "skill-in-means." Although generally associated with the Mahāyāna tradition and the perfections of a *Bodhisattva*, it also refers to the Buddha's ability to suit his teachings to the capacity of his disciples and his audiences in order to bring them to enlightenment.

Vajrayāna: Literally, "diamond or thunderbolt vehicle," in Sanskrit, this third form of Buddhism emphasizes ritual and devotional practices, and is found today in the Tantric traditions of Tibet. As a form of Buddhism, it combines elements of Mahāyāna philosophy with esoteric Tantric practices in order to help its practitioners achieve enlightenment. Special emphasis is placed on the role of the *guru* or spiritual master, who utilizes *mantras*, *maṇḍalas*, and *mudrās* to help his followers realize their inner Buddha-nature.

Varṇa: Literally, "color," this term refers to the four main social classes in ancient India: the priestly Brahmins, the warrior Kshatriyas, the merchant Vaishyas, and the peasant Shūdras. This term is often mistaken for *jāti* (birth status), which refers to one's caste or station in society.

Vedas: From the Sanskrit word, "*veda*," meaning "knowledge," this term refers to the earliest collections of Indian religious texts. Strictly speaking, the *Vedas* include the Ṛg Veda (hymns to gods), the *Sāma Veda* (songs and instructions based on the Ṛg Veda), the *Yajur Veda* (ritual verses and mantras), the *Atharva Veda* (hymns and magical formulae for ordinary life), the *Brāhmaṇas* (ritual rules), and the *Upanishads*.

Vimalakīrti Sūtra: An important and influential Mahāyāna Sutra named after its main character, the layman Vimalakīrti. Its primary subject is the method and means to the perfection of insight.

Vinaya: Name of the basket of teachings concerned with the monastic rules and discipline of the Buddhist community. These rules, which vary in number between 227 (for men) and 311 (for women), cover the day-to-day activities of the monastic community.

Wu-wei: Chinese for "no action." It refers to non-coercive, spontaneous action in accord with one's true nature.

Yāna: Sanskrit term for "vehicle." It refers to the various spiritual paths one follows. It is most commonly found conjoined with other terms to designate particular paths, i.e., Hīnayāna (Lesser vehicle), Mahāyāna (Greater vehicle), and Ekayāna (One vehicle).

Yoga: Literally, "to yoke, or bind," this term refers to ascetic meditative techniques for disciplining the mind and body in order to achieve "higher" knowledge and escape the bondage and suffering of *saṃsāra*.

Yogācāra: Indian Mahāyāna Buddhist school, whose name means, "Practice of yoga," and also known as the *Vijñānavāda* or "Way of Consciousness" school, it focused on the nature and activities of consciousness in understanding reality.

Bibliography

Primary sources

Bodhi, Bhikkhu (trans.) (2000) *The Connected Discourses of the Buddha: A Translation of the Samyutta Nikaya*, Boston: Wisdom Publications.

  (trans. and ed.) (2005) *In the Buddha's Words: An Anthology of Discourses from the Pali Canon*, Boston: Wisdom Publications.

Nanamoli, Bhikkhu and Bodhi, Bhikkhu (trans.) (2001) *The Middle Length Discourses of the Buddha: A Translation of the Majjhima Nikaya*, Second Edition, Boston: Wisdom Publications.

Price, A. F. and Mou-lam, Wong (trans.) (1990) *The Diamond Sutra & The Sutra of Hui-Neng*, Boston: Shambhala Publications.

Radhakrishnan, Sarvepalli and Moore, Charles A. (eds.) (1957) *A Sourcebook in Indian Philosophy*, Princeton: Princeton University Press.

Thanissaro, Bhikkhu (trans.) (1998) *Dhammapada: A Translation*, Barre, MA: Dhamma Dana Publications.

Thera, Nyanaponika and Bodhi, Bhikkhu (trans. and ed.) (1999) *Numerical Discourses of the Buddha*, Walnut Creek, CA: Altamira Press.

Walshe, Maurice (trans.) (1995) *The Long Discourses of the Buddha: A Translation of the Digha Nikaya*, Boston: Wisdom Publications.

Watson, Burton (trans.) (1993) *The Lotus Sutra*, New York: Columbia University Press.

  (1997) *The Vimalakirti Sutra*, New York: Columbia University Press.

Secondary sources

Armstrong, Karen (2001) *Buddha*, New York: Penguin Putnam.

Arnold, Edwin (1890) *The Light of Asia*, Boston: Roberts Brothers.

Broughton, Jeffrey L. (1999) *The Bodhidhamma Anthology: The Earliest Records of Zen*, Berkeley: University of California Press.

Carrithers, Michael (1983) *The Buddha*, Oxford: Oxford University Press.

Ch'en, Kenneth (1964) *Buddhism in China: A Historical Survey*, Princeton: Princeton University Press.

(1968) *Buddhism: The Light of Asia*, New York: Barron's Educational Series, Inc.

(1973) *The Chinese Transformation of Buddhism*, Princeton: Princeton University Press.

Collins, Steven (1982) *Selfless Persons: Imagery and Thought in Theravada Buddhism*, Cambridge: Cambridge University Press.

Conze, Edward (1951) *Buddhism: Its Essence and Development*, Birmingham, UK: Windhorse Publications.

Eppsteiner, Fred (ed.) (1985) *The Path of Compassion: Writings on Socially Engaged Buddhism*, Berkeley: Parallax Press.

Feldmeier, Peter (2006) *Christianity Looks East: Comparing the Spiritualities of John of the Cross and Buddhaghosa*, New York: Paulist Press.

Fitzgerald, Timothy (2000) *The Ideology of Religious Studies*, New York: Oxford University Press.

Gethin, Rupert (1998) *The Foundations of Buddhism*, Oxford: Oxford University Press.

Gombrich, Richard (1988) *Theravada Buddhism: A Social History from Ancient Benares to Modern Colombo*, London: Routledge & Kegan Paul.

Gowans, Christopher W. (2003) *Philosophy of the Buddha*, New York: Routledge.

Griffiths, Paul J. (1986) *On Being Mindless: Buddhist Meditation and the Mind-Body Problem*, Illinois: Open Court.

(1994) *On Being Buddha: The Classical Doctrine of Buddhahood*, Albany: State University of New York Press.

Gruzalski, Bart (2000) *On the Buddha*, Belmont, CA: Wadsworth Publishing Company.

Gyatso, Tenzin, Fourteenth Dalai Lama (1995) *The World of Tibetan Buddhism*, Boston: Wisdom Publications.

Gyatso, Tenzin, Fourteenth Dalai Lama (2005a) "Our Faith in Science," *The New York Times*, November 12, 2005.

(2005b) *The Universe in a Single Atom: The Convergence of Science and Spirituality*, New York: Morgan Road Books.

Hamilton, Sue (2001) *Indian Philosophy: A Very Short Introduction*, Oxford: Oxford University Press.

Harris, Elizabeth J. (2000) *What Buddhists Believe*, Oxford: Oneworld Publications.

Harvey, Peter (1990) *An Introduction to Buddhism: Teachings, History and Practices*, Cambridge: Cambridge University Press.

(1995) *The Selfless Mind: Personality, Consciousness and Nirvana in Early Buddhism*, Richmond: Curzon Press.

Hawkins, Bradley K. (1999) *Buddhism*, New Jersey: Prentice Hall Inc.

Hershock, Peter D. (1996) *Liberating Intimacy: Enlightenment and Social Virtuosity in Ch'an Buddhism*, Albany: State University of New York Press.

(2005) *Chan Buddhism*, Honolulu: University of Hawai'i Press.

Hiriyanna, M. (1985) *Essentials of Indian Philosophy*, London: George Allen & Unwin.

Honderich, Ted (ed.) (1995) *The Oxford Companion to Philosophy*, Oxford: Oxford University Press.

Jayatilleke, K. N. (1963) *Early Buddhist Theory of Knowledge*, London: George Allen & Unwin.

Kalupahana, David J. (1975) *Causality: The Central Philosophy of Buddhism*, Honolulu: University of Hawai'i Press.

(1976) *Buddhist Philosophy: A Historical Analysis*, Honolulu: University of Hawai'i Press.

(1987) *The Principles of Buddhist Psychology*, Albany: State University of New York Press.

(1992) *A History of Buddhist Philosophy: Continuities and Discontinuities*, Honolulu: University of Hawai'i Press.

Kalupahana, David J., and Kalupahana, Indrani (1982) *The Way of Siddhartha: A Life of the Buddha*, Boulder: Shambhala Publications.

Keown, Damien (1996) *Buddhism: A Very Short Introduction*, Oxford: Oxford University Press.

(ed.) (2003) *Dictionary of Buddhism*, Oxford: Oxford University Press.

King, Richard (1999) *Indian Philosophy: An Introduction to Hindu and Buddhist Thought*, Washington, D.C.: Georgetown University Press.

Kitagawa, Joseph and Cummings, Mark D. (1989) *Buddhism and Asian History*, New York: Macmillan Publishing Company.

Klostermaier, Klaus K. (1999) *Buddhism: A Short Introduction*, Oxford: Oneworld Publications.

Knipe, David M. (1991) *Hinduism: Experiments in the Sacred*, New York: HarperCollins Publishers.

Knott, Kim (1998) *Hinduism: A Very Short Introduction*, Oxford: Oxford University Press.

Koller, John M. (2006) *The Indian Way: An Introduction to the Philosophies and Religions of India*, Second Edition, New Jersey: Pearson Prentice Hall.

Kupperman, Joel J. (1999) *Learning from Asian Philosophy*, New York: Oxford University Press.

(2001) *Classic Asian Philosophy: A Guide to the Essential Texts*, Oxford: Oxford University Press.

LaFleur, William R. (1988) *Buddhism: A Cultural Perspective*, New Jersey: Prentice Hall Inc.

Lopez, Donald S., Jr. (2001) *The Story of Buddhism: A Concise Guide to its History and Teachings*, New York: HarperCollins Publishers.

(ed.) (2005) *Critical Terms for the Study of Buddhism*, Chicago: University of Chicago Press.

Mitchell, Donald W. (2002) *Buddhism: Introducing the Buddhist Experience*, New York: Oxford University Press.

Mohanty, J. N. (2000) *Classical Indian Philosophy*, Maryland: Rowan & Littlefield Publishers.

Nanamoli, Bhikkhu (1972) *The Life of the Buddha: According to the Pali Canon*, Pariyatti Edition, Kandy, Sri Lanka: Buddhist Publication Society.

Nhat Hanh (1975) *The Miracle of Mindfulness: A Manual on Meditation*, Revised Edition, Boston: Beacon Press.

(1995) *Living Buddha, Living Christ*, New York: Riverhead Books.

(2005) *Thich Nhat Hanh: Essential Writings*, edited by Robert Ellsberg, New York: Orbis Books.

Pine, Red (trans.) *The Zen Teachings of Bodhidhamma*, San Francisco: North Point Press.

Polkinghorne, John (1995) *Serious Talk: Science and Religion in Dialogue*, Valley Forge: Trinity Press.

Prebish, Charles S. (2001) *The A to Z of Buddhism*, Maryland: The Scarecrow Press.

Rahula, Walpola (1974) *What the Buddha Taught*, Revised Edition, New York: Grove Press.

Rajapakse, Reginton (1986) "Buddhism as Religion and Philosophy," *Religion*, 16, 51–55.

Reichenbach, Bruce R. (1990) *The Law of Kamma: A Philosophical Study*, Honolulu: University of Hawai'i Press.

Renard, John (1999) *101 Questions and Answers on Buddhism*, New York: Gramercy Books.

(1999) *101 Questions and Answers on Hinduism*, New York: Gramercy Books.

Robinson, Richard H., Johnson, Willard L. and Thanissaro, Bhikkhu (2005), *Buddhist Religions*, Fifth Edition, Belmont, CA: Wadsworth Publishing Company.

Sen, K. M. (1961) *Hinduism*, London: Penguin Books.

Shattuck, Cybelle (1999) *Hinduism*, New Jersey: Prentice Hall Inc.

Smith, Huston and Novak, Philip (2003) *Buddhism: A Concise Introduction*, New York: HarperCollins Publishers.

Stcherbatsky, Th. (1922) *The Central Conception of Buddhism: And the Meaning of the Word "Dhamma"*, Delhi: Motilal Banarsidass Publishers.

Strong, John S. (2001) *The Buddha: A Short Biography*, Oxford: Oneworld Publications.

(2002) *The Experience of Buddhism: Sources and Interpretations*, Second Edition, Belmont, CA: Wadsworth Publishing Company.

Tanabe, George J., Jr. and Tanabe, Willa Jane (1989) *The Lotus Sutra in Japanese Culture*, Honolulu: University of Hawai'i Press.

Thomas, Edward J. (2002) *The History of Buddhist Thought*, New York: Dover Publications.

Williams, Paul (1989) *Mahayana Buddhism: The Doctrinal Foundations*, London: Routledge.

Williams, Paul and Tribe, Anthony (2000) *Buddhist Thought: A Complete Introduction to the Indian Tradition*, London: Routledge.

Wright, Arthur F. (1959) *Buddhism in Chinese History*, Stanford: Stanford University Press.

Yao, Xinzhong (2000) *An Introduction to Confucianism*, Cambridge: Cambridge University Press.

Index